MW01102638

Maria Grasso's masterful comparative analysis provides a fresh look on the study of political participation and, more broadly, on the functioning of democracy. Her book fits squarely with a long-standing research tradition in sociology and political science, namely the study of generations and political engagement. She shows that both conventional and unconventional forms of participation have declined, and will continue to fall in the future with new, less politicized generations replacing older, more civic ones.

Marco Giugni, *Professor and Director of the Institute of Citizenship Studies, University of Geneva, Switzerland*

A truly wonderful and deeply original book which demonstrates, as never before, the profound influence of cohort effects and socialisation on political participation and the continuing significance of domestic political factors. Theoretically innovative, methodologically sophisticated and thoroughly convincing, Maria Grasso puts down a very significant marker in a debate whose importance can scarcely be exaggerated.

Colin Hay, *Professor of Political Science, Sciences Po, Paris, France*

In this important book, Maria Grasso carefully employs a rich body of data to uncover the continued importance of political generation and national context: while our formative experiences do not determine our future political behaviour, they do have a long-lasting influence throughout our lives – with long term implications for our politics.

Charles Pattie, *Professor of Geography, University of Sheffield, UK*

This is one of the best sustained analyses of political generations and democratic participation to date. Grasso's analysis is both theoretically nuanced and rigorously empirical. Her careful methodology allows her to disentangle the effects of generation, age, and period in ten Western European democracies. Analyzing five political generations, Grasso convincingly shows the lasting effects of formative experiences and the ongoing centrality of the 1960s 'protest generation' to new social movements. The book has important implications for democratic engagement: as younger generations replace Baby Boomers, Western European democracies are likely to see declining participation in social movements and in conventional politics.

Nancy Whittier, *Professor of Sociology, Smith College, USA*

Events of May 1968 in Paris: Demonstrations (Photo by Georges Melet/*Paris Match* via Getty Images)

Generations, Political Participation and Social Change in Western Europe

This new comparative analysis shows that there are reasons to be concerned about the future of democratic politics. Younger generations have become disengaged from the political process. The evidence presented in this comprehensive study shows that they are not just less likely than older generations to engage in institutional political activism such as voting and party membership – they are also less likely to engage in extra-institutional protest activism.

Generations, Political Participation and Social Change in Western Europe offers a rigorously researched empirical analysis of political participation trends across generations in Western Europe. It examines the way in which the political behaviour of younger generations leads to social change. Are younger generations completely disengaged from politics, or do they simply choose to participate in a different way to previous generations?

The book is of key interest to scholars, students and practitioners of political sociology, political participation and behaviour, European politics, comparative politics and sociology.

Maria T. Grasso is a Lecturer in Politics and Quantitative Methods at the Department of Politics, University of Sheffield, UK, and Deputy Editor for Western Europe of *Mobilization: An International Quarterly.*

Routledge Research in Comparative Politics

Generations, Political Participation and Social Change in Western Europe

Maria T. Grasso

Routledge
Taylor & Francis Group

LONDON AND NEW YORK

First published 2016
by Routledge
2 Park Square, Milton Park, Abingdon, Oxon OX14 4RN

and by Routledge
711 Third Avenue, New York, NY 10017

Routledge is an imprint of the Taylor & Francis Group, an informa business

© 2016 Maria T. Grasso

The right of Maria T. Grasso to be identified as author of this work has
been asserted by her in accordance with sections 77 and 78 of the
Copyright, Designs and Patents Act 1988.

All rights reserved. No part of this book may be reprinted or reproduced or
utilised in any form or by any electronic, mechanical, or other means, now
known or hereafter invented, including photocopying and recording, or in
any information storage or retrieval system, without permission in writing
from the publishers.

Trademark notice: Product or corporate names may be trademarks or
registered trademarks, and are used only for identification and explanation
without intent to infringe.

British Library Cataloguing in Publication Data
A catalogue record for this book is available from the British Library

Library of Congress Cataloging in Publication Data
A catalog record for this book has been requested

ISBN: 978-1-138-92499-4 (hbk)
ISBN: 978-1-315-68403-1 (ebk)

Typeset in Times New Roman
by Wearset Ltd, Boldon, Tyne and Wear

To Nick and Max

Contents

Figures

Tables

Acknowledgements

My work on this project began with the start of my doctoral research at Nuffield College, University of Oxford almost ten years ago. There are many people to whom I am grateful for reading my work, discussing ideas, for their comments, feedback and encouragement along the way. They have all contributed to this book in some way or another even though they might not even know it. In particular, I would like to thank Stephen Fisher for all the feedback and the many conversations on the subject matter of this research, and Marco Giugni, for comments and suggestions and for encouraging me to publish this work. I mention here a few other names in a list which is not exhaustive but hopefully serves to show how indebted I am to the many discussions and exchanges that I have been lucky enough to have had with others in various settings, from e-mail exchanges, to internal presentations, to workshops and conferences, to Nuffield College high table dinners: Robert Andersen, David Armstrong, Nan Dirk de Graaf, Geoffrey Evans, Mark Franklin, Colin Hay, Anthony Heath, James Laurence, Chaeyoon Lim, Peter Mair, Anja Neundorf, Richard Niemi, Charles Pattie, David Robertson, James Tilley, Andries van den Broek, Nancy Whittier and all the participants of the "Beyond Political Socialization: New Approaches in Age, Period, Cohort Analysis" workshop, Nuffield College, University of Oxford, 16–17 March, 2012. It goes without saying that all remaining errors are entirely my own and the usual disclaimers apply.

I would also like to express my gratitude to my family: my husband, Nick, for always being supportive, and my son, Maximilian, who arrived while this project was in progress and has kept me wonderful company throughout the various stages leading to its completion. I also want to thank my mother and my father, Laura and Paolo, and my younger sister, Anna, for somehow always being there for me despite us being based in three different countries.

At Routledge, I am particularly grateful to Andrew Taylor who first discussed the book plan with me and encouraged me to proceed and to Charlotte Endersby and Sophie Iddamalgoda for masterfully keeping me on track with deadlines and always providing informative answers to my e-mails.

I would also like to acknowledge the UK Economic and Social Research Council (ESRC) for fully funding me throughout the MSc and DPhil at the University of Oxford (Economic and Social Research Council "1+3" Studentship

Award: PTA-031–2005–00145), and also the national election studies teams and centres, particularly the Istituto Cattaneo in Italy and the Centre de Données Socio-Politiques (CDSP) in France, for allowing me access to the data, as well as the World Values Study/European Values Study (WVS/EVS) and European Social Survey (ESS) research teams for providing the cross-national survey data on which most of the analyses in this study are based.

Abbreviations

CSES   Comparative Study of Electoral Systems
EB   Eurobarometer
EES   European Election Study
ESS   European Social Survey
EVS   European Values Study
ISSP   International Social Survey Programme
NSMs   New Social Movements
SMOs   Social Movement Organisations
WVS/EVS   World Values Study/European Values Study

1 Introduction

This book is about democracy. It is about the way in which Western European citizens' popular political engagement has evolved since the end of the 1970s to the onset of the 2008 financial crisis. The key conclusions of the book point to a slow but steady decline of democratic politics. A central argument of this book is that we have witnessed the hollowing out of democracy over the last few decades. In particular, this is expressed in the decline of political participation and popular involvement in political activism. The book presents empirical evidence to show how democratic publics have increasingly become alienated from their own political systems and both institutional and extra-institutional means to influence the organisation of our societies. At the end of the twenty-first century, Western publics have become the objects, rather than the subjects, of history.

This new comparative analysis shows how the decline of political involvement in Western Europe occurs through generational change. Social change comes about as older generations die out and are replaced by younger generations exhibiting new patterns of behaviour. Increasingly, the democratic representative mechanisms in advanced democracies are breaking down since citizens – and younger ones in particular – no longer see politics as a means to change the world for the better. Rather, they see politicians as distant and selfish, careerists trapped – in the words of Pitkin (2004), "inside the beltway" not just physically, but also mentally. More and more citizens reject politics by not voting. This is most dramatically seen in the decline of youth voter turnout, not just in Britain, but across advanced democracies. For some, the decline of what is termed 'conventional' political participation – voting, engaging with politics parties and other traditional institutions of politics – is offset to some extent at least by protest activism and new social movements that have become more widespread since the 1960s. Evidence presented in this book however suggests that the observed rise in protest activism is no panacea for our hollowed out democracies. First, participation in protest activities and new social movements, while useful for democratic dialogue, cannot replace engagement with a functioning representative democratic system. Second, evidence presented in this book suggests that just like with conventional participation, unconventional engagement and protest activism will also commence to decline in the future as the politically active 1960s–1970s generation of baby-boomers begins to age and comes to be replaced in the population by the more politically passive younger generations coming of age in the 1980s and 1990s.

In the future, the only hope to revitalise our democracies lies with the emergence of a newly politicised generation of young people developing progressive answers for contemporary problems. Only time will tell if the current financial crisis and the steep toll it is exerting, including deepening inequality across the globe, is sowing the conditions for the development of a new politicised younger generation that can inject fresh life into democratic politics. It has been said that social change "cannot take its poetry from the past but only from the future" (*The Eighteenth Brumaire of Louis Bonaparte*. Karl Marx 1852). This book provides an analysis of how the political participation patterns of Western European democracies have evolved since the end of the 1970s to the onset of the 2008 financial crisis in order to contribute to our understanding of the forces that have shaped the present.

Data and methods

In order to investigate the state of popular political involvement and the health of democratic society in Western Europe, this book draws on analyses of data from established cross-national surveys. For the most part, we focus on the period 1981–2006 – from the great transformations of the age of affluence and the emergence of 'new social movements' to just before the start of the financial crisis. This time frame allows us to assess the extent of changes in the political participation patterns of Western European democracies as predicted by prominent theories of social change. Excluding the most recent years allows us first to focus on specific explanations without including confounding factors; second, this is necessary in order to analyse generational change since we need to examine periods that allow for the youngest generations to have 'come of age'. We rely in particular on the well-established cross-national surveys of the European Values Study (EVS) and the European Social Survey (ESS). Both provide high quality data on the participation patterns of European publics over time.

While the results of this investigation are widely generalisable to advanced industrial societies, we focus on ten Western European countries in particular in order to allow a manageable amount of variation for developing explanatory narratives. These ten Western European democracies that this study will focus on are Belgium, Denmark, France, Germany (West), Great Britain, Ireland, Italy, the Netherlands, Spain and Sweden. They are all established European democracies that have roughly similar political systems and historical trajectories; most importantly, they can be understood to have similar political generations (Van Deth and Elff 2000). Importantly, analysing empirical survey data on political participation allows for the examination of the extent to which 'conventional', or elite-directed, formal, institutional, political participation, associated with traditional institutions such as political parties and trade unions, is in decline. At the same time, it also allows for examining the question of the extent to which 'unconventional', or elite-challenging, informal, extra-institutional, political participation related to new social movements (NSMs) and protest is on the rise.

In order to understand the processes of social change underpinning declining popular political involvement in Western Europe, we examine the extent to which these changes are driven by the replacement of older with younger generations in the population. Since social change comes about through intergenerational replacement, it is often argued that the above patterns should be most prominent amongst the youngest generations (Grasso 2013a). In other words, that the youngest generation is the least likely to participate in conventional political activities, while at the same time being the most likely to engage in unconventional political activities, including getting involved in new social movements (Grasso and Giugni 2013, Grasso and Giugni 2015, Giugni and Grasso 2015, Grasso and Giugni 2016). In the course of this book, we will conduct analyses of survey data and examine evidence to determine whether this is indeed the case when we look at the landscape of political participation in Western Europe.

The results presented in this book show that the patterns of political participation across Western Europe are remarkably varied, partly owing to diverse histories and political cultures. The book also presents evidence that it is not the case that younger generations are completely detached from conventional politics, parties and trade unions. We also show that it is also not the case that all older generations are less engaged in protest and other types of unconventional activism than the youngest cohorts. One of the key conclusions of this study is to show that the generation socialised in the tumultuous political period of the late 1960s and 1970s are the most active in protest activism. They are still 'the protest generation' (Grasso 2011). The results presented in this study provide clear evidence that the divergent formative experiences of the five political generations identified in diverse and specific historical and political contexts matter, and that they differentiate generations in their patterns of participation many years later (Grasso 2013b). This finding in particular has important implications for the future of our democracies and we elaborate on these wider conclusions in the final chapter.

Since political participation is a complex, multi-dimensional concept, its patterns exhibit substantial cross-national and over-time variation (Pattie *et al.* 2004). This means it should be both understood and measured across a spectrum of different activities (Grasso 2016) and for each country in turn, at least for the starting analyses. For this reason, for most of the book, country-by-country analyses are conducted. We are interested in examining the extent to which declining political involvement is a process common to Western European democracies or rather whether there are important cross-national differences. We are also interested in examining whether patterns are similar for indicators grouped into the same conventional/unconventional theoretical categories. As such we do not collapse indicators into scales, but rather examine them each on their own terms to more clearly see over time and generational patterns.

In order to convincingly argue that the observed differences in participation between older and younger generations will lead to social change through intergenerational replacement, we must show that these are indeed 'generational' differences due to divergent socialisation experiences and not simply 'age' differences related to the different life-stages that respondents are in at the time of their observation. Moreover, we need to isolate 'period effects' relating to the historical moment of observation. For example, we know that younger people tend to be more likely to attend demonstrations and that older people are generally more likely to vote and to become party members (Grasso 2011, Grasso 2014). Moreover, these activities have been more or less popular in different time periods. A detailed account of the data and methods underpinning this study is provided in the Appendix, but here we just note that care has been taken in the empirical analysis underlying this research to develop statistical methods and models to disentangle age, generational and period, or time, effects in order to isolate 'pure' socialisation differences that are likely to support processes of social change through intergenerational replacement.

Participation and democracy

Why does political participation matter? Political participation is at the heart of democratic practice. The way in which scholars conceptualise its relation to democracy and the implications they draw from the patterns they observe, reveal their preferences for different types of democratic government. For some, all that matters is for a minimum number of people to vote to legitimise governments (Schumpeter 1952), whilst for others, democracy is unthinkable without parties (Schattschneider 1942). Yet more consider 'cyber-activism' (Pickerell 2003) and e-petitions just as worthwhile, since all that is important is that people are somehow 'engaged' with the processes of government.

For popular theorists of democracy, participation is important because it is the dominant method for developing and critically examining political ideas, as well as providing the demos with a means to keep government to account (Barber 1984; Habermas 1975; Mill 1861). Radical democrats take this a step further in arguing that "social objectivity is ultimately political" and in fact "constituted through acts of power" (Laclau and Mouffe 1985: 6). On this reading, political participation is necessary for democracy since it is only through political struggle that society creates meaning and decides how it should be organised (Furedi 2005; Mouffe 2000). Political practice itself, on this reading, is understood as constituting social identities; the "ineradicability of antagonism" in democracy implies that the absence of participation simply preserves the power relations that are already in place (Mouffe 2000: 13).

On the other side of the spectrum, elite competition theorists, while also granting that political participation is necessary for democracy, see it, mostly in the form of voting, as primarily a means for legitimising elite decision-making (Almond and Verba 1963; Berelson *et al.* 1954; Rosema 2006; Schumpeter 1952). The important difference between elite competition theorists and those who defend a more participatory approach concerns whether mass political involvement is either desirable or a realistic expectation. Theorists of participatory democracy argue that the more vibrant and engaged the polity, the more dynamic and truly democratic society will be. On the other side of the debate, elite competition theorists are more pessimistic about people, considering them in the main ignorant, emotional and prone to 'crowd mentality'. These theorists fear mass participation for its potential to be radically destabilising. In other words: some participation is important for legitimising democratic systems, but in general it is best left to the experts.

While different theories of democracy may disagree on the extent to which participation is desirable and the centrality of the function it is meant to fulfil in modern democracies, they all invariably agree that at least some degree of participation is essential for functioning democratic government.

How scholars conceptualise participation and the meaning they attach to different activities carries implications for the conclusions they draw concerning the importance of declining popular political participation in Western democracies. For Mair (2006), following Schattschneider's (1942) classical account, democracy is unthinkable without parties. Hence, the steep decline in party membership is concerning since it is a symptom of the demise of representative, accountable democratic government. Contrary to Mair (2006), others understand the demise of traditional parties in less pessimistic terms. For Norris (2002), it is less concerning that traditional agencies have become less popular, since activism has been 'reinvented' through the rise of alternative avenues; participation has simply evolved from the 'politics of loyalties' to the 'politics of choice'.

Whilst the elite competition argument has been criticised for being too pessimistic about the citizenry, the emphasis on the progressive potential of any kind of participatory democracy has also been problematised. Authors such as Mair (2006) emphasise the changing role of political parties as they become more managerial to suggest that the current political context is in many respects different from those of the past and that other types of participation, namely unconventional ones, cannot substitute parties in representative political systems. This brings the social significance of the various forms of political participation into focus, which is in turn fundamental to understanding the dynamic potential of participation, since it occurs within specific social contexts. Individuals are situated in society and in distinct socio-historical contexts and react to what is out there; they do not act in a vacuum. Without taking stock of this, the participatory citizenship argument runs the risk of equating participation per se with the heart and soul of democracy. This would be an overly reductionist view: the ideals of both democracy and politics involve ideas, arguments, confrontation and the creation of specific kinds of meaning and broader orientations towards the organisation and future of society, not simply activism for its own sake.

While participation can be understood as both legitimising and as challenging, both problematic and as desirable, as world-shaking or as world-affirming, or as potentially superficial depending on context and the theoretical conceptualisations adopted, it is useful to point out that very same political activities can mean and have meant very different things in different historical and national contexts. Even the most cursory knowledge of political sociology provides evidence for the constantly evolving nature of political participation. While theorists broadly agree on definitions of political participation, the transformation of participatory repertoires though time and across national contexts creates challenges for theorising about democratic practice, and for measurement and conceptualisations (Van Deth 1986). At the same time, while the meaning of participation has changed over time, so too have the democratic 'virtues' of the public also ebbed and flowed. In contrast to today's worries over declining voter turnout, in the late 1960s, Butler and Stokes (1969: 26) wrote of Britain that "blurred ideas of popular sovereignty and universal suffrage are so interwoven in prevailing conceptions of British government that the obligation to vote becomes almost an aspect of the citizen's national identity". In contrast to this, today it is not suffrage, but new social movements and protest campaigns that are becoming increasingly synonymous with vibrant popular engagement in politics, in turn leading to the development of conflicting narratives on the state of democratic politics. It is to these that we now turn.

Conflicting narratives

The casual observer reading about politics in the newspapers or watching the television today is confronted with a number of conflicting narratives concerning political participation and the state of democratic politics. More specifically, the view that 'conventional' participation is declining is supported by pointing out that we are also experiencing a decline of civic culture and civic virtue, that 'social capital stocks' are being irreversibly eroded. For proponents of this view, these deeper and particularly pervasive social consequences are signalled by the decline in voter turnout and party membership observed in a number of advanced Western democracies over the past few decades. Conversely, we are also told that 'new' channels of political engagement are becoming increasingly prevalent and influential within society. Instead of participating in the old party-style politics, representatives of this perspective argue that people are in reality engaged in a growing number of grassroots campaigns, that these concern specific issues that really matter to them, and which more often than not give rise to 'new social movements'. Similarly dissonant images of political participation are conjured up when young people are presented as the litmus test for the resilience of democratic norms in advanced democracies. Again, two broad camps emerge. One tells the story of apathetic young people being disengaged from both traditional forms of political engagement and also society more widely. On this reading, today's young people have simply 'lost the knack' of protest. This claim seems thrown into sharper focus when comparing younger generations to their more radical baby-boomer parents of 'the protest generation' coming of age in the 1960s–1970s. Meanwhile, others argue that this reading is myopic. Instead, they tell a story of very much politicised young people, who are busy spearheading the 'new politics' and its wave of different single-issue campaigns.

In this context of conflicting narratives, it has become increasingly commonplace to argue that what ultimately gives rise to such contradictory views is an overly narrow conception of 'the political' coupled with a broad-brushed nostalgia for a 'romantic Golden Age' of political participation (Norris 2002).

Following this line of thought, many authors highlight the way that the realm of politics itself has widened considerably in post-industrial societies, and especially within advanced Western European democracies. Consequently, these authors tend to hold that political participation itself must be reconceptualised to include the resultant 'new forms of engagement' that have emerged, such as online petitions, Internet discussion groups and 'cyber-activism'.

As a result, arguments concerning the relationship between young people's political behaviour and the implications for the future of democratic societies abound. Once more, two broad and opposing perspectives are developed concerning the relationship between young people and democracy or politics more broadly. On the one hand, some argue that young people are particularly apolitical since they have entered politics in a peculiarly depoliticised political context. Unlike the 1970s and previous decades, this perspective understands the contemporary political climate as being characterised primarily by the significant absence of ideological debate and meaningful alternatives in the realm of party competition. However, on the other hand, others say that there is nothing special about young people today. On this view, the perceived radicalism of the protesting baby-boomers is in fact a romanticised, impressionistic account. Consequently, if young people participate less than older cohorts, this is simply because today, like yesterday, they are more preoccupied with other concerns, such as completing university, finding a house, a partner and a job, and generally finding their place in an increasingly complicated and diversified world.

In the academic literature, scholars studying 'conventional' political participation such as voting and party membership generally show that participation is falling and more so amongst the youngest cohorts. Others, studying 'unconventional' participation and 'new social movements' suggest that while 'conventional' participation may be declining, 'unconventional' participation will continue to rise. This is because more 'cognitively mobilised' and 'post-materialist' younger cohorts prefer to participate in other, 'elite-challenging' repertoires.

It is in particular the 'protest generation', those coming of age in the tumultuous 1960s and 1970s that engage in various kinds of protest activism including demonstrating and joining occupations as well as engagement in new social movements. Stressing the distinctiveness of this generation, Della Porta and Diani (2006) argue that this generation was unique in that it came of age in a particularly radicalising context, and therefore was especially active in the new social movements and protest activities emerging in these decades. In the course of this study, we will examine the extent to which different 'political generations' show distinctive patterns of participation and the extent to which younger generations match the highly politicised 1960s–1970s generation in their patterns of political engagement – both in new and old political activities.

Why do citizens participate (or fail to do so)?

As Franklin (2004) highlights, the early voting studies (Boechel 1928; Gosnell 1927; Merriam and Gosnell 1924; Tingsten 1937) took it for granted that turnout would be higher when "issues of vital concern [were] presented" (Boechel 1928: 517), and therefore "low voter turnout would be blamed on parties and politicians for failing to present issues of vital concern ... not on the characters of those who failed to vote" (Franklin 2004: 2). Today, on the other hand, scholars often see low turnout as bad for democracy because it is seen as calling into question citizens' civic duty and their commitment to democracy (Norris 1999; Patterson 2002; Wattenberg 2002).

However, it appears simplistic to generalise and describe citizens who do not turn out to vote as necessarily apathetic without attempting to understand the reasons why they choose not to participate (Hay 2007). While some might be political dropouts others might be political protestors (Milner 2005). Dropouts can be characterised as those people who do not participate because they are generally apathetic and uninformed, whereas protestors are politically knowledgeable people that consciously choose not to participate in conventional politics for any of a number of reasons, and may turn to unconventional forms of participation. Historically, political participation emerged from the need to make compelling decisions about how to organise society. It appears mistaken to place the blame for declining levels of participation squarely on atomised individuals existing in a vacuum. Rather, it seems that what drives citizens to participate cannot be captured in terms of static individual characteristics, but should rather be understood as flowing from the dynamic interaction of individuals and their wider institutional and political contexts. Franklin (2004: 179) discusses the depressing effect of globalisation on turnout since "a globalised world in which governments surrender powers to bodies such as the WTO is also a world in which elections are less meaningful as vehicles for achieving or blocking policy change". As the world changes, so does the social significance of different means of participation and their perceived effectiveness for influencing political outcomes on the part of citizens. In a world where governments surrender more and more powers to external bodies, political participation relating to the selection of representatives could start to appear increasingly ineffective as a means for social change.

Against the idea that it is individual-level influences that are driving falling turnout, a different type of explanation argues that what matters are changes in political context (Heath and Taylor 1999). Evidence for these arguments is generally adduced by reference to the declining ideological differences between parties and coalitions competing for power in advanced Western democracies (Gray and Kittilson 2005; Mair 2000; Pattie and Johnston 2001; Poguntke 2002; Rogers 2005). Some have argued that narrowing party or coalition differences lead voters to feel indifferent (Bara 2006; Bara and Budge 2001). Mair (2006: 25) argues that what is driving declining political engagement are the "twin processes of popular and elite withdrawal from mass electoral politics" with particular reference to the transformation of political parties. This process can be understood as largely self-reinforcing at the individual level: as politicians retreat from civil society, democratic citizens feel that politics has increasingly less bearing on their lives (Gray and Kittilson 2005; Mair, 2006; Pattie and Johnston,

2001). Through party politics, participation had a specific contextual significance. It was about advancing the interests of specific groups (traditionally, classes) in society. Mair (2006) shows how the decline of parties leads to the hollowing out of democratic sovereignty, since parties have traditionally acted as the drivers of the conflict of ideas in democratic government. He reminds us of Schattschneider's (1942: 1) classical argument that democracy was unthinkable without parties:

> Political parties created democracy and ... modern democracy is unthinkable save in terms of parties.... The parties are not therefore merely appendages of modern government; they are in the centre of it and play a determinative and creative role in it.

As organisations that reflected specific and well-delineated interests within society, traditional mass parties were immersed in a complex network of trade unions, churches, business associations, mutual societies and social clubs in civil society (Johnston 2006; Walsh *et al.* 2004). Mass parties were rooted in society, whilst their electorates were relatively stable and easy to distinguish (De Sio 2006; Evans and Andersen 2004). Over the past few decades, however, these broader networks have largely disintegrated across Western Europe with the increasing individualisation of society, traditional collective identities and organisations have weakened (Beck 1994; Beck and Beck-Gernsheim 2001; Clarke and Stewart 1998; Giddens 2000; Piven and Cloward 2000). While parties were usually understood to integrate and mobilise the citizenry (to articulate collective interests, translate them into public policy and organise the institutions of government) they now instead focus on the procedural aspects of democracy (Rogers 2005). The weakening of the role of parties implies that we are increasingly moving toward a situation where neither elections nor the struggle between parties, and by extension, politics, are seen to be very important (Mair 2006: 32). Politicians are seen as so distant, so removed from the real concerns of 'the people' to lose any relevance. As Pitkin (2004: 339) argues:

> The representatives act not as agents of the people but simply instead of them.... They are professionals, entrenched in office and in party structures. Immersed in a distinct culture of their own, surrounded by other specialists and insulated from the ordinary realities of constituents' lives.

As such, "they live not just physically but also mentally 'inside the beltway'" (Pitkin 2004: 339).

The structure of the book

The book is structured as follows. First we focus on political participation as a multi-dimensional concept (Chapter 2). Next we examine generations and their role for social change (Chapter 3). In Chapter 4 we consider over-time change in political participation in Western Europe for a number of different types of activities. We show that there is considerable diversity by country, time period and indicator. In particular, we analyse whether survey evidence shows that people are participating less in 'conventional' forms of participation and more in 'unconventional' modes, and whether there are any important cross-national differences.

These results lay the groundwork for dealing with the more fundamental question of whether there are generational differences in conventional participation in the direction postulated by prominent theories and what might explain these, by conducting country-by-country analyses (Chapter 5). Next, we examine generational differences in 'unconventional' participation, again by conducting country-by-country analyses (Chapter 6). In the last empirical chapter, findings from the country-by-country analyses in Chapter 5 and 6 are generalised for the whole of Western Europe (Chapter 7). The results show that once more the baby-boomers are very active in protests such as demonstrations and occupations and also activism in new social movements as well as consumer-politics such as boycotts. Taken as a whole, the evidence presented shows that formative experiences matter: the baby-boomers, coming of age in the radicalising period of the late 1960s and 1970s, stand out as 'the protest generation'.

In the final chapter (Chapter 8), a discussion of the results and their implications for the future of political participation as well as for future research in political participation is presented. Crucially, the fact that the baby-boom generation was so large, and that the key works predicting an intergenerational shift in political participation emerged when this cohort was still young, seems to have led scholars to confuse the distinctive political participatory proclivities of 'the protest generation' with an emerging societal trend, one that would be extended and expanded by each successive younger cohort. The results of this study challenge this conclusion and show instead that unless a new 'protest generation' emerges, unconventional participation will also begin to decline as the baby-boomers come to be replaced by less active cohorts in the population.

References

Almond, G. and S. Verba (1963). *The Civic Culture: Political Attitudes and Democracy in Five Nations*. London, Sage.

Bara, J. (2006). Do Parties Reflect Public Concerns? *Democratic Politics and Party Competition*. J. Bara and A. Weale. London, Routledge.

Bara, J. and I. Budge (2001). "Party Policy and Ideology: Still New Labour?" *Parliamentary Affairs* 54: 590–606.

Barber, B. (1984). *Strong Democracy: Participatory Politics for a New Age*. Berkeley, University of California Press.

Beck, U. (1994). The Reinvention of Politics: Towards a Theory of Reflexive Modernisation. *Reflexive Modernisation: Politics, Tradition, and Aesthetics in the Modern Social Order*. U. Beck, A. Giddens and S. Lash. Cambridge, Polity.

Beck, U. and E. Beck-Gernsheim (2001). *Individualisation: Institutionalised Individualism and its Social and Political Consequences*. London, Sage.

Berelson, B., P. Lazarsfeld and W. McPhee (1954). *Voting: A Study of Opinion Formation in a Presidential Campaign*. Chicago, University of Chicago Press.

Boechel, R. (1928). *Voting and Non-Voting in Elections*. Washington, DC, Editorial Research Reports.

Butler, D. and D. Stokes (1969). *Political Change in Britain: Forces Shaping Electoral Choice*. New York, St Martin's Press.

Clarke, H. and M. Stewart (1998). "The Decline of Parties in the Minds of Citizens". *Annual Review of Political Science* 1: 357–78.

De Sio, L. (2006). Political Involvement and Electoral Competition. *Center for the Study of Democracy*, University of California, Irvine.

Della Porta, D. and M. Diani (2006). *Social Movements: An Introduction, 2nd Edition*. Oxford, Blackwell.

Evans, G. and R. Andersen (2004). "Do Issues Decide? Partisan Conditioning and Perceptions of Party Issue Positions across the Electoral Cycle". *British Elections and Parties Review* 14: 18–39.

Franklin, M. N. (2004). *Voter Turnout and the Dynamics of Electoral Competition in Established Democracies since 1945*. Cambridge, Cambridge University Press.

Furedi, F. (2005). *The Politics of Fear: Beyond Left and Right*. London, Continuum.

Giddens, A. (2000). *The Third Way and Its Critics*. Cambridge, Polity.

Giugni, M. G. and M. T. Grasso (2015). Environmental Movements in Advanced Industrial Democracies: Heterogeneity, Transformation, and Institutionalization. *Annual Review of Environment and Resources*, 40: 337–361.

Gosnell, H. (1927). Getting Out the Vote: An Experiment in the Simulation of Voting. Chicago, Chicago University Press.

Grasso, M. T. (2011). *Political Participation in Western Europe*. Nuffield College, University of Oxford. D. Phil. Thesis.

Grasso, M. T. (2013a). The Differential Impact of Education on Young People's Political Activism: Comparing Italy and the United Kingdom. *Comparative Sociology*, 12: 1–30.

Grasso, M. T. (2013b). "What Are the Distinguishing Generational, Life Course, and Historical Drivers of Changing Identities? Future Identities: Changing Identities in the UK – The Next 10 Years". *Foresight: The Future of Identity in the UK*. London, The Government Office for Science.

Grasso, M. T. (2014). "Age-Period-Cohort Analysis in a Comparative Context: Political Generations and Political Participation Repertoires". *Electoral Studies* 33: 63–76.

Grasso, M. T. (2016). Political Participation. *Developments in British Politics 10*. R. Heffernan, P. Cowley and C. Hay, Eds. Basingstoke, Palgrave Macmillan.

Grasso, M. T. and M. Giugni (2013). Anti-austerity movements: Old wine in new vessels? Working Paper, XXVII Meeting of the Italian Political Science Association (SISP), University of Florence. Florence, September 12–14.

Grasso, M. T. and M. Giugni (2015). Are Anti-Austerity Movements Old or New? In: Giugni, M. G. and Grasso, M. T., Eds. *Austerity and Protest: Popular Contention in Times of Economic Crisis*. Farnham, Surrey Ashgate.

Grasso, M. T. and M. Giugni (2016). "Do Issues Matter? Anti-Austerity Protests' Composition, Values, and Action Repertoires Compared". *Research in Social Movements, Conflicts and Change* 39.

Gray, M. and M. Kittilson (2005). Feeling Left Out by the Left? Left Party Economic Performance and Voter Turnout in Comparative Perspective, 1950 to 2000. *American Political Science Association*. Washington, DC.

Habermas, J. (1975). *Legitimation Crisis*. Boston, Beacon Press.

Hay, C. (2007). *Why We Hate Politics*. Cambridge, Polity Press.

Heath, A. and B. Taylor (1999). New Sources of Abstention? *Critical Elections: British Parties and Elections in Long-Term Perspective*. G. Evans and P. Norris. London, Sage.

Johnston, R. (2006). "Party Identification: Unmoved Mover or Sum of Preferences?" *Annual Review of Political Science* 9: 329–51.

Laclau, E. and C. Mouffe (1985). *Hegemony and Socialist Strategy: Towards a Radical Democratic Politics*. London, Verso.

Mair, P. (2000). "Partyless Democracy: Solving the Paradox of New Labour?" *New Left Review* 2: 21–35.

Mair, P. (2006). "Ruling the Void? The Hollowing of Western Democracy". *New Left Review* 42: 25–51.

Marx, K. (1852). *The Eighteenth Brumaire of Louis Bonaparte*. London: Lawrence and Wishart.

Merriam, C. and H. Gosnell (1924). *Non-Voting*. Chicago, University of Chicago Press.

Mill, J. S. (1861). *On Liberty*. London, Random House.

Milner, H. (2005). "Are Young Canadians Becoming Political Dropouts? A Comparative Perspective". *IRRP Choices* 11(3): 1–26.

Mouffe, C. (2000). Deliberative Democracy or Agonistic Pluralism. *Political Science Series*. G. Hafner. Vienna Institute for Advanced Studies 72.

Norris, P., Ed. (1999). *Critical Citizens: Global Support for Democratic Governance*. Oxford, Oxford University Press.

Norris, P. (2002). *Democratic Phoenix: Reinventing Political Activism*. Cambridge, MA, Cambridge University Press.

Patterson, T. (2002). *The Vanishing Voter: Public Involvement in an Age of Uncertainty*. New York, Knopf.

Pattie, C. and R. Johnston (2001). "A Low Turnout Landslide: Abstention in the General Election of 1997". *Political Studies* 49: 286–305.

Pattie, C., P. Seyd and P. Whiteley (2004). *Citizenship in Britain: Values, Participation and Democracy*. Cambridge, Cambridge University Press.

Pickerell, J. (2003). *Cyberprotest: Environmental Activism Online*. Manchester, Manchester University Press.

Pitkin, H. (2004). "Representation and Democracy: Uneasy Alliance". *Scandinavian Political Studies* 27(3): 335–42.

Piven, F. and R. Cloward (2000). *Why Americans Still Don't Vote: and Why Politicians Want it That Way*. Boston, Beacon Press.

Poguntke, T. (2002). Parties Without Firm Social Roots? *Keele European Parties Research Unit Working Paper* 13: 1–31.

Rogers, B. (2005). "From Membership to Management? The Future of Political Parties as Democratic Organisations". *Parliamentary Affairs* 58(3): 600–10.

Rosema, M. (2006). "Low Turnout: Threat to Democracy or Blessing in Disguise? Consequences of Citizens' Varying Tendencies to Vote". *Electoral Studies* XX: 1–12.

Schattschneider, E. (1942). *Party Government*. New York, Greenwood Press.

Schumpeter, J. A. (1952). *Capitalism, Socialism and Democracy*. London, Allen and Unwin.

Tingsten, H. (1937). *Political Behaviour*. London, King and Son.

Van Deth, J. W. (1986). "A Note on Measuring Political Participation in Comparative Research". *Quality and Quantity* 120: 261–72.

Van Deth, J. W. and M. Elff (2000). Political Involvement and Apathy in Europe 1973–1998. *Mannheimer Zentrum für Europäische Sozialforschung Working Paper* 33: 1–47.

Walsh, K., M. Jennings and L. Stoker (2004). "The Effects of Social Class Identification on Participatory Orientations Towards Government". *British Journal of Political Science* 34: 469–95.

Wattenberg, M. (2002). *Where Have All the Voters Gone?* Cambridge, MA, Harvard University Press.

2 Studying political participation in Western Europe

This chapter focuses on some of the key issues in research on political participation. In particular it looks at questions of definition and measurement of political participation in Western Europe.

Definitions and the expanding domain of participation

In this study, political participation is taken to consist in activities – including joining a political organisation – that are enacted specifically to influence the political decision-making processes on some level or other. This therefore includes attempting to influence the activity of government and the selection of officials, trying to affect the values and preferences which guide the political decision-making process, and seeking to include new issues on the agenda (Morales 2009: 57–8). Nearly all definitions of political participation include four basic concepts: "actions by ordinary citizens directed toward influencing some political outcomes" (Brady 1999: 737). In the classic definition, Verba and Nie (1972: 72) define political participation as "those activities by private citizens that are more or less directly aimed at influencing the selection of governmental personnel and/or the actions they take". Meanwhile, Kaase and Marsh (1979: 42) define political participation as "all voluntary activities by individual citizens intended to influence either directly or indirectly political choices at various levels of the political system". Parry *et al.* (1992: 16) hold that participation includes "actions by citizens which are aimed at influencing decisions which are, in most cases, ultimately taken by public representatives and officials". For Clarke *et al.* (2004: 219), participation is "a voluntary activity done by an individual acting alone or with others ... a means by which citizens express their political attitudes, beliefs and opinions", and that which "requires resources or skills, conveys information to public officials, and is purposive, that is, it attempts to achieve goals or implement policies".

Definitions of political participation therefore include some element of action, however, the category can be ambiguous. For example, in their seminal study, Almond and Verba (1963) treated political discussion as one of many forms of political participation. Similarly, Barnes and Kaase (1979) grouped political discussion under the heading of 'political participation', together with reading about politics and working with parties and voluntary organisations.

Verba *et al.* (1978: 46) further posited an important distinction between: (1) political interest, measured through subjective reported levels, or via indirect utterances in terms of political discussion, and (2) political participation proper, or those activities directed at influencing the processes of government. Therefore, political involvement comprises two related but distinct dimensions. On the one hand lies political participation, constituted by those activities that supplement the established democratic representative process. On the other hand lies political interest, "the degree to which politics arouses a citizen's curiosity" (Van Deth 1990: 278), understood in terms of subjective political interest (Van Deth and Elff 2000: 2).

Verba *et al.* (1995: 39) stress that they "focus on activity: we are concerned with doing politics, rather than with being attentive to politics". I follow Brady (1999) and Verba *et al.* (1995) in focusing specifically on doing politics. This is as opposed to being attentive to politics, which I take frequency of political discussion to indicate; more so, since frequency of political discussion is often used as an indirect measure of political interest. As such, this indicator is not included in the analyses of political participation.

Amongst the many activities that political participation includes, since the mid-to-late 1960s, researchers have increasingly tended to contrast more 'orthodox' or 'conventional' political participation, such as voting, party membership and contacting politicians, with what they see as more 'unorthodox' or 'unconventional' involvement, "such as protests, demonstrations, marches and even 'terrorist' violence" (Evans 2003: 83). Early studies instead generally understood participation as a uni-dimensional phenomenon, though they also recognised some problems with this approach (Milbrath 1965). In contrast, more recent studies tend to draw multidimensional distinctions (Verba *et al.* 1978). The most significant development in the conceptualisation of political participation is thus seen in the growth of protest movements since the mid-to-late 1960s, which drew specific attention to the distinction between 'conventional' and 'unconventional' political participation (Barnes and Kaase 1979). The two forms of participation were not seen as necessarily mutually exclusive; rather, authors concluded that the two types were complementary and cumulative (Barnes and Kaase 1979: 149–52). Recently, scholars have also considered civic participation, particularly in respect to theories of 'social capital' (Hall 1999; Putnam 1993, 2000). Van Deth (2001: 2) clearly elucidates the expansion of the realm of political participation:

> starting with a strong focus on voting and electoral participation in the 1940s and 1950s, by now the repertoire of gaining influence includes such activities as casting a vote, visiting the burgomaster, signing petitions, donating money, or fighting with the police.

Not only has the repertoire expanded, but:

> Since the scope of government activities and responsibilities has been expanded too in the last few decades, the domain of political participation

grew considerably. The combined increase in both the repertoire and the domain of political participation implies that these activities affect virtually all aspects of social life in advanced societies.

(Van Deth 2001: 2)

In other words: "the study of political participation has become the study of everything" (Van Deth 2001: 2).

The issue of what counts as political participation is particularly important when examining participation in associations. Morales (2009: 48) argues that

> 'social' or non-political associations are ... either those that pursue private goods (sports associations, religious associations, many youth associations, etc.) or those which, while pursuing public goods, do not primarily aim at influencing the public arena (health-care associations, artistic cultural associations, etc.).

On the other hand, political organisations are defined as groups that are formally organised

> that seek collective goods ... and which have as their main goal to influence political decision-making processes, either by trying to influence the selection of government personnel or their activities, to include issues on the agenda, or to change the values and preferences which guide the decision making process.

(Morales 2009: 47–8)

Here we follow Morales (2009: 52–3), alongside the classic works of Olson (1965) and Wilson (1974), in examining union membership as a form of political participation in Chapter 4. While it is true that

> several studies have shown that Scandinavian unions, in particular, are organisations with little political activity ... there can be little doubt that ... trade unions ... (i) fundamentally pursue collective goods and (ii) have as one of their main objectives the influencing of political decision-making.

(Morales 2009: 52)

Moreover, Dekker *et al.* (1997) make the important point that excluding strikes and union membership from cross-national studies of political participation underestimates working class political activism, and this would be particularly true in countries with strong left-wing subcultures such as Italy, Spain, Portugal and France (Sperber 2009).

In defining more specifically what it means to participate in political associations, this study follows the distinction made in the literature between 'old' or 'traditional' and 'new' memberships of organisations (Dekker *et al.* 1997; Morales 2009). On this reading, participation in 'old' political associations is understood as a form of 'conventional' political participation, whereas participation in 'new' political associations is a form of 'unconventional' political participation. However, this research does not construct repertoire scales. Consequently, the theoretical distinction is subjected to critical scrutiny in the empirical chapters. Further, 'old' and 'new' organisations have been differentiated by several criteria in the literature: ideology (distributive versus libertarian values), logics of participation (instrumental versus expressive), organisational structures (centralised versus decentralised) and the types of repertoires associated with them (conventional versus unconventional participation). However, this research concurs with Morales (2009: 26–7) that these criteria "are not particularly useful when establishing a criterion for classifying specific organisations into the categories of 'new' or 'traditional'". Instead, here we follow Morales' (2009: 27–8) criterion for distinguishing 'old' and 'new' organisations based on the nature of the representative link between those organisations and the wider society: (1) 'new' political organisations are characterised by the

> lack of a representative link with specific sectors of the population … they do not run for elections and they cannot claim representative mandates for any subset of citizens … the issues they stand for are universalist in their aims: … environmental, peace or human rights organisations … are not claiming to represent a … constituency;

(2) 'old' political organisations (political parties, unions) on the other hand "are the political actors *par excellence* in the representation of the interests and demands of specific sectors of society … political parties represent their voters, unions represent the workers who vote for them".

In a similar way, Kriesi (1996: 152–4) also distinguishes between social movement organisations (SMOs) on the one hand and traditional political organisations on the other. Developing the understanding of political memberships as a "specific form of political participation", Morales (2009: 29) notes that participation in a political association could imply "militancy, activism" but also that "it is not essential to be particularly active in a political association in order to be a political participant: merely joining or paying fees supports the organisation in its attempt to influence the political process". This means that being a member of a party, or of an environmental or other 'new' politics organisation, fulfils the criteria of political action (Brady 1999: 737).

Barnes and Kaase (1979) classically understood conventional political participation as being both 'traditional' and 'institutionalised', whereas they see unconventional political participation as 'extra-institutional' or as some type of 'direct political action'. On this reading, it would seem that all memberships should count as conventional participation. However, if we understand 'extra-institutional' as meaning unrelated to the traditional organs of representation such as parties and trade unions, and as such, lacking a representative link with specific sectors of the population, then belonging to or doing unpaid work for environmental or third world development organisations, can be seen as fitting into the 'unconventional' or 'new' category. Hence, when levels of conventional and unconventional participation are analysed over time in Chapter 4, the theoretical subdivision is employed between 'conventional' or 'traditional' political participation (voting, contacting a politician, joining a party, joining a labour union, doing unpaid voluntary work for a political party or a political group, doing unpaid voluntary work for a union) and 'unconventional' or 'new' political participation (signing a petition, joining a boycott, joining an environmental organisation, joining a development organisation, doing unpaid voluntary work for an environmental organisation, doing unpaid work for a development organisation, attending a demonstration, occupying buildings or factories, joining an unofficial strike). Moreover, since we are interested in testing whether over-time patterns for different indicators and cohort differences in participation follow those suggested in the literature, analyses are conducted indicator by indicator avoiding the construction of scales (Grasso 2014). Therefore, this subdivision remains open to empirical scrutiny in this study. Only indicators for new social movement participation are combined in Chapters 6–7; they are kept separate in Chapter 4 where we examine over-time trends.

Categorisations of political participation

There are multiple categorisations of participation in the literature that resemble the 'conventional'/'unconventional' distinction (Grasso 2016). Inglehart (1990) proposes what is perhaps the most comprehensive categorisation in distinguishing between (1) *elite-directed activities:* voting, party membership, other party-mediated activities, union membership and (2) *elite-directing activities:* political discussion, participation in new social movements and protest activities such as demonstrations, boycotts, signing petitions, occupations, unofficial strikes, etc. (Inglehart 1990: 335–6). In later work, he uses the term *elite-challenging* (Inglehart and Catterberg 2002) instead of *elite-directing*, and political discussion is no longer referred to in this work. As such, here *elite-challenging activities* is taken to designate all the activities mentioned above with the exclusion of political discussion. In this study, the conventional-unconventional, formal-informal and institutional-extra-institutional distinctions are understood as mapping onto the elite-directed-elite-challenging distinction, and the terms are used interchangeably, since the activities included in these repertoires are the same.

Other than the conventional-unconventional dichotomy, the literature also distinguishes between activities that are done with others, and those activities that one does on one's own (Milbrath 1965; Verba *et al.* 1978). Activities that can be done on one's own are known as 'individualised' (voting, contacting a politician, signing a petition, joining a boycott), and 'social' those activities which one does in conjunction with others (working for a party, working for a union, working for an environmental organisation, working for a development or human rights organisation, demonstrating, occupying buildings or factories, and joining an unofficial strike); membership, or joining political organisations, however, do not clearly fit in either grouping since these could be social or individualised (joining a party, a union, an environmental or a third world development or human rights organisation).

Table 2.1 shows how the indicators under analysis in this study subdivide based on both the conventional/unconventional and individualised/social/membership dimensions. Voting and contacting a politician are conventional-individualised activities (only available in the ESS); signing a petition, joining a boycott are unconventional-individualised activities (available in both the EVS and ESS); working for a party and working for a union are conventional-social activities (the former is available in both surveys, the latter only in the EVS); demonstrating, occupying, joining an unofficial strike, working for an environmental organisation or for a development or humanitarian organisation are unconventional-social activities (only demonstrating is available in both surveys, the other indicators are only available in the EVS); as for the memberships, they are divided into 'old' and 'new' (party and union membership are available in both surveys, but new memberships are only in the EVS), as explained above.

Table 2.1 Indicators of political participation in the EVS and ESS by type

	Individualised actions	*Social political actions*	*Memberships*
'Conventional' or 'traditional', or 'elite-directed'	• Voting • Contacting a politician	• **Working for a party** • Working for a union	• **Member of a party** • **Member of a union**
'Unconventional' or 'new', or 'elite-challenging'	• **Signing a petition** • **Joining a boycott**	• **Demonstrating** • Occupying buildings or factories • Joining an unofficial strike • Working for an environmental organisation • Working for a development or human rights organisation	• Member of an environmental organisation • Member of a development or human rights organisation

Notes
Indicators marked in **bold** are available in both the EVS 1981, 1990 and 1999 *and* ESS 2002, 2004 and 2006 surveys.

This table only includes indicators of political participation available in EVS 1981, 1990 *and* 1999. The 1981 EVS also includes E030 'damaging things, breaking windows, street violence' and E031 'personal violence'. The 1990 and 1999 EVS also include indicators for belonging and unpaid voluntary work in other 'new' organisations: women's groups (A075, A092) and the peace movement (A076, A093).

This table only includes indicators of political participation available in ESS 2002, 2004 *and* 2006. The ESS 2002 also includes other types of activities, such deliberately buying products for political, ethical or environmental reasons, and other memberships, e.g. 'environmental, protection, peace and animal rights'.

Measuring political participation

Comparative research into participation faces many challenges. After the initial problem of defining what should count as political participation, one must decide how to measure it. Any study that relies on survey analysis must also deal with the practical restriction of what data are available for the different types of participation. This is a particular issue when examining both conventional and unconventional political participation side by side. Above we defined political participation as those activities, including participation in political associations, which are enacted to influence the political decision-making processes on some level. This includes attempting to influence the activity of government and the selection of officials, trying to affect the values and preferences which guide the political decision-making process and attempting to include new issues on the agenda (Morales 2009: 47–8). This study also agreed with Morales' (2009: 29) argument that participation in political associations is a specific type of political participation and that it can be distinguished into 'conventional' or 'traditional' and 'unconventional' or 'new' types. Following Morales (2009: 29), this research also holds that while participation in political associations could imply "militancy, activism", that nevertheless "it is not essential to be particularly active in a political association in order to be a political participant: merely joining or paying fees supports the organisation in its attempt to influence the political process". This means that being a member of a party, a member of a union or of an environmental, development or human rights or other 'new' politics organisation, are understood here to fulfil the criteria of political action (Brady 1999: 737). As such, they will be included in the set of indicators of political participation.

Party membership is the key indicator of conventional participation in this study. Many studies include membership in political associations as an indicator of participation (e.g. Dekker *et al.* 1997; Morales 2009; Norris 2002). Using survey data implies that we define membership of a political organisation based on what survey respondents say about themselves. An alternative would be to use organisation registers. However, this is not helpful if one wishes to conduct individual-level analyses of participants. We do use data from official party membership rolls in Chapter 4 to compare results and show that there are some differences between these estimates (Mair and Van Biezen 2001) and those from the EVS data. This could be due to the slightly different time frames analysed or other issues discussed below. A further problem could be that conceptions of what makes a party member or an activist vary cross-nationally (Morales 2009). For example, in some countries people may equate party membership simply with feelings of party attachment or commitment. This also applies to other types of organisations: for many people, simply paying a fee makes them a member, whereas for others this is not an important sign of commitment. Jordan and Maloney (1997) discuss 'chequebook activism', which describes a process where organisations conduct campaigns through an activist minority whilst the majority of 'members' simply pay fees in support of the cause. Despite these limitations, survey data make it possible to conduct individual-level analyses to examine who joins political organisations. More specifically, it makes it possible to examine whether the youngest cohorts are the least likely to join traditional organisations and more likely to join 'new' organisations. In turn, this facilitates analyses of social change. Hence, while aggregate data sources exist for measuring levels of party membership and turnout, and these are considered in Chapter 4 which examines patterns of activism, survey data are the only focus of Chapters 5–7 where the individual-level analyses are conducted.

When considering other forms of participation, and particularly individualised forms of participation such as boycotting a certain product for ethical or political reasons, surveys are the only available source of data for examining the characteristics of participants, and as such key to analysing the bases of social change. Throughout this study, and following Brady (1999: 737), participants are identified as those who have said that they have actually participated in a specific activity. This includes those who report that they are members of – or in other words, participate in – a specific political organisation. This is because we are interested in who participated in a specific activity, and more generally, in patterns of participation by type of activity. In this study, we do not, like other authors, include action potential questions or treat these action potential answer options for participation questions as approximating a continuous variable ranging from 1 'would never do', through 2 'might do', to 3 'have done'. All the dependent variables in this study are dichotomous – in other words they distinguish between those that participated and those that did not. We also do not construct combined measures of participation including several different actions, except for NSM participation.

Political participation in Western Europe

This study investigates political participation in Western Europe. As such, it consciously applies a research design of the 'most similar' systems. The ten Western European countries included in the analyses are Belgium, Denmark, France, Germany (West, in the EVS), Great Britain, Ireland, Italy, the Netherlands, Spain and Sweden. All share broadly similar political systems and sociohistorical legacies. With the exception of Spain – where Franco's regime persisted until 1975 – the other nine Western European countries have been democracies at least since the end of WWII. Moreover, all these countries have been exposed to similar economic, political and social processes and have been economically, politically and culturally interdependent throughout the last century (Morales 2009: 34). They have similar political systems, and during the period covered by the surveys (1981–2006) equally provided their citizens with political rights. They are 'post-industrial' democracies (cf. Inglehart 1990; Inglehart and Catterberg 2002; Norris 2002), and so share the degree of economic development. As such, levels of participation, individual-level sources of variation and the meanings of participation are broadly equivalent (Morales 2009: 35). Whereas my research design is one of the 'most similar' systems, studies which instead include many different countries must assume that the meaning of different forms of participation is the same in varied cross-national contexts

(Morales 2009: 35), and further face the difficulty of distinguishing between different country types. Norris (2002: 11), who employs a research design of the 'most different' systems, faces the problem of having to classify types of nations into "post-industrial societies", "other highly developed nations", "older democracies", "newer democracies", and so on. Moreover, the different types of participation analysed in this study are all available to citizens in these countries. These broad similarities allow me to assess more accurately the causes for variation and, in particular, by selecting a group of countries with relatively similar historical trajectories, to focus on intergenerational differences in participation without introducing too much 'noise' from other variables.

Indeed, since one of the purposes of this study is to understand social change processes driving declining participation, it is particularly important that the histories of the various countries, and therefore the generational experiences of the same cohorts in different countries (as discussed in more detail in the next chapter), be broadly similar. Previous empirical research has shown that political variables have diverging implications in ex-Soviet nations due to different socio-historical legacies and, in particular, the experience of communism in the second half of the twentieth century. As such, restricting the analysis to Western European democracies allows for participation in the different activities to be broadly equivalent across countries and eases the comparison of results. This also means that the categorisation of cohorts based on the socio-historic context of their formative years is broadly applicable to all the nations under analysis in this study. It is of course understood that this restriction means that the conclusions will only be generalisable for the set of countries included in this study and other nations that are very similar to these.

Individual-level influences and aggregate-level change

The rational choice approach to the study of political participation has historically highlighted the role of individual characteristics. In their seminal work, *Participation in America*, Verba and Nie (1972) found their analysis on the 'baseline model' which, later renamed as the 'resource model', dominated explanations of voter turnout (Parry *et al.* 1992; Verba *et al.* 1995; Wolfinger and Rosenstone 1980). To this was later added the 'mobilisation model' that took into account the role of parties, interest groups and candidates in mobilising people to vote (Rosenstone and Hansen 1993). While the mobilisation model added some important elements for the understanding of individual voting decisions, Franklin (2004: 17) points out a fundamental problem arising from the extension of the idea that resources and mobilisation affect turnout to the idea that turnout depends on the social makeup of society since: "quite large changes in the structure of the population do not necessarily have important effects on turnout in established democracies". His argument is, instead, that

> turnout appears to vary because of variations in the character or elections, not because of variations in the character of society (except for its age

structure), and individual-level relationships between voting and social characteristics are conditioned by the level of turnout rather than the other way
round.

(Franklin 2004: 206)

Turnout started declining in many countries during the 1960s, precisely when
"most countries [saw] a huge expansion of secondary and tertiary education",
these "anomalies" "call into question the causal primacy of education in determining turnout (Brody 1978) – a primacy established firmly at the individual
level" (Franklin 2004: 19).

Despite this, a prominent narrative on declining voter turnout and other forms of
conventional participation has been to understand them as a manifestation of public
disillusionment and mistrust in the political system (Levi and Stoker 2000). Survey
evidence showing high levels of dissatisfaction with the way democracy works;
increasing public cynicism towards politicians (Grasso 2011); low opinions of
Members of Parliament; low trust in politicians; the widespread belief that the
British government places party interests above the national interest have been
used to support this conclusion (Curtice and Jowell 1997). Furthermore, building
on this, a number of explanations have been offered in the literature for why voters
may have become more cynical about formal party politics. One of these is that
society has become more individualistic thus leading to the erosion of collective
duties such as voting, especially amongst the young (Clarke *et al.* 2004). Another
is that as education levels have risen, so have public expectations on government
while the latter's capacities to deliver have remained the same, leading the public
to become cynical of what can be achieved through politics (Dalton 2004).

Resources, attitudes and cross-national differences in participation

Alongside age, gender and education have historically been identified as
important socio-economic predictors of political participation (Almond and
Verba 1963; Inglehart 1990; Milbrath 1965). As politics has historically been the
domain of men, the literature argues that political interest and participation
should be affected by gender roles (Almond and Verba 1963; Berelson *et al.*
1954; Verba *et al.* 1978). However, others have argued that with the growing
liberalisation of gender roles, the gender differences for political involvement
should attenuate, and more so amongst the young (Inglehart 1990; Van Deth and
Elff 2000). Additionally, since Almond and Verba (1963), survey evidence has
generally confirmed that education is linked to a citizen's level of political
knowledge, interest and sophistication (Milbrath 1965; Van Deth and Elff 2000)
and the better educated have been found to be more likely to have the time,
money, access to political information, knowledge and ability to become politically
involved (Grasso 2013; Dalton 2008; Parry *et al.* 1992; Verba and Nie 1972).

The literature identifies two other kinds of predictors of political participation: group effects and political attitudes (Dalton 2008). In the first group, party

attachment and membership in voluntary organisations represent possible influences on participation (Dalton 2008: 55). For example, party attachment can promote party membership and party work as well as stimulate to action because of group-based partisan forces in elections. Moreover, it has historically been argued that membership in voluntary organisations offers the opportunity to develop skills which play a key role in prompting more overtly political participation (Clark 2001; Olsen 1972; Verba and Nie 1972) as well as providing a useful heuristic for determining whether participation in political activities is worthwhile (Uhlaner 1989). However, Theiss-Morse and Hibbing (2005) find that membership in non-political voluntary associations does not lead to overt political participation. In the second group, ideological identification, satisfaction with the way democracy works in one's country and other political values may help explain variations in levels of political involvement (Dalton 2008; Van Deth 2000; Van Deth and Elff 2000). While dissatisfaction with the way democracy works in one's country has been said to influence participation patterns (Farah 1979) its causal role is debated in the literature. Some argue that satisfaction increases support for the political process and thereby participation, whereas others suggest that dissatisfaction might stimulate efforts for change (the social deprivation hypothesis) (Dalton 2008: 77). Indeed, both these theories may be correct but only apply to certain forms of participation. Additionally, the literature also discusses the role of ideological differences (Verba *et al.* 1978; Verba *et al.* 1995), with the general argument being that if participation influences the law-making processes, then the question of whether activists are drawn equally from different political camps has implications for democracy (Dalton 2008: 56).

Cross-national differences in political involvement have been found to persist even when controlling for the relevant socio-economic factors (Inglehart 1990: 352). One possible explanation is that cultural attitudes vary systematically in different national contexts (Westholm and Niemi 1992). Social movement scholars have traditionally emphasised cross-national differences in opportunity structures (Kriesi and Wisler 1996).

Conclusions

This chapter has drawn out the key themes to help contextualise the analyses in the main empirical chapters (4–7) and provided a theoretical backdrop for discussing the implications and significance of the results. In the next chapter, I move to discussing generations and social change, age groups and cohort classifications, based on theory, that allow for dealing with the identification problem.

References

Almond, G. and S. Verba (1963). *The Civic Culture: Political Attitudes and Democracy in Five Nations*. London, Sage.
Barnes, S. and M. Kaase (1979). *Political Action: Mass Participation in Five Western Societies*. Thousand Oaks, CA, Sage.

Berelson, B., P. Lazarsfeld and W. McPhee (1954). *Voting: A Study of Opinion Formation in a Presidential Campaign*. Chicago, University of Chicago Press.

Brady, H. (1999). Political Participation. *Measures of Political Attitudes*. J. Robinson, P. Shaver and L. Wrightsman. Burlington, VA, Academic Press.

Brody, R. (1978). The Puzzle of Political Participation in America. *The New American Political System*. A. King. Washington, DC, American Enterprise Institute: 287–324.

Clark, W. (2001). *Activism in the Public Sphere: Exploring the Discourse of Political Participation*. Ashgate, Aldershot.

Clarke, H., D. Sanders, M. Stewart and P. Whiteley (2004). *Political Choice in Britain*. Oxford, Oxford University Press.

Curtice, J. and R. Jowell (1997). Trust in the Political System. *British Social Attitudes: the 14th Report. The End of Conservative Values?* R. Jowell, J. Curtice, A. Park and L. Brook. Ashgate, Aldershot.

Dalton, R. (2004). *Democratic Challenges, Democratic Choices*. Oxford, Oxford University Press.

Dalton, R. (2008). *Citizen Politics: Public Opinion and Political Parties in Advanced Industrial Democracies*. Washington, DC, CQ Press.

Dekker, P., R. Koopmans and A. van den Broek (1997). Voluntary Associations, Social Movements and Individual Political Behaviour in Western Europe. *Private Groups and Public Life: Social Participation and Political Involvement in Representative Democracies*. J. Van Deth. Abingdon, Routledge.

Evans, G. (2003). Political Culture and Voting Participation. *Developments in British Politics 7*. P. Dunleavy, A. Gamble, R. Heffernan and G. Peele. Basingstoke, Palgrave Macmillan.

Farah, B. (1979). Political Dissatisfaction. *Political Action: Mass Participation in Five Western Democracies*. Barnes and Kaase. Beverly Hills, CA, Sage.

Franklin, M. N. (2004). *Voter Turnout and the Dynamics of Electoral Competition in Established Democracies since 1945*. Cambridge, Cambridge University Press.

Grasso, M. T. (2011) [with the assistance of J. Rose and the Committee's Research Advisory Board]. Survey of Public Attitudes Towards Conduct in Public Life 2010. *Surveys of Public Attitudes Towards Conduct in Public Life*. London, Committee on Standards in Public Life.

Grasso, M. T. (2013). "The Differential Impact of Education on Young People's Political Activism: Comparing Italy and the United Kingdom". *Comparative Sociology* 12: 1–30.

Grasso, M. T. (2014). "Age-Period-Cohort Analysis in a Comparative Context: Political Generations and Political Participation Repertoires". *Electoral Studies* 33: 63–76.

Grasso, M. T. (2016). Political Participation. *Developments in British Politics 10*. R. Heffernan, P. Cowley and C. Hay, Eds. Basingstoke, Palgrave Macmillan.

Hall, P. (1999). "Social Capital in Britain". *British Journal of Political Science* 29: 417–61.

Inglehart, R. (1990). *Culture Shift in Advanced Industrial Society*. Princeton, Princeton University Press.

Inglehart, R. and G. Catterberg (2002). "Trends in Political Action: The Developmental Trend and the Post-Honeymoon Decline". *International Journal of Comparative Sociology* 43: 300–16.

Jordan, G. and W. Maloney (1997). *The Protest Business? Mobilising Campaign Groups*. Manchester, Manchester University Press.

Kaase, M. and A. Marsh (1979). Political Action: A Theoretical Perspective. *Political Action: Mass Participation in Five Western Democracies*. S. Barnes and M. Kaase. Beverly Hills, CA, Sage: 27–56.

Kriesi, H. (1996). The Organizational Structure of New Social Movements in a Political Context. *Comparative Perspectives on Social Movements: Political Opportunities,*

Mobilizing Structures, and Cultural Framings. D. McAdam, J. McCarthy and M. N. Zald. Cambridge, Cambridge University Press.

Kriesi, H. and D. Wisler (1996). "Social Movements and Direct Democracy in Switzerland". *European Journal of Political Research* 30(1): 19–40.

Levi, M. and L. Stoker (2000). "Political Trust and Trustworthiness". *Annual Review of Political Science* 3(1): 475–507.

Mair, P. and I. Van Biezen (2001). "Party Membership in Twenty European Democracies, 1980–2000". *Party Politics* 7(1): 5–21.

Milbrath, L. (1965). *Political Participation: How and Why Do People Get Involved in Politics?* Chicago, Rand McNally College Publishing Company.

Morales, L. (2009). *Joining Political Organisations: Institutions, Mobilisation and Participation in Western Democracies*. Colchester, Essex, ECPR Press.

Norris, P. (2002). *Democratic Phoenix: Reinventing Political Activism*. Cambridge, MA, Cambridge University Press.

Olsen, M. E. (1972). "Social Participation and Voting Turnout: A Multivariate Analysis". *American Sociological Review* 37: 317–33.

Olson, M. (1965). *The Logic of Collective Action*. Cambridge, MA, Harvard University Press.

Parry, G., G. Moyser and N. Day (1992). *Political Participation and Democracy in Britain*. Cambridge, Cambridge University Press.

Putnam, R. (1993). *Making Democracy Work*. Princeton, Princeton University Press.

Putnam, R. (2000). *Bowling Alone: The Collapse and Revival of American Community*. New York, Simon & Schuster.

Rosenstone, S. and J. Hansen (1993). *Mobilization, Participation, and Democracy in America*. New York, Macmillan.

Sperber, N. (2009). "Three Million Trotskyists? Explaining Extreme Left Voting in France in the 2002 Presidential Election". *European Journal of Political Research* 4(3): 359–92.

Theiss-Morse, E. and J. Hibbing (2005). "Citizenship and Civic Engagament". *Annual Review of Political Science* 8: 227–49.

Uhlaner, C. (1989). "Rational Turnout". *American Journal of Political Science* 33: 390–422.

Van Deth, J. (2001). Studying Political Participation: Towards a Theory of Everything? *Joint Sessions Workshops, ECPR*. Grenoble, France, 6–11 April, 2001.

Van Deth, J. W. (1990). Interest in Politics. *Continuities in Political Action: A Longitudinal Study of Political Orientations in Three Western Democracies*. M. Jennings and J. W. Van Deth. Berlin, De Gruyter and Aldine: 275–312.

Van Deth, J. W. (2000). "Interesting but Irrelevant: Social Capital in Western Europe". *European Journal of Political Research* 37: 115–47.

Van Deth, J. W. and M. Elff (2000). Political Involvement and Apathy in Europe 1973–1998. *Mannheimer Zentrum für Europäische Sozialforschung Working Paper* 33: 1–47.

Verba, S. and N. Nie (1972). *Participation in America: Political Democracy and Social Equality*. New York, Harper Row.

Verba, S., N. H. Nie and J. Kim (1978). *Participation and Political Equality*. Cambridge, Cambridge University Press.

Verba, S., K. Schlozman and H. Brady (1995). *Voice and Equality: Civic Voluntarism in American Politics*. Cambridge, MA, Harvard University Press.

Westholm, A. and R. G. Niemi (1992). "Political Institutions and Political Socialization: A Cross-National Study". *Comparative Politics* 25(1): 25–41.

Wilson, J. Q. (1974). *Political Organisations*. Princeton, Princeton University Press.

Wolfinger, R. and S. Rosenstone (1980). *Who Votes?* New Haven, Yale University Press.

3   Generations and social change

This chapter examines the role of generations for social change, particularly in relation to political participation. We discuss the question of age, cohort and period effects and how this relates to making sense of social change. We also examine theories of social change with specific reference to the patterns of participation of Western publics.

Young people and political disengagement

It is often argued that advanced Western democracies have entered a period of political disengagement, where politics has become increasingly irrelevant to the lives of Western citizens (Grasso 2011, Grasso 2014; Dalton and Wattenberg 2000; Mair 2006; Mulgan 1994). It is also common for social commentators to point to low levels of turnout, party membership and political participation as evidence for these theories (Mair and Van Biezen 2001; Sloam 2014; Van Biezen *et al.* 2012). In some cases, these findings have led to talk of an 'anti-political' zeitgeist (Mulgan 1994), and ignited concerns for the supposedly widespread apathy and cynicism of democratic citizens.

With very few exceptions (Rosema 2006; Schumpeter 1952; Theiss-Morse and Hibbing 2005), low, or at the very least, very low, participation levels are almost universally understood to have negative implications for democratic practice (Almond and Verba 1963; Barber 1984; Dahl 1989; Dalton 2008). This issue is exacerbated if considered in the context provided by the argument that young people, socialised into a new depoliticised climate, could be the ones driving falling participation levels (Blais *et al.* 2004; Franklin 2004; Henn *et al.* 2005). The dominant concern here is that if declining political participation is caused by the distinctive socialisation circumstances of new generations, then political involvement will continue to fall as older, politically involved cohorts die out and are replaced by new, increasingly disengaged cohorts (Grasso 2011, Grasso 2014). As Hooghe (2004: 333) points out: "An implicit assumption in most of the current literature on youth and politics is that youth studies have a wider relevance for the field of political science in general". While "structural social changes ... are expected to have an impact on the political attitudes and behaviours of the entire population ... for adults these effects are mitigated by the fact that their initial political orientations were shaped decades ago" (Hooghe 2004: 333). On the other hand, since young people are undergoing their political socialisation at the time when these changes are taking place, their political attitudes and behaviours will be more deeply influenced by them.

The implications of this argument are substantial. Because the specific political orientations of older cohorts were shaped in some definitive way or other in the past, these orientations then more or less persist throughout their life-cycles (Jennings 1987). In turn, the political behaviours of older cohorts reflect their formative experiences in the past much more than any influences of the present political or social context. Still further, this has significant consequences for younger cohorts, since both the altered political context and "these structural transformations [are] not just easier to detect and observe, [they] might also have a stronger impact as they were experiences in the formative period of their lives" (Hooghe 2004: 333). Franklin (2004: 216) explains this point clearly:

> the future lies in the hands of young people. Young people hold the key to the future because they are the ones who react to new conditions. Older people are, on the whole, too set in their ways ... so most long-term change comes about by way of generational replacement.

However, while young people are often considered the least politically engaged age group compared to all other age groups – at least when it comes to conventional participation – theorists continue to disagree as to why this is the case. Some have argued that lower levels of political involvement amongst the young are merely reflections of their life-cycle stage (Parry *et al.* 1992; Verba and Nie 1972). Others suggest that what really matters for political involvement is the distinctive socialisation experiences of a generation (Alwin and Krosnick 1991; Beck and Jennings 1991; Bennett 1986; Hooghe and Stolle 2003; Inglehart 1990; Van Den Broek 1996; Van Deth and Elff 2000). If the generational argument is correct, we would expect that different cohorts exhibit diverging patterns of political participation, influenced by their 'formative experiences' (Mannheim 1928) and that these should be durable through their life-cycle. If, on the other hand, life-cycle theories are correct, different age groups should exhibit diverging patterns of participation, but these differences would attenuate and become negligible as younger cohorts mature and enter adulthood. In this context, it is only the generational argument that carries implications for social change. Therefore, to assess whether the patterns of participation of younger cohorts spell out anything of interest for the future of political participation in advanced Western democracies, one must apply the correct methods (see Appendix) to disentangle age and cohort effects.

The remainder of this chapter focuses on why different socialisation experiences might have implications for diverging cohort patterns of participation. Following Pilcher (1994: 481), I argue that to understand social change we should pay more attention to the socio-political concept of generations as suggested by Mannheim in his 1928 essay 'The Problem of Generations'. In addition, I discuss existing explanations for over-time change in turnout, party membership and other forms of conventional political participation. I also present arguments for the rise of 'unconventional' participation and new repertoires in relation to theories of generational change. I propose a synthesis that attempts to take into account arguments for diverging patterns in terms of a changing political context and the divergent socialisation experiences of specific cohorts. As such, I also examine the question of cohorts and generations and explore some of the generational distinctions offered in the literature.

The evolution of political participation?

A number of studies argue that political involvement in Western Europe has declined over recent decades, and that citizens are less politicised than ever before. For one author, we are witnessing the transformation of party democracy into 'audience democracy' (Manin 1997). For another, whilst politics used to "belong to the citizen and something in which the citizen could, and often did, participate in", today it has instead become "an external world which people watch from outside: a world of political leaders, separate from that of the citizenry" (Mair 2006: 44). Many related analyses of falling political involvement in Western Europe focus on declining party membership and turnout in particular (Dalton 2008; Dalton and Wattenberg 2000; Franklin 2004). However, scholars studying unconventional political participation, which is often associated with new social movements, claim that participation is actually going up (Inglehart 1990; Inglehart and Welzel 2005; Norris 2002). For example, Inglehart (1990: 340) argues that while "union membership rates ... have been falling in most Western countries, and traditional political party ties have been weakening" with "the effect of depressing certain types of participation such as voting that are heavily dependent on elite-directed mobilisation", it is also true that "at the same time, elite-directing types of participation, aimed at influencing specific policy decisions are becoming more widespread".

Indeed, the well-established association between higher education levels and conventional political participation at the individual level (Verba 1993; Verba and Nie 1972), coupled with the expansion of education in the latter part of the twentieth century, would seem to suggest an overall rise in participation in Western Europe, at least since the 1970s. This idea is best captured by the 'puzzle' of voter turnout (Franklin 2004). Adapted for conventional political involvement more generally, counter to theoretical expectations, the well-established individual-level association between education and participation (Verba 1993) has not translated into the aggregate level of the population. Rather, empirical evidence supports a decline in conventional participation in the latter part of the twentieth century. Inglehart (1990) also discusses the influence of education on participation. He argues that economic development in advanced industrial societies "should lead to rising levels of mass political participation for three good theoretical reasons". These are: (1) 'cognitive mobilisation': since educational levels have risen dramatically in the second half of the twentieth century, people have developed enhanced abilities to participate; (2) the liberalisation of gender roles means more women can participate; (3) the value priorities have shifted from materialist to post-materialist: "being freed from the need to focus their energies primarily on the struggle for economic and physical security should enable them to devote more attention to post-materialist concerns – such as politics" (Inglehart 1990: 335).

For Inglehart (1990: 335–6) since "in most Western nations, the public in general and students in particular seem much less politicised than they were in the late 1960s and early 1970s ... or so it seems", "common sense and theory point in opposite directions" in the fact that

> the immediate consequences of [the] three long term changes ... have been partially masked by the fact that, while the individual level preconditions for political participation have been improving, external mobilisation has been in decline, as a result of the decay of political party machines, labour unions and religious institutions.

However, "the stagnation of electoral turnout and other forms of elite-directed participation" is matched by an "increase in unconventional forms of participation, and the rise of new social movements ... all manifestations of the rise of elite-directing participation" (Inglehart 1990: 335–6).

Declining 'conventional' political participation?

The core body of evidence supporting the argument for declining political engagement is found in the literature on conventional political participation. 'Conventional' participation is understood in the literature as involvement in political activities that are mediated by the traditional organs of participation, or membership of these organisations (Dekker *et al.* 1997; Morales 2009), such as political parties and trade unions and related to class-based cleavages (Mair 2006). Dalton (2000: 29) argues that what matters here is not just the magnitude but also the universality of the decline: "the similarity of trends for so many nations forces us to look beyond specific and idiosyncratic explanations ... something broader and deeper must be occurring". Others warn that politics has become a 'spectator sport' (Dalton 2000). Mair (2006) suggests that the seeds for this process lie in the transformation of political parties, and in particular their withdrawal from civil society and decreased mediation and representation of group-based interests in favour of managerialism (Sartori 1969; Whiteley and Seyd 2002). Others focus on individualisation, structural change and the blurring of the old left-right class-based cleavage on which the parties used to compete and from which trade unions drew their popular support (Beck 1994; Beck and Beck-Gernsheim 2001; Clark and Lipset 1991; Pakulski 1993).

Voting is the most common form of conventional political participation. However, several theorists show that turnout has been declining and that perhaps national elections have become increasingly less important for the citizens of modern Western democracies (Blais *et al.* 2004; Dalton and Wattenberg 2000; Mair 2006). In the 1990s, average turnout fell from 82 to 78 per cent across Western Europe. This was the lowest turnout recorded in any post-war decade; eleven out of fifteen advanced Western democracies recorded their lowest ever decade averages in this period (Mair 2006). The decline in voter turnout has been especially acute in the United Kingdom, where it has fallen from 77 per cent in 1992, to 71 per cent in 1997, to 59 per cent in 2001, registering only a small rise (61 per cent) in more recent elections.

Franklin (2004) shows that turnout rises in Malta, rises slightly in Belgium, Denmark, Sweden, Norway, Australia and Israel, but that all the other countries show declines of various magnitudes. With data for 1950–1997, Gray and Caul (2000: 1097) show that turnout has declined in Belgium, France, Germany, Ireland, Italy, the Netherlands and Great Britain, but not in Denmark and Sweden. They do not examine Spain. However, in her 2002 study, Norris argues that "concerns that post-industrial societies are inevitably experiencing a deep secular erosion of voting participation during the last half century are greatly exaggerated" (2002: xii). She argues that in the period 1945–2000 only eight post-industrial nations experienced declining turnout (Austria, France, Switzerland, the Netherlands, Australia, Canada, the United States and New Zealand) whereas four experienced rising turnout (Sweden, Israel, Greece and Malta).

Theorists also argue that plunging party membership shows the extent to which the citizens of advanced democratic nations have grown increasingly disenchanted with politics (Dalton and Wattenberg 2000). The ratio of party membership to the electorate across Western European democracies fell between the 1980s and the end of the 1990s (Mair 2000; Mair and Van Biezen 2001; Scarrow 2000). Mair and van Biezen (2001) claim that since the 1990s parties have been 'haemorrhaging members'. Studies show that participation in other party-mediated activities is also declining (Dalton 2008; Mulgan 1994; Parry *et al.* 1992). The majority of Europeans have little or no contact with political bodies or organisations. The British studies have tended to conclude that the pressure on people's time had made party activism undesirable and that since major parties have become more managerial in style, they are less in need for volunteers and have thus reduced joining incentives (Mair 2006; Whiteley and Seyd 2002).

A number of political changes that appear across advanced industrial democracies during the second half of the twentieth century could have implications for political participation. Theorists discuss the breakdown of the traditional left-right polarisation. Some find a resultant shift in the axis of political contestation to include preferences on social values, particularly concerning the libertarian-authoritarian dimension and the emergence of new parties (Kitschelt 1988). Others highlight partisan dealignment and the declining influence of political parties and increasing voter volatility (Mair 2006; Wattenberg 2000); or premise the rise of new political cleavages (Heath *et al.* 1990). A prominent argument is that the 'old' politics of class has given way to what some researchers term the 'New Politics'. These: "develop around questions common to most highly industrialised societies, such as environmental pollution, the dangers of nuclear energy, the question of women's equality and human rights, the need for peaceful international co-existence and for helping the third world" (Baker *et al.* 1981: 141). As Della Porta and Diani (2006: 6) point out:

> even the most superficial observer of the 1960s could have not helped noticing that many of the actors engaged in those conflicts (youth, women, and professional groups) were only partially related to the class conflicts, which had constituted the principal component of political cleavages in industrial societies.

The paradox envisaged by some authors is that pressure for social change no longer comes from the working class struggle for material interests and socioeconomic equality, but rather from a struggle for 'recognition' of culture and identity groups disproportionately drawn from the highly educated middle classes (Habermas 1975, 1981; Touraine 1971, 1981).

Rising 'unconventional' political participation?

Several studies argue that demonstrations and other forms of unconventional political participation originally associated with the rise of new social movements and the new politics in the late 1960s, and more recently the rise of consumer politics, are commonplace today (Norris 2002, 2004; Van Aelst and Walgrave 2001). By 1975, Tilly argued that protest had simply become another way of mobilising public opinion and influencing governmental agendas. Dalton (2008: 69) argued that protest has become common amongst the educated and politically sophisticated middle classes. Rather than being spontaneous outbreaks aimed at overthrowing the established political order, modern demonstrations are consciously organised by new social movements and lobby groups and aimed at influencing the political agenda. As Della Porta and Diani (2006: 6) point out, these political events are not just the stuff of history textbooks. They have important implications for the study of political participation today, since, while

> the excitement and optimism of the 1960s may be long gone ... social movements, protest actions, and, more generally, political organisations unaligned with major political parties or trade unions have become permanent components of Western democracies. It is no longer possible to describe protest politics, grassroots participation, and symbolic challenges as 'unconventional'.

Several other studies have argued that political participation has simply changed and that people today are more likely to be involved in unconventional political participation and other types of grassroots activism or social forms of engagement (Henn *et al.* 2005; Inglehart and Welzel 2005; Norris 2004). For Inglehart (1990: 339), this is a positive change:

the institutions that mobilised political participation in the late 19th and 20th centuries – labour union, church, and mass political party – were hierarchical organisations in which a small number of leaders or political bosses led a mass of disciplined troops.... A newer elite-directing mode of participation expresses the individual's preferences with far greater precision and in much more details than the old.

Topf (1995) reports trends based on data from the Civic Culture (1959), Political Action (1973–1976) studies and European Values Survey (1981–1990). He shows that unconventional participation rose in all thirteen Western European democracies studied except Finland in the period 1981–1999 (Topf 1995: 69). Dalton (2008: 65) also shows a rise in unconventional forms of participation in the United States, Germany, France and Great Britain for the period 1974–1990. In a more recent study which uses the same data as Topf's (1995), Norris (2002: 198) also finds evidence of rising unconventional political participation in Britain, Germany, the Netherlands, Austria, the United States, Italy, Switzerland and Finland between the early 1980s and early 1990s. She concludes that "protest politics is on the rise as a channel of political expression and mobilisation" (Norris 2002: 221). Limiting our investigation to conventional political participation would therefore underestimate participation levels (Norris 2002, 2004; Grasso 2013, Grasso 2016).

Figure 3.1 summarises the arguments concerning the evolution of political participation that in advanced, post-industrial societies 'conventional' political participation, typical of older cohorts, should be declining (or stagnant), whereas 'unconventional' political participation, typical of younger cohorts, relating to protest politics, consumer politics and participation in new social movements, should be rising. Whereas people used to join 'traditional' political organisations such as political parties and labour unions and participated in citizen-oriented actions, such as voting and volunteering with parties (and therefore older cohorts should engage in this more), people today are said to be increasingly joining 'new', NSM organisations (environment, development, anti-racist, anti-nuclear, etc.) and engaging in unconventional political actions, such as demonstrating, doing unpaid voluntary work for NSMs, signing petitions and engaging in consumer politics (Grasso and Giugni 2013, Grasso and Giugni 2015; Giugni and Grasso 2015, Grasso and Giugni 2016). The youngest, 'cognitively mobilised', cohorts are said to typify these new trends and thus to be the most active in 'new' organisations and in unconventional repertoires. Chapter 4 explores the questions of whether 'conventional' political participation is declining across Western Europe and of whether 'unconventional' participation is on the rise. Chapters 5–7 explore cohort differences in participation in various activities to examine if they conform to patterns suggested in the literature. For this purpose, the next few sections turn to the issue of age differences in political participation and to the question of life-cycle versus generation, or cohort, effects. The following sections also examine Mannheim's (1928) theory of generations and the classification of cohorts, based on the socio-historic period of their formative years, used in this study.

Social and individualised political actions

'Conventional', or 'citizen-oriented' (Norris 2002), including voting, working for a party (or a union), contacting a politician

'Unconventional', or 'cause-oriented' (Norris 2002), including demonstrating, working for an NSM, signing a petition, consumer politics

'CONVENTIONAL' or 'ELITE-DIRECTED'
Declining, or 'stagnant'
Typical of older cohorts

'UNCONVENTIONAL' or 'ELITE-CHALLENGING'
Rising, since late 1960s
Typical of younger cohorts

'Old', or 'traditional', organisations, mainly ('old') political parties and labour unions

Memberships

'New', NSM/SMO-type, including environmental, animal rights, third world development and human rights organisations

Figure 3.1 Summary of arguments on the evolution of political participation.

Note
This figure is adapted from Norris (2004: 22); the distinction between 'elite-directed' and 'elite-challenging' repertoires is from Inglehart and Catterberg (2002). In previous work, Inglehart (1990) distinguishes between 'elite-directed' and 'elite-directing' repertoires. 'Elite-directing' and 'elite-challenging' are roughly equivalent categories, except that the latter does no longer seem to include political discussion.

Age differences in political participation

It is often argued that young people are particularly detached from conventional politics (Mulgan 1994; Park 1995; Rubenson *et al.* 2004; Wilkinson and Mulgan 1995). In the United Kingdom in particular, young people's disengagement from politics is well documented and young people are the least likely age group to register to vote (Grasso 2013a). Interviews with young people also reveal a profound cynicism about politics: politicians tend to be perceived as sleazy and untrustworthy, Parliament is considered obscure and ritualistic, whilst political coverage is said to be incomprehensible and dull (Coughlan 2003). The fact that young people are less likely than older cohorts to vote and to participate in other conventional activities leads some authors to describe young people as an age group who are mainly distinctive in their lack of interest in traditional politics (Park 1995) and to argue in turn that for this generation politics has become a dirty word (Wilkinson and Mulgan 1995).

Arguments about age differences in participation generally rely on life-course explanations for lower levels of participation amongst the young. Theorists in this school (Parry *et al.* 1992; Verba and Nie 1972) often argue that the lowest levels of political involvement can be expected amongst young people because they are more concerned with "the struggle for partners, house, career opportunities, and the like" (Van Deth 1990: 302). Several other explanations are offered for why young people are less engaged in conventional politics than other age groups. One is that following the professionalisation of politics and the introduction of increasingly marketing-led campaigning methods, the campaigning strategies adopted by political parties tend to be geared more towards middle aged voters, therefore marginalising young people leading them to consider formal politics as remote and irrelevant (Kimberlee 1998). However, it may also (or instead) be the case that parties tend to cater less for young people's interests, since they perceive them as a lost constituency (Keiser 2000). Another theory is that young people espouse a 'new politics' value agenda which leads them to prioritise new social movements and consumer-style single-issue campaigns over mainstream political participation (Abramson and Inglehart 1992; Inglehart 1990).

Generational differences in political participation

Whilst different groups might exhibit different patterns of behaviours because of their age, this might also be due to the specific experiences of their formative years. Generational theories share the idea that some attitudes are formed early in one's life and remain relatively stable over time (Alwin and Scott 1996; Whittier 1997). So, for example, if baby-boomers protest more than other cohorts, this would be due to their socialisation experiences, not their younger age. Mannheim (1928) argued that adolescence and young adulthood are critical periods for the development of values, attitudes and beliefs and that once established, these beliefs and values tend to crystallise and stabilise, persisting throughout people's lives. On this reading, 'formative experiences' leave a lasting imprint on the political behaviour of generations coming of age in specific periods.

Alwin and Krosnick (1991: 171) suggest that the unique political characteristics of certain eras "provide a basis for the assumption that birth cohorts achieving political awareness during the ascendancy of one particular political party will be affected by the different popularity of parties". Russell *et al.* (1992) show that socialisation during Thatcher's ascendancy meant that first-time electors in 1979 and 1987 were more Conservative relative to other cohorts in their youth. Similarly for Italy, Mattei *et al.* (1990) show how the strong PCI showing in the 1979 election meant that new voters in this period became more strongly Communist and politically involved than previous cohorts. Inglehart's (1977) theory of post-materialism is also based on the idea of distinctive generations but his argument is that growing up in a period of relative affluence and stability makes younger cohorts less materialistic than previous generations, and therefore that growing up with rising living standards leads younger cohorts to display post-materialist values emphasising freedom of expression, quality of life, protection of the environment, and so on.

In his classic study of voter turnout in Western Europe, Franklin (2004: 6) argues that turnout depends not on how individuals approach elections, but on how elections appear to people. For this reason, he focuses on factors such as the rules under which elections are conducted (electoral system characteristics), the party system structure (fractionalisation and cohesion) and features of elections (in particular, competitiveness of the race) (Franklin 2004: 6). Franklin (2004: 210) then finds that these factors cause declining voter turnout by way of a cohort mechanism, since new cohorts of voters are more impressionable to changes in the character of electoral competition. Franklin (2004) draws evidence for the resilience of political habits from Butler and Stokes (1969) who found that the first three elections was the length of time needed for people to firmly become habitual supporters of a certain party; using Jennings and Niemi's (1991) data, Plutzer (2002) also found that people made the transition from habitual non-voting to habitual voting during the span of three elections. The main argument is that "older people, who learned the habit of voting when turnout was high, will vote at higher rates that younger people, who are learning the habit of voting in less competitive elections" (Franklin 2004: 207). In this sense then, turnout change is constrained by the fact that for older people, voting becomes a habit, and these cohorts are less responsive to changes in the character of electoral competition. The implication of Franklin's (2004: 205) argument is that generational replacement will cause a substantial decline in turnout in the long run.

An important consideration raised by the discussion above is that while Mannheim conceived of generations as reflecting different socio-historic contexts of socialisation, there are various other ways of distinguishing between cohorts. For Franklin, what matters is socialisation into voting when turnout was high or not; for Inglehart, the key issue is that younger cohorts were socialised in a period of greater affluence and stability. Therefore, different research questions will require different cohort schemas ranging from the purely demographic to the socio-historical type.

Classifications of political generations

Different categorisations of socio-historic generations are available in the literature, though most tend to be developed within specific national contexts. For example, Heath and Park (1997: 4) divide British generations into four groups: (1) the pre-war generation born before 1926 and mostly socialised during the 1920s and early 1930s; (2) the post-war generation, born between 1927 and 1945 and mostly socialised during the 1940s and 1950s; (3) the '60s generation, born between 1946 and 1960 and mostly socialised during the 1960s and early 1970s; (4) the '80s generation, born after 1960 and mostly socialised during the 1970s and 1980s. Clarke *et al.* (2004: 270–1) distinguish between (1) the post-WWII generation, people who reached the age of adulthood before 1950; (2) the Macmillan generation, people who reached the age of majority between 1951 and 1964; (3) the Wilson/Callaghan generation, those who became adults between 1964 and 1979, an era of Labour government interrupted by the 1970–1974 Conservative interregnum; (4) the Thatcher generation, who entered the electorate between 1979 and 1992 during a period of Conservative hegemony; (5) the Blair generation, becoming eligible to vote after 1992, the last year in which the Conservatives won a general election.

Van Den Broek (1996) and Van Deth and Elff (2000) employ for the Netherlands, and for Europe, respectively, Becker's (1990, 1992) distinction between generations. Becker (1990: 2; 1992: 222) defined a generation as "the grouping of a number of cohorts characterised by a specific historical setting and by common characteristics". As Van Den Broek (1996: 4) explains, Becker "contended that the formative periods of members of successive cohorts took place in historical eras that differed to such an extent that five distinct generations emerged, diverging in biographical characteristics, value orientations and behavioural patterns". These generations were characterised as: (1) the pre-war generation, born 1910–1930, experiencing economic depression, and seen as industrious, law-abiding, those who fought in the war; (2) the silent generation, born 1931–1940, experiencing post-war reconstruction, an industrious, law-abiding generation; (3) the protest generation, born 1941–1955, the affluent, self-actualisation generation, engaging in protest activity; (4) the lost generation, born 1956–1970, experiencing economic crises, focused on self-actualisation; (5) the pragmatic generation, born 1970–, characterised by pragmatism.

In this study we will distinguish between the following generations:

1   *The pre-WWII generation*, born between 1909 and 1925 and experiencing their formative years before 1945;
2   *The post-WWII generation*, born between 1926 and 1945 and experiencing their formative years between 1946 and 1965;

3   *The baby-boom or '60s–70s generation*, born between 1946 and 1957 and experiencing their formative years between 1966 and 1977;
4   *The '80s generation*, born between 1958 and 1968 and experiencing their formative years between 1978 and 1988; and
5   *The '90s generation*, born between 1969 and 1981 and experiencing their formative years in the post-Cold War period 1989–2001.

Formative experiences and generational differences in participation

If Mannheim's (1928) account that generations are firmly located within socio-historical contexts is correct, then we would expect different generations to exhibit different patterns of participation based on the period of their 'formative years' (2013b). The generations coming of age in the classic period of party cleavage congealment (Lipset and Rokkan 1967), broadly, before the mid-to-late 1960s, should be more likely to be members of political parties, to vote and engage in conventional participation more generally, than those generations which came of age in subsequent historical periods. On the other hand, the generation that came of age in the radicalising period of the mid-to-late 1960s and 1970s, the baby-boomers, or 'the protest generation', should be more likely than older cohorts to engage in demonstrations, and possibly to be involved in new social movements. The '80s and '90s generations instead, coming of age in periods witnessing the end of left-right polarisation, could be seen to be more apathetic relative to the baby-boomers. As Della Porta and Diani (2006: 1) recognise: "in the late 1960s, the world was apparently undergoing deep, dramatic transformations, even a revolution, some thought". Events such as

> American civil rights and antiwar movements, the Mai 1968 revolt in France, students' protests in Germany, Britain, or Mexico, the worker-student coalitions of the 1969 'Hot Autumn' in Italy ... all these phenomena ... suggested that deep changes were in the making.

Thus, the authors argue: "social transformations and events of particular relevance ... produced an irreversible change in conceptions of social and political life, and that a new generation of citizens ... was formed" (Della Porta and Diani 2006: 69). Therefore, "It would thus be possible to speak of a 1960s generation, just as one speaks of generations when referring to the events of 1848, of the post-Victorian era, or of the Great Depression of the 1920s and 1930s" (Della Porta and Diani 2006: 69).

Inglehart and Catterberg (2002: 303) also propose that younger cohorts will be more elite-challenging than those born before 1945, but they do not emphasise the distinctiveness of the baby-boomers in arguing that:

> Intergenerational value change has important implications concerning the changes we can expect over the coming decades. As younger, better-educated,

and more post-materialist cohorts replace older ones in the adult population, intergenerational population replacement will tend to bring a shift toward increasingly participant publics.

Several studies in the literature have tested Inglehart's (1977, 1990) post-materialism thesis. For example, Brooks and Manza (1994: 541) test two of his central propositions, that: (1) post-materialism characterises a distinct type of values commitment and that (2) the commitment to post-materialism leads to a rejection of the state as a means of accomplishing policy objectives and show that neither argument is supported by evidence. Rather, they argue for an altern-ative account which they characterise as "value pluralism" (Brooks and Manza 1994). Similarly, Evans and De Graaf (1996) show that it is more likely that it is progressive liberalism, and not post-materialism, that is spreading amongst younger cohorts. While tests of Inglehart (1977, 1990) have focused on the notion of post-materialist values, less attention has been paid to testing the thesis with respect to generational differences in political participation. In this study we provide a test for whether it is the case that participation in new social move-ments and unconventional forms of participation rises, particularly amongst more recent cohorts and whether more recent cohorts participate in these types of activities more than older cohorts.

Indeed, while there are good reasons to think that the 1960s generation might be more radical than previous generations due to the period of their formative years, this is not so for the '80s and '90s generations. Since as Della Porta and Diani (2006: 69) say "political contexts subsequently differed greatly", then so would have the socialisation experiences of cohorts coming of age after the radi-calising period of the late 1960s and 1970s. Since the social process which Ingle-hart and Catterberg (2002: 303) propose is one which centres on rising education levels, while the socialisation experiences of the '80s and '90s cohorts might not in and of themselves encourage higher levels of elite-directing activities, their higher education levels could nonetheless have led to their higher levels of parti-cipation, relative to the pre-1960s cohorts, in these activities. Inglehart and Catterberg (2002) do not directly study generational differences in participation, but they report rising levels of unconventional activity in the population as a whole. These could be due to period effects affecting the population as a whole and not cohort effects with younger generations involving themselves in these activities more than older cohorts.

Moreover, there are other arguments that characterise the socialisation period of the 1980s and 1990s as potentially having a depressing effect on the political participation of these generations. In his classic essay *The End of History?* Fuku-yama (1989) wrote that "In watching the flow of events over the past decade or so, it is hard to avoid the feeling that something very fundamental has happened in world history" and that this "end of history will be a very sad time" since:

> The struggle for recognition, the willingness to risk one's life for a purely abstract goal, the worldwide ideological struggle that called forth daring,

courage, imagination, and idealism, will be replaced by economic calculation, the endless solving of technical problems, environmental concerns, and the satisfaction of sophisticated consumer demands.

(1989: 1)

For Fukuyama then, the end of the Cold War and the ideological struggle between Left and Right marks the replacement of "the willingness to risk one's life for a purely abstract goal" with more mundane, managerial-practical preoccupations. One might conclude from this that the end of the Cold War also marked the demise of some of the strongest motivations driving individuals to participate in politics. Without widespread ideological struggle, it seems, a key element of what has traditionally motivated individuals to participate in politics dissipates. Therefore, one would expect that this new political context would have some influence on the political socialisation process of young adults coming of age in the wake of this historical period. It is worth noting here that several theorists have argued that the left-right dimension has traditionally been a central aspect of political life mainly because it establishes a primary line of ideological division, and facilitates the debate required for democracy. Mouffe (2005) argues that the left-right dimension is normatively important because it represents a recognition of the antagonism inherent in the sphere of politics, and provides the partisan dimension that in turn politics requires to politicise and mobilise the citizenry. She contends that "to be able to mobilize passions towards democratic designs, democratic politics must have a partisan character. This is indeed the function of the left/right distinction" (Mouffe 2005: 6). Most importantly, Mouffe contends that "what is at stake in the left/right opposition is not a particular content ... but the recognition of social division and the legitimisation of [political] conflict" (Mouffe 2005: 119). Based on this, if Fukuyama and Mouffe are right then, cohorts socialised in the end of the twentieth century, in other words the '80s and '90s generations, would be less politicised and therefore potentially less participatory than previous cohorts. There is some evidence for this. Clarke *et al.* (2004: 270–1) show how:

> the Thatcher era – a period characterised by insistent advocacy of market rather than government solution to societal problems, and a more general emphasis on the individual rather than collective good – had important negative effects on public attitudes towards electoral participation

and that "these effects have not abated since New Labour came to power in 1997".

There is thus some evidence that in Britain at least, the '80s and '90s generations are less likely to vote than older generations. In this study we will investigate the patterns of engagement of political generations across Western Europe to examine the extent to which the political context at the time of socialisation influences generational differences across time and space.

Classifications of generations based on formative years

A central question of this study relates to the extent to which social change in patterns of political participation is underpinned by processes of inter-generational replacement and what this means for the future of democratic societies. Table 3.1 summarises the classification of political generations used in this study and compares it to other similar classifications developed in the literature. As can be seen, these categorisations are broadly similar despite the fact that they are developed for different nation-specific contexts. The cohort classification scheme we use is for the whole of Western Europe. Van Deth and Elff (2000) also applied a scheme for the whole of Western Europe.

In order to draw temporal boundaries between birth cohorts and in keeping with Mannheim's (1928) classic theory of generational differences as based in the socio-historic context of formative years, we treat mid-to-late adolescence (15–25 years of age) as the key moment of political socialisation, in other words, the 'formative years'. These are the political 'impressionable years'. Each respondent is assigned to a particular political generation based on the historic formative period during which they have spent the majority of their formative years (i.e. lived through at least six out of their eleven formative years during the historic formative period of their generation). So, for example, someone born in 1946 would have spent six out of eleven formative years in the period 1966–1971, which falls in the historic formative period 1966–1977, placing them in the baby-boom generation. Similarly, someone born in 1957 would have spent six out of their eleven formative years in the period 1972–1977, also placing them in the baby-boom generation (the majority of the formative years, again were in the 1966–1977 period). In the same way, someone born in 1948 would have lived through eight out of eleven formative years in the period 1966–1973; someone born in 1954 would have lived through nine out of eleven formative years in the period 1969–1977. Since all these individuals experienced the majority of their formative years (at least six out of eleven years in the span between fifteen and twenty-five years of age) during the formative period 1966–1977, they are all categorised as members of the baby-boom generation for the analysis. This method of classifying individuals based on the historical context of the majority of their formative years is similar to Nikolayenko's (2008) method for classifying political generations in Russia. While an individual born in 1960 turned seventeen in 1977, it would be misleading to categorise this person as a member of the baby-boom generation since they only spent the first two formative years in the 1966–1977 period. Instead, based on this method, which emphasises the historical setting of socialisation for the majority of their formative years, this person would be assigned to the '80s generation in this study.

This method of categorising political generations based on formative years emphasises the commonality of experiences, grounded in the politico-historical context of socialisation, which the individuals grouped into a cohort share. As such, it is particularly appropriate for testing whether the socio-historic context of the formative years of a generation has an impact on their participation. So, for example, the members of the pre-WWII generation share the fact that they all came of age (i.e. experienced the majority of their formative years) before the end of WWII and as such lived through war and the economic depression. The members of the post-WWII generation have in common the fact that they all came of age in the post-war reconstruction period and the early 1960s economic boom. The baby-boomers all came of age in the radicalising political period of the mid-late 1960s and 1970s and experienced growing levels of affluence and the expansion of education. The '80s generation came of age during the period of Thatcher's rise in Britain and the final stages of the Cold War and the ascendancy of neoliberalism in Europe and the world more widely. The '90s generation, finally, came of age after the fall of the Berlin Wall, during the time of the demise of traditional left-wing parties accompanied by party-system restructuring in many European countries, a phase that some have dubbed 'the End of History'.

Of course one could argue that one cross-national typology misses some key differences in formative experiences between members of the same 'generations' in different countries. For example, one could easily see that the end of the Cold War (and unification) could have possibly meant quite different things in Germany compared to somewhere like the Netherlands. And Spain, as mentioned, had a proto-fascist regime until the mid-1970s. Moreover, Ireland and Spain lived through civil wars in the interbellum period. However, following Mannheim (1928), Becker (1990: 2; 1992: 222) defined a generation as "the grouping of a number of cohorts characterised by a specific historical setting and by common characteristics". As Van Den Broek (1996: 4) explains, Becker "contended that the formative periods of members of successive cohorts took place in historical eras that differed to such an extent that five distinct generations emerged, diverging in biographical characteristics, value orientations and behavioural patterns". Therefore, while drawing boundaries between cohorts is always arbitrary, the emphasis on 'historical eras' implies that the differences between successive generations (even within a given country) should be greater than those between members of the same generation across Western European countries.

It is also telling that all the typologies presented in Table 3.1 are strikingly similar in their designation of generations. This implies that scholars see these generations as forming relatively distinct groupings in the way suggested by Becker. Moreover, the descriptive terms which Becker used to describe the formative experiences of these generations characterise the various cohorts in each schema. For example, Thatcher's generation, or the '80s generation, in Britain is generally seen to be characterised by more individualistic values owing to the rise of neoliberalism in the 1980s; the '60s generation or the baby-boomers/protest generation (or even the Wilson/Callaghan generation) is generally seen to be the most radical and left-wing. These broad generational groupings are also common in popular parlance. We often speak of the '80s generation or the '60s generation or Generation X and Y.

Table 3.1 Cohort classification based on socio-historic period of formative years compared to others in the literature

The categorisation employed in this study:

	Pre-WWII	Post-WWII	Baby-boomers	'80s generation	'90s generation	Context
Formative years	1929–1945	1946–1965	1966–1977	1978–1988	1989–2001	Western Europe
Year of birth	1909–1925	1926–1945	1946–1957	1958–1968	1969–1981	

Heath and Park (1997)

	Pre-war	Post-war gen.	'60s generation	'80s generation		Context
Formative years*	1920s/1930s	1940s/1950s	1960s/1970s	1970s/1980s		Great Britain
Year of birth	Before 1926	1927–1945	1946–1960	After 1960		

Clarke et al. (2004)

	Post-WWII	Macmillan gen.	Wilson/Callaghan	Thatcher generation	Blair generation	Context
Formative years**	Before 1950	1951–1964	1964–1979	1979–1992	Post-1992	Great Britain
Year of birth	Before 1932	1933–1946	1946–1961	1961–1974	Post-1975	

	Pre-war gen.	Silent generation	Protest generation	Lost generation	Pragmatic gen.	Context
						Becker (1990, 1992), Van Den Broek (1996)
Formative years*** Year of birth	Depression, war 1910–1930	Reconstruction 1931–1940	Affluence, radicalism 1941–1955	Crisis, individualism 1956–1970	Pragmatism Post-1970	Netherlands and Western Europe (in Van Deth and Elff 2000)

Notes

* While the years of birth of my cohorts and Heath and Park's (1997) are very similar, the 'formative years' intervals do not match up between the two classifications because they are defined differently due to the different nature of the research questions. Heath and Park (1997) divide cohorts by year of birth; their 'socialisation period' is then deduced from this – e.g. when the birth cohorts in question would have been in their pre-adult years. On the other hand, following Mannheim (1928), my classification, based on the historic period in which individuals spent the majority of their formative years (15–25 years of age), starts with the historic periods and ends up with cohorts.

** Clarke et al. (2004) do not give formative years, but simply say "those who became adults between 1951–1964", etc. As such, I derived 'formative years' by subtracting eighteen from the boundaries for the periods which they specify for each generation.

*** Similarly to Mannheim (1928), Becker (1990: 2, Becker, 1992: 222) defined a generation as "the grouping of a number of cohorts characterised by a specific historical setting and by common characteristics". As Van Den Broek (1995: 4) explains, Becker "contended that the formative periods of members of successive cohorts took place in historical eras that differed to such an extent that five distinct generations emerged, diverging in biographical characteristics, value orientations and behavioural patterns".

Moving on, since the changing historic context of political socialisation means that generations have undergone different formative experiences, one would expect these differences to be reflected in divergent levels and patterns of political participation, both traditional and new, between the cohorts identified here. For example, one would expect that the baby-boom generation, coming of age in the ascendancy period of new social movements and protest politics, would exhibit higher levels of participation in these kinds of activities, despite the depressing effect of ageing and nation-specific period effects. Events such as the student revolts of 1968 would have had an important impact on the socialisation experience of the baby-boomer, or 1960s–70s generation, in many European countries (Grasso 2011, Grasso 2014). In the regression analyses, I will use the post-WWII cohort as the reference category (which is also, conveniently, the largest cohort group) to highlight differences between older and younger cohorts. However, it may also be the case that since, as mentioned above, nation-based contexts of socialisation vary, even for the same generation, baby-boomers in France (where 1968 was a very influential historical landmark) might behave differently from baby-boomers in Denmark (where no such major student/labour movement-led revolts and agitation took place). Similarly, because of the different experiences associated with the end of the Cold War, the '90s generation in Germany might exhibit different patterns of behaviour to that in the Netherlands, for example. Indeed, in Chapters 5–6 it will be interesting to test whether the (assumed) commonalities understood to unite members of specific generations (coming of age in the same historic period), despite diverse national contexts, do really stand the test of country-by-country analysis. Is it really the case, as generational theorists such as Mannheim would argue, that intergenerational differences in participation show remarkably similar patterns across European nations?

Conclusion

This chapter discussed the evolution of political participation in Western Europe and young people's disengagement from politics. We also examined generational theory and the implication of socialisation in diverse political contexts for the participation patterns of different cohorts. In the next chapter we turn to examining empirical trends and then move on to analysing generational differences in participation in later chapters.

References

Abramson, P. and R. Inglehart (1992). "Generational Replacement and Value Change in Eight Western European Societies". *British Journal of Political Science* 22(2): 183–228.

Almond, G. and S. Verba (1963). *The Civic Culture: Political Attitudes and Democracy in Five Nations*. London, Sage Publications.

Alwin, D. and J. Krosnick (1991). "Aging, Cohorts and the Stability of Socio-political Orientations over the Life Span". *American Journal of Sociology* 97: 169–95.

Alwin, D. and J. Scott (1996). Attitude Change: Its Measurement and Interpretation Using Longitudinal Surveys. *Understanding Change in Social Attitudes*. B. Taylor and K. Thomson. Dartmouth, Aldershot.

Baker, K., R. Dalton and K. Hildebrandt (1981). *Germany Transformed: Political Culture and the New Politics*. Cambridge, MA, Harvard University Press.

Barber, B. (1984). *Strong Democracy: Participatory Politics for a New Age*. Berkeley, University of California Press.

Beck, P. A. and M. K. Jennings (1991). "Family Traditions, Political Periods, and the Development of Partisan Orientations". *The Journal of Politics* 53(3): 742–63.

Beck, U. (1994). The Reinvention of Politics: Towards a Theory of Reflexive Modernisation. *Reflexive Modernisation: Politics, Tradition, and Aesthetics in the Modern Social Order*. U. Beck, A. Giddens and S. Lash. Cambridge, Polity.

Beck, U. and E. Beck-Gernsheim (2001). *Individualisation: Institutionalised Individualism and its Social and Political Consequences*. London, Sage.

Becker, H. A. (1990). Dynamics of Life Histories and Generations Research. *Life Histories and Generations*. H. A. Becker. Utrecht, ISOR.

Becker, H. A. (1992). A Pattern of Generations and its Consequences. *Dynamics of Cohorts and Generations Research*. H. A. Becker. Amsterdam, Thesis Publishers.

Bennett, S. E. (1986). *Apathy in America 1960–1984: Causes and Consequences of Citizen Political Indifference*. New York, Transnational Publishers.

Blais, A., E. Gidengil and N. Nevitte (2004). "Where Does Turnout Decline Come From?" *European Journal of Political Research* 43: 221–36.

Brooks, C. and J. Manza (1994). "Do Changing Values Explain the New Politics? A Critical Assessment of the Postmaterialist Thesis". *The Sociological Quarterly* 35(4): 541–70.

Butler, D. and D. Stokes (1969). *Political Change in Britain: Forces Shaping Electoral Choice*. New York, St Martin's Press.

Clark, T. N. and S. M. Lipset (1991). "Are Social Classes Dying?" *International Sociology* 6(4): 397–410.

Clarke, H., D. Sanders, M. Stewart and P. Whiteley (2004). *Political Choice in Britain*. Oxford, Oxford University Press.

Coughlan, S. (2003). "Young People Vote Against Politics". *BBC News Online*, from http://news.bbc.co.uk/1/hi/education/2699275.stm (accessed 16 November 2015).

Dahl, R. A. (1989). *Democracy and its Critics*. New Haven; London, Yale University Press.

Dalton, R. (2000). The Decline of Party Identification. *Parties without Partisans: Political Change in Advanced Industrial Democracies*. R. J. Dalton and M. P. Wattenberg. Oxford, Oxford University Press: xiv, 314p.

Dalton, R. (2008). *Citizen Politics: Public Opinion and Political Parties in Advanced Industrial Democracies*. Washington, DC, CQ Press.

Dalton, R. and M. Wattenberg (2000). *Parties without Partisans: Political Change in Advanced Industrial Democracies*. Oxford, Oxford University Press.

Dekker, P., R. Koopmans and A. van den Broek (1997). Voluntary Associations, Social Movements and Individual Political Behaviour in Western Europe. *Private Groups and Public Life: Social Participation and Political Involvement in Representative Democracies*. J. Van Deth. Abingdon, Routledge.

Della Porta, D. and M. Diani (2006). *Social Movements: An Introduction, 2nd Edition*. Oxford, Blackwell.

Evans, G. and N. D. De Graaf (1996). "Why Are the Young More Postmaterialist? A Cross-National Analysis of Individual and Contextual Influences on Postmaterial Values". *Comparative Political Studies* 28(4): 608–35.

Franklin, M. N. (2004). *Voter Turnout and the Dynamics of Electoral Competition in Established Democracies since 1945*. Cambridge, Cambridge University Press.

Fukuyama, F. (1989). "The End of History?" *The National Interest*.

Giugni, M. G. and M. T. Grasso (2015). "Environmental Movements in Advanced Industrial Democracies: Heterogeneity, Transformation, and Institutionalization". *Annual Review of Environment and Resources* 40: 337–61.

Grasso, M. T. (2011). *Political Participation in Western Europe*. Nuffield College, University of Oxford. D. Phil. Thesis.

Grasso, M. T. (2013a). "The Differential Impact of Education on Young People's Political Activism: Comparing Italy and the United Kingdom". *Comparative Sociology* 12: 1–30.

Grasso, M. T. (2013b). "What Are the Distinguishing Generational, Life Course, and Historical Drivers of Changing Identities? Future Identities: Changing Identities in the UK – The Next 10 Years". *Foresight: The Future of Identity in the UK*. London, The Government Office for Science.

Grasso, M. T. (2014). "Age-Period-Cohort Analysis in a Comparative Context: Political Generations and Political Participation Repertoires". *Electoral Studies* 33: 63–76.

Grasso, M. T. (2016). Political Participation. *Developments in British Politics 10*. R. Heffernan, P. Cowley and C. Hay, Eds. Basingstoke, Palgrave Macmillan.

Grasso, M. T. and M. Giugni (2013). Anti-austerity movements: Old wine in new vessels? Working Paper, XXVII Meeting of the Italian Political Science Association (SISP), University of Florence. Florence, September 12–14.

Grasso, M. T. and M. Giugni (2015). Are Anti-Austerity Movements Old or New? *Austerity and Protest: Popular Contention in Times of Economic Crisis*. M. G. Giugni and M. T. Grasso, Eds. Farnham, Surrey, Ashgate.

Grasso, M. T. and M. Giugni (2016). "Do Issues Matter? Anti-Austerity Protests' Composition, Values, and Action Repertoires Compared". *Research in Social Movements, Conflicts and Change* 39.

Gray, M. and M. Caul (2000). "Declining Voter Turnout in Advanced Industrial Democracies, 1950–1997. The Effects of Declining Group Mobilisation". *Comparative Political Studies* 33: 1091–1122.

Habermas, J. (1975). *Legitimation Crisis*. Boston, Beacon Press.

Habermas, J. (1981). "New Social Movements". *Telos* 49: 33–7.

Heath, A. and A. Park (1997). Thatcher's Children? *British Social Attitudes: The End of Conservative Values? (the 14th Report)*. R. Jowell. London, Sage: 1–22.

Heath, A., R. Jowell, J. Curtice and G. Evans (1990). "The Rise of the New Political Agenda?" *European Sociological Review* 6(1): 31–48.

Henn, M., M. Weinstein and S. Forrest (2005). "Uninterested Youth? Young People's Attitudes towards Party Politics in Britain". *Political Studies* 53(3): 556–78.

Hooghe, M. (2004). "Political Socialisation and the Future of Politics". *Acta Politica* 39: 331–41.

Hooghe, M. and D. Stolle (2003). "Age Matters: Life-cycle and Cohort Differences in the Socialisation Effect of Voluntary Participation". *European Political Science* 3(2): 49–56.

Inglehart, R. (1977). *The Silent Revolution: Changing Values and Political Styles among Western Publics*. Princeton, Princeton University Press.

Inglehart, R. (1990). *Culture Shift in Advanced Industrial Society*. Princeton, Princeton University Press.

Inglehart, R. and G. Catterberg (2002). "Trends in Political Action: The Developmental Trend and the Post-Honeymoon Decline". *International Journal of Comparative Sociology* 43: 300–16.

Inglehart, R. and C. Welzel (2005). *Modernization, Cultural Change and Democracy: The Human Development Sequence*. Cambridge, Cambridge University Press.

Jennings, M. K. (1987). "Residues of a Movement: The Aging of the American Protest Generation". *The American Political Science Review* 81(2): 367–82.

Jennings, M. K. and R. G. Niemi (1991). *The Youth-Parent Socialisation Panel Study*. Princeton, Princeton University Press.

Keiser, M. (2000). "Young Adults and Civic Participation". *National Civic Review* 89(1): 33–8.

Kimberlee, R. (1998). "Young People and the 1997 General Election". *Renewal* 6(2): 87–90.

Kitschelt, H. (1988). "Left-Libertarian Parties: Explaining Innovation in Competitive Party Systems". *World Politics* 40(2): 194–234.

Lipset, S. and S. Rokkan (1967). *Party Systems and Voter Alignments: Cross-national Perspectives*. London, Collier-Macmillan.

Mair, P. (2000). "Partyless Democracy. Solving the Paradox of New Labour?" *New Left Review* 2: 21–35.

Mair, P. (2006). "Ruling the Void? The Hollowing of Western Democracy". *New Left Review* 42: 25–51.

Mair, P. and I. Van Biezen (2001). "Party Membership in Twenty European Democracies, 1980–2000". *Party Politics* 7(1): 5–21.

Manin, B. (1997). *The Principles of Representative Government*. Cambridge, Cambridge University Press.

Mannheim, K. (1928). The Problem of Generations. *Essays on the Sociology of Knowledge*. London, Routledge.

Mattei, F., R. G. Niemi and G. Powell (1990). "On the Depth and Persistence of Generational Change: Evidence from Italy". *Comparative Political Studies* 23(3): 334–54.

Morales, L. (2009). *Joining Political Organisations: Institutions, Mobilisation and Participation in Western Democracies*. Colchester, Essex, ECPR Press.

Mouffe, C. (2005). *On the Political*. Abingdon, Routledge.

Mulgan, G. (1994). *Politics in an Antipolitical Age*. Cambridge, Polity.

Nikolayenko, O. (2008). "Life-cycle, Generational, and Period Effects on Protest Potential in Yeltsin's Russia". *Canadian Journal of Political Science* 41(2): 437–60.

Norris, P. (2002). *Democratic Phoenix: Reinventing Political Activism*. Cambridge, Cambridge University Press.

Norris, P. (2004). Young People and Political Activism: From the Politics of Loyalties to the Politics of Choice? *Civic Engagement in the 21st Century: Toward a Scholarly and Practical Agenda*. University of Southern California.

Pakulski, J. (1993). "The Dying of Class or of Marxist Class Theory?" *International Sociology* 8(3): 279–92.

Park, A. (1995). Teenagers and their Politics. *British Social Attitudes: The 12th Report*. R. Jowell. Dartmouth, Aldershot.

Parry, G., G. Moyser and N. Day (1992). *Political Participation and Democracy in Britain*. Cambridge, Cambridge University Press.

Pilcher, J. (1994). "Mannheim's Sociology of Generations: An Undervalued Legacy". *British Journal of Sociology* 45(3): 481–95.

Plutzer, E. (2002). "Becoming a Habitual Voter: Inertia, Resources, and Growth in Young Adulthood". *American Political Science Review* 96: 41–56.

Rosema, M. (2006). "Low Turnout: Threat to Democracy or Blessing in Disguise? Consequences of Citizens' Varying Tendencies to Vote". *Electoral Studies* XX: 1–12.

Rubenson, D., A. Blais, P. Fournier, E. Gidengil and N. Nevitte (2004). "Accounting for the Age Gap in Turnout". *Acta Politica* 39: 407–21.

Russell, A. T., R. J. Johnston and C. J. Pattie (1992). "Thatcher's Children: Exploring the Links between Age and Political Attitudes". *Political Studies* 40(4): 742–56.

Sartori, G. (1969). "From the Sociology of Politics to Political Sociology". *Government and Opposition* 4(2): 195–214.

Scarrow, S. (2000). Parties without Members? *Parties without Partisans: Political Change in Advanced Industrial Democracies*. R. J. Dalton and M. P. Wattenberg. Oxford, Oxford University Press: xiv, 314p.

Schumpeter, J. A. (1952). *Capitalism, Socialism and Democracy*. London, Allen and Unwin.

Sloam, J. (2014). "New Voice, Less Equal". *Comparative Political Studies* 47: 663–88.

Theiss-Morse, E. and J. Hibbing (2005). "Citizenship and Civic Engagament". *Annual Review of Political Science* 8: 227–49.

Tilly, C. (1975). Collective Violence in European Perspective. *Violence in America*. H. D. Graham and T. R. Gurr. New York, Bantam.

Topf, R. (1995). Beyond Electoral Participation. *Citizens and the State*. H. D. Klingemann and D. Fuchs. Oxford, Oxford University Press: 52–91.

Touraine, A. (1971). *The Post-Industrial Society*. New York, Random House.

Touraine, A. (1981). *The Voice and the Eye*. Cambridge, Cambridge University Press.

Van Aelst, P. and S. Walgrave (2001). "Who is that (Wo)man in the Street? From the Normalisation of Protest to the Normalisation of the Protester". *European Journal of Political Research* 39: 461–86.

Van Biezen, I., P. Mair and T. Poguntke (2012). "Going, Going, … Gone? The Decline of Party Membership in Contemporary Europe". *European Journal of Political Research* 51(1): 24–56.

Van Den Broek, A. (1996). *Politics and Generations. Cohort Replacement and Generation Formation in Political Culture in the Netherlands*. Tilburg, Tilburg University Press.

Van Deth, J. W. (1990). Interest in Politics. *Continuities in Political Action: A Longitudinal Study of Political Orientations in Three Western Democracies*. M. Jennings and J. W. Van Deth. Berlin, De Gruyter and Aldine: 275–312.

Van Deth, J. W. and M. Elff (2000). Political Involvement and Apathy in Europe 1973–1998. *Mannheimer Zentrum für Europäische Sozialforschung Working Paper* 33: 1–47.

Verba, S. (1993). "Citizen Activity: Who Participates? What Do They Say?" *American Political Science Review* 87(2): 303–18.

Verba, S. and N. Nie (1972). *Participation in America: Political Democracy and Social Equality*. New York, Harper Row.

Wattenberg, M. (2000). The Decline of Party Mobilisation. *Parties without Partisans: Political Change in Advanced Industrial Democracies*. R. J. Dalton and M. P. Wattenberg. Oxford, Oxford University Press.

Whiteley, P. and P. Seyd (2002). *High-Intensity Participation: The Dynamics of Party Activism in Britain*. Ann Arbor, University of Michigan Press.

Whittier, N. (1997). "Political generations, micro-cohorts, and the transformation of social movements." *American Sociological Review* 62(5): 760–778.

Wilkinson, H. M. and G. Mulgan (1995). *Freedom's Children*. London, Demos.

4   The evolution of political participation in Western Europe

This chapter examines the patterns of popular political involvement in Western Europe to analyse whether there has been a progressive hollowing out of democracy's popular component over time. In particular, this chapter scrutinises whether conventional or 'elite-directed' political participation has been falling, whilst unconventional or 'elite-challenging' participation has been on the rise in Western European democracies. While studies of voter turnout and party membership suggest that Western publics are becoming increasingly disengaged, scholars studying 'unconventional' participation associated with the rise of new social movements and the 'New Politics', argue that political involvement is not universally declining. Rather, a new type of engagement is becoming more influential as younger, more 'cognitively mobilised' (Inglehart 1990) 'critical citizens' (Norris 1999, 2011) with 'new' value priorities shun 'elite-directed' forms of engagement in favour of 'elite-challenging' ones (Inglehart and Catterberg 2002; Inglehart and Welzel 2005). Given these conflicting narratives on political engagement, and the fact that studies tend to focus on only one type of participation or the other, this chapter examines over-time patterns for all the available indicators of both 'conventional' and 'unconventional' participation side by side. In this way, it tries to trace as unified a picture of possible of participation patterns in Western Europe in the last thirty years or so. It analyses over-time cross-national indicators of political participation from three aggregate data sources, two large cross-national surveys and seven national election studies.

Key themes and previous research

A number of studies have argued that Western European political involvement has been falling, and that citizens are less politicised than ever before. According to one author, we are witnessing the transformation of party democracy into "audience democracy" (Manin 1997). The arguments and analyses on declining political involvement in Western Europe have focused on declining party membership and turnout (Blais *et al.* 2004; Franklin 2004; Mair 2006; Van Biezen *et al.* 2012) whereas scholars studying unconventional participation, often associated with new social movements, say that participation should be rising (Inglehart 1977, 1990; Inglehart and Catterberg 2002; Inglehart and Welzel 2005; Norris 1999, 2002, 2011).

Conventional participation is made up of political activities mediated by the traditional organs of participation, or membership of these organisations, such as political parties and trade unions (Mair 2006). Mair (2006) suggests that political parties have withdrawn from civil society. They have turned away from both their mediation and representation of group-based interests in favour of a more managerial orientation (Whiteley and Seyd 2002). Voting is the most common form of conventional political participation and studies have shown that turnout has been dropping away. Franklin (2004) shows that since 1945 turnout rises in Malta, rises slightly in Belgium, Denmark, Sweden, Norway, Australia and Israel, but that all the other established democracies show decline of various magnitudes. Others show that plunging party membership reflects citizen disenchantment with politics (Dalton and Wattenberg 2000). Participation in other party-mediated activities is also declining (Norris 2004).

In contrast, unconventional political participation originally associated with the rise of new social movements and the new politics in the late 1960s, and, more recently, the rise of consumer politics, are said to be on the rise (Norris 2002; Norris *et al.* 2005). In the remainder of this chapter we will examine evidence for the patterns of participation in Western Europe to examine whether the data show growing unconventional participation and declining conventional engagement.

Findings

'Elite-directed' or 'conventional' participation: over-time patterns

Turnout

Figure 4.1 and Figure 4.2 show the Lowess[1] smoothed curves for turnout at legislative elections 1945–2008 and 1970–2008, respectively. Figure 4.1 shows declining turnout in France, Ireland, Italy, the Netherlands and Great Britain for the period 1945–2008. It also shows that France, Ireland and Britain begin at lower turnout levels than Italy and the Netherlands. On the other hand, Figure 4.2, for the period 1970–2008, shows declining turnout in France, Germany, Ireland, Italy, Great Britain and Sweden.

Table 4.1 shows that the coefficients for turnout regressed on time (measured in election years) are negative and significant for both 1945–2008 and 1970–2008 in six nations: France, Germany, Ireland, Italy, the Netherlands and Great Britain. The coefficient is only significant and negative in the period 1970–2008 in Sweden. In all nations except for the Netherlands, the coefficient is greater in 1970–2008 and the greatest turnout falls occur in France, Germany and Ireland. This is contrary to expectations since the Netherlands abolished compulsory voting in 1967 and the first election without compulsory voting was in 1971 (Gratschew 2004). Italy also relaxed its compulsory voting rules in this

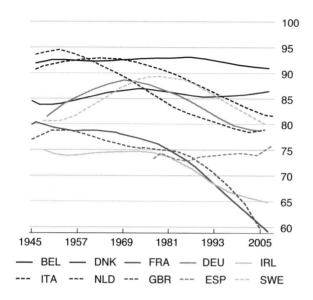

Figure 4.1 Turnout at legislative elections since 1945, %.

Note
Lowess smoothed lines.

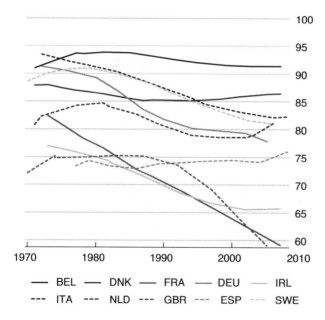

Figure 4.2 Turnout at legislative elections since 1970, %.

Note
Lowess smoothed lines.

Table 4.1 The evolution of political participation? Participation regressed on time[a]

		BEL	DNK	FRA	DEU	IRL	ITA[b]	NLD	GBR	ESP[c]	SWE
'ELITE-DIRECTED'											
Turnout	[1945–2008]	-0.01	0.03	-0.29**	-0.13*	-0.15**	-0.18**	-0.33**	-0.24**	n.a.	0.05
	[1970–2008]	-0.01	-0.05	-0.67**	-0.45**	-0.41**	-0.35***	-0.18	-0.37*	0.03	-0.31**
	[2002–2006]	0.05	0.19***	-0.22***	-0.12***	-0.16***	-0.37***	-0.10*	0.001	-0.01	0.05
Party membership[a]	[1978–2000]	-0.02**	-0.02**	-0.06**	-0.02**	-0.03**	-0.05**	-0.03**	-0.05**	0.05**	-0.02**
	[1964–2004]	n.a.	-0.001	-0.003**	-0.001**	n.a.	-0.002**	-0.002**	-0.001**	n.a.	-0.002**
	[1981–1990]	0.69**	0.14	0.001	0.17	0.17	0.29	-0.06	-0.29	-0.76***	-0.30*
	[1990–1999]	0.20	0.001	-0.34	-1.05***	0.11	-0.27	-0.02	-0.85***	0.38	0.07
	[2002–2006]	-0.02	0.10	-0.04	0.08	-0.05	0.03	0.05	-0.02	-0.12	-0.14*
Unpaid work party	[1981–1990]	-0.12	-0.14	-0.15	-0.32	0.10	-0.33	0.04	0.43	-0.96***	0.73*
	[1990–2000]	0.51*	0.29	-0.80*	-1.24***	-0.29	-0.43*	0.17	-0.27	0.35	0.09
	[2002–2006]	0.03	0.04	-0.14	-0.01	-0.10	0.28	0.09	-0.16	-0.09	0.001
Contacted politician	[2002–2006]	0.02	0.04	-0.06	-0.03	0.03	0.13	0.001	-0.05	0.001	-0.06
Union membership	[1981–1990]	-0.08	0.24**	-0.75***	-0.11	-0.60***	-0.44**	0.18	-0.58***	-0.85***	0.51***
	[1990–1999]	0.13	0.17	-0.30	-0.88***	0.10	0.02	0.17	-0.60***	0.20	0.23*
	[2002–2006]	0.07*	-0.07	-0.04	-0.23***	-0.01	-0.23	-0.08	-0.07	0.05	-0.04
Unpaid work union	[1981–1990]	0.23	0.11	-0.35	-0.12	-0.48	-0.56**	0.24	-0.001	-0.70**	0.99***
	[1990–1999]	0.14	0.12	-0.60*	-1.71**	0.30	-0.14	0.28	0.57	-0.19	0.54**
'ELITE-CHALLENGING'											
Joining unofficial strikes	[1981–1990]	0.75***	0.68***	-0.09	0.20	-0.37	0.91***	0.45	0.02	-0.31*	0.64*
	[1990–1999]	0.15	0.28*	0.25	-0.16	0.48*	-0.06	0.47	0.15	0.50***	0.42
Occupying buildings or factories	[1981–1990]	0.41	-0.20	0.04	-0.09	0.01	0.34*	0.42	-0.04	-0.22	-0.53
	[1990–1999]	0.31	0.28	0.14	-0.45	0.16	0.19	0.46	-0.14	0.21	2.57***

Attending demonstrations	[1981–1990]	0.70***	0.59***	0.31**	0.51***	0.21	0.41***	0.81***	0.41**	-0.15*	0.49***
	[1990–1999]	0.48***	0.06	0.27**	0.10	0.26*	0.04	0.31**	-0.02	0.26**	0.62***
	[2002–2006]	-0.06	-0.06	0.001	-0.23***	-0.17*	0.06	0.03	0.001	0.001	-0.13*
Joining in boycotts	[1981–1990]	1.23***	0.22	0.12	0.46***	0.05	0.45**	0.30	0.82***	-0.69***	0.75***
	[1990–1999]	-0.01	1.00***	0.04	0.11	0.12	0.10	1.08***	0.15	0.14	0.91***
	[2002–2006]	-0.12*	0.05	0.00	-0.08*	-0.07	-0.08	-0.07	-0.06	0.11*	-0.04
Signing petitions	[1981–1990]	1.12***	0.25**	0.29***	0.41***	0.55***	0.15	0.60***	0.61***	-0.13	0.75***
	[1990–1999]	0.75***	0.21*	0.59***	-0.37***	0.66**	0.33***	0.34***	0.18	0.34***	1.01***
	[2002–2006]	-0.09*	0.18***	0.01	-0.07*	-0.07	-0.30**	-0.05	0.02	-0.05	0.07*
Member environment, animal rights	[1981–1990]	1.38***	0.99***	1.02***	0.97***	0.16	0.64*	1.11***	0.44**	0.37	1.62***
	[1990–1999]	-0.16	-0.13	-0.64**	-1.18***	-0.19	0.06	0.68***	-1.62***	0.23	-0.30*
Unpaid work environment, a. r.	[1981–1990]	0.55*	1.57**	0.82*	1.01**	0.57	0.66	1.10**	0.82*	-0.01	-0.31
	[1990–1999]	-0.08	0.64	-0.94**	-1.15**	0.06	-0.12	-0.43	1.39***	-0.40	0.16
Member development/ human rights	[1981–1990]	2.37***	-0.22	0.85*	0.37	0.22	-0.001	1.50***	0.51	0.20	1.09***
	[1990–1999]	0.38**	0.36	-0.67*	-1.04*	0.48	0.96***	0.63***	0.11	0.85**	0.55**
Unpaid work development, h.r.	[1981–1990]	2.32***	-0.39	1.12*	-0.04	0.77	0.10	0.92*	0.34	-0.56	0.74*
	[1990–1999]	0.14	0.27	-0.65	-1.34*	0.24	0.98**	0.37	1.35***	0.55	0.36

Notes
Significance levels:
* $p \leq 0.05$.
** $p \leq 0.01$.
*** $p \leq 0.001$.
Cell entries are unstandardised beta (B) OLS (for turnout) or logistic regression coefficients for the activities regressed on time; these models are not meant to be properly specified but to give a sense of over-time change in participation.
a The data sources are the same as in Figures 4.1–4.24.
b European Social Survey data (2002–2006) for Italy are only for the period 2002–2004.
c Elections in Spain start in 1977.

period (Gratschew 2004). Here, indeed, the decline in turnout is as expected greater for 1970–2008. Turnout does not decline in either period in Belgium, Denmark or Spain. Due to enforced and strict compulsory voting rules, it is not surprising that turnout in Belgium stays above 90 per cent for the whole period. Italy and the Netherlands begin at similar turnout levels to Belgium, but register turnout closer to 80 per cent by the end of the period, probably due to the end of compulsory voting. Denmark is relatively stable, with about 85 per cent turnout for the whole period. In the low-turnout group, France, Ireland and Great Britain begin with turnout below 80 per cent and end with 60–65 per cent turnout. Using data for the period 1950–1997, Gray and Caul (2000: 1097) have shown declining turnout in Belgium, France, Germany, Ireland, Italy, the Netherlands and Great Britain, but not in Denmark and Sweden. They do not consider Spain. Evidence presented here confirms the importance of looking at different time frames. It does not support the conclusion that turnout is declining in Belgium. It also shows that turnout is indeed declining in Sweden, if we take into account updated turnout data until 2008 (Gray and Caul (2000) report a +4.3 point rise in turnout in Sweden for 1950–1997). For Denmark, Gray and Caul (2000) show a rise in turnout in the period 1950–1997. Evidence presented here shows that there is no significant turnout change in this nation.

Norris (2002) reports evidence that in 1945–2000, only eight post-industrial nations experienced declining turnout: Austria, France, Switzerland, the Netherlands, Australia, Canada, the United States and New Zealand. On the other hand, four nations experienced rising turnout: Sweden, Israel, Greece and Malta. Based on these findings, Norris (2002: xii) argues that "concerns that post-industrial societies are inevitably experiencing a deep secular erosion of voting participation during the last half century are greatly exaggerated". However, contrary to this conclusion, evidence reported here shows that the addition of turnout data until 2008 means that a further five post-industrial nations must be added to the eight Norris (2002) identifies with declining turnout. This brings the total up to thirteen. With the exception of Belgium, Denmark and Spain, turnout declined significantly in the period 1970–2008 in seven out of ten countries under analysis. The contradictory evidence for Sweden depending on the period, alongside the greater magnitude of coefficients in 1970–2008, would suggest that turnout decline sharpens since the 1970s.

Party membership

Figure 4.3 shows that aggregate party membership 1978–2000 (Mair and Van Biezen 2001) fell in all nations except Spain. In Belgium, Denmark, Italy and Sweden, party membership fell from about 5–10 per cent in this period, whereas in Germany, Ireland, the Netherlands and Great Britain it fell from about 2–5 per cent. Figure 4.4 for party membership with National Election Studies data 1964–2002 shows a decline in self-reported party membership in six out of seven nations analysed (except Denmark). However, the decline is small in Germany where party membership is low throughout. In Italy, the spike in party

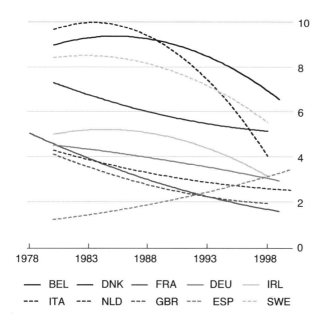

Figure 4.3 Party membership (aggregate), %, over time.

Note
Best fit quadratic smoothed lines; data are from Mair and van Biezen (2001) from party registers.

membership corresponds to the highly politicised period of the early 1970s. Figure 4.5 for self-reported party membership 1981–1999 (EVS) shows that it fell in France, Germany, Italy, Great Britain and Sweden and rose in Belgium and the Netherlands. Figure 4.6 for self-reported party membership 2002–2006 (ESS) shows largely stable patterns that follow on almost perfectly from levels reported in Figure 4.5 for 1999 (in the Netherlands, however, levels are almost 5 points lower).

Table 4.1 where participation is regressed on time shows that the regression coefficients over time for all four available indicators of party membership, including 2002–2006, are negative. Three are significant in Sweden, three out of four in Germany and Great Britain, two out of four in France, Italy and the Netherlands, and one out of three in Ireland. In Denmark, only the aggregate indicator of party membership is significant and negative, whereas in Spain, the only significant coefficient, for aggregate party membership is positive. In Belgium, aggregate party membership 1978–2000 is declining, whereas self-reported party membership 1981–1999 is rising. Hence, aggregate party membership 1978–2000 is declining in all nations except Spain, and self-reported party membership for the period 1981–1999 is only declining in four countries. This evidence perhaps confirms the argument in the literature that survey data for party

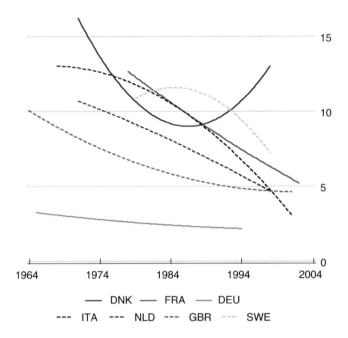

Figure 4.4 Party membership (self-reported), National Election Studies, %, over time.

Note
Best fit quadratic smoothed lines; data are from different time periods and are only available for the following seven countries: National Election Study data on self-reported party membership for Denmark (1971–1998), Germany (1965–1994), Netherlands (1971–1998), Great Britain (1964–2001) and Sweden (1979–1998) are all from the European Voter Database; data for Italy (1968–2001) are from the ITANES; data for France (1978–2002) are from EPF 1978–1997 and PEF 2002 (CSDP); data from National Election Studies for Belgium, Ireland and Spain were not available.

membership generally over-estimate levels due to respondents' confusion concerning what party membership means (Mair and Van Biezen 2001). The evidence may also support the claim that people who tend to answer surveys on political attitudes are also more likely to be politically active.

Evidence presented here therefore confirms that while party membership may be declining across Western Europe, there remains substantial variation across countries (Scarrow 2000). Using different data sources, the evidence presented also shows that at least one indicator of party membership is negative and significant in all nations except for Spain. However, the new data for the period 2002–2006 show that party membership has only continued to decline in Sweden in this later period. Given the finding in the section on turnout, that decline was only significant for 1970–2008 in Sweden, this could mean that conventional participation started falling later here.

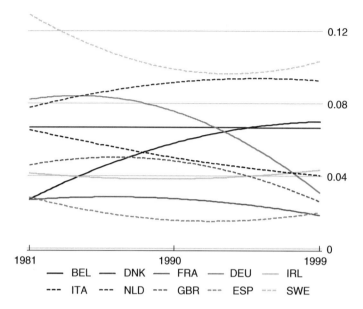

Figure 4.5 Party membership (self-reported), EVS (proportion saying 'yes'), over time.

Note
Best fit quadratic smoothed lines.

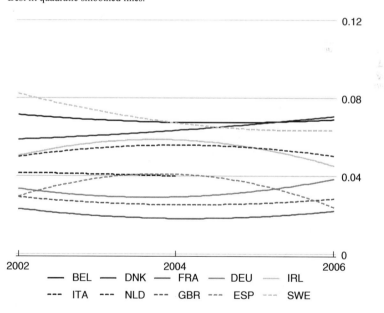

Figure 4.6 Party-membership (self-reported), ESS (proportion saying 'yes'), over time.

Note
Best fit quadratic smoothed lines.

Other party-mediated activities

Party work falls in France, Germany and Italy in 1990–1999 and in Spain in 1981–1990. Party work rises in Sweden in 1981–1990 (Figure 4.7), despite the fact that party membership fell. Figure 4.8 for respondents saying they worked for a party or political group in the last twelve months (2002–2006) shows that this indicator reports higher levels. Unfortunately, data for other forms of party-mediated participation are only available in the European Social Survey, for 2002–2006. This means it is difficult to reach firm conclusions about extended over-time patterns for these activities. Table 4.1 shows that none of the regression coefficients are significant for the ESS 2002–2006 indicators. Figure 4.9 for respondents saying they contacted a politician or government official in the last twelve months shows a decline in France, Germany and Sweden, and a rise in Denmark, Ireland and Italy. Between 10 and 20 per cent of respondents reported having contacted a politician or government official.

Union membership and unpaid work

Figure 4.10 shows that doing unpaid work for a union fell sharply in Germany and France in 1990–1999 and in Italy and Spain in 1981–1990. It rose, in both

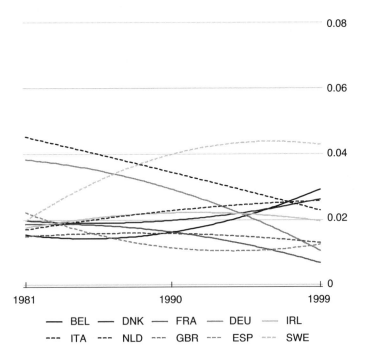

Figure 4.7 Unpaid work for a party, EVS (proportion saying 'yes'), over time.

Note
Best fit quadratic smoothed lines.

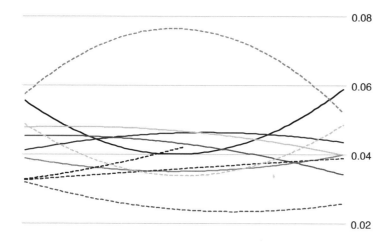

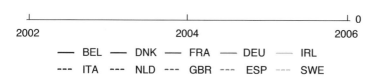

Figure 4.8 Work for a party/group last twelve months, ESS (proportion saying 'yes'), over time.

Note
Best fit quadratic smoothed lines.

periods, in Sweden. Figures 4.11 and 4.12 show self-reported labour union membership 1981–1999 and 2002–2006. In all countries where striking and occupying factories rose (except for France and Italy) union membership also rose. This suggests that these forms of activism could be understood as part of the repertoire of class-based political action, relating to the old labour movement.

Taken together, the evidence presented in this section shows that the various types of 'elite-directed' participation are not declining across the board. This type of participation rises in some countries but falls in others. Patterns for turnout and party membership for the aggregate and national election study data show that these activities are declining across the ten countries. However, the evidence presented from the EVS 1981–1999 and ESS 2002–2006 surveys actually shows overwhelming stability. Out of sixteen regression coefficients for elite-directed participation reported in Table 4.1 for each country, the majority are not significant, and thus, decline does not seem universal.

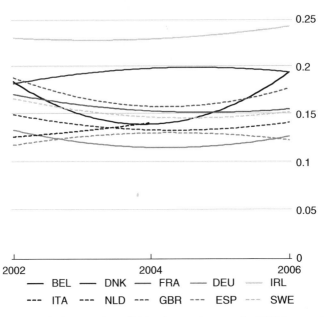

0.25

0.2

0.15

0.1

0.05

0

2002   2004   2006

— BEL — DNK — FRA — DEU ⋯ IRL

--- ITA --- NLD --- GBR --- ESP --- SWE

Figure 4.9 Contacted a politician last twelve months, ESS (proportion saying 'yes'), over time.

Note
Best fit quadratic smoothed lines.

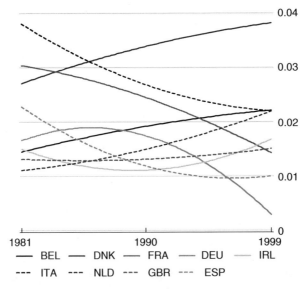

0.04

0.03

0.02

0.01

0

1981   1990   1999

— BEL — DNK — FRA — DEU ⋯ IRL

--- ITA --- NLD --- GBR --- ESP

Figure 4.10 Unpaid work for a union, EVS (proportion saying 'yes'), over time.

Note
Best fit quadratic smoothed lines; Sweden is not shown on Figure 4.10 since it was an outlier with levels >10 per cent in 1999.

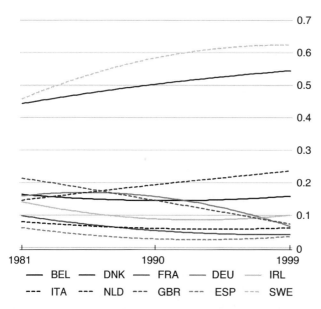

Figure 4.11 Union membership (self-reported), EVS (proportion saying 'yes'), over
time.

Note
Best fit quadratic smoothed lines.

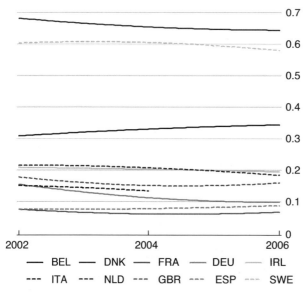

Figure 4.12 Union membership (self-reported), ESS (proportion saying 'yes'), over
time.

Note
Best fit quadratic smoothed lines.

'Elite-challenging' or 'unconventional' participation: over-time patterns

Striking and occupying

Figure 4.13 shows over-time patterns for the proportion of respondents saying they had joined an unofficial strike in 1981–1999. Figure 4.14 is for occupying buildings. Table 4.1 shows that these activities go up in Belgium, Denmark, Ireland, Italy, Spain and Sweden. The steepest rise in striking occurs in Denmark across this period. The proportion of respondents saying they joined a strike is also the highest in Denmark: rising from 10 per cent in 1981 (in average with other nations), to about 18 per cent in 1989 and 22 per cent in 1999. This can be attributed to the deregulation conflict amongst bus drivers in Esbjerg 1994–1995, and in Copenhagen in 1997, the 'RiBus-konflikten', one of the longest disputes in post-war Danish industrial relations, resulting in 1,740 strikes in 1995 alone (EIRO 1997; Gill *et al.* 1998).

Attending a demonstration

Figure 4.15 shows a rise in the proportion of respondents saying they had attended a demonstration 1981–1999 in all ten nations; Table 4.1 shows that the rise was particularly steep in Belgium, France, the Netherlands and Sweden. Italy and France stand out as the two nations with the highest proportion of

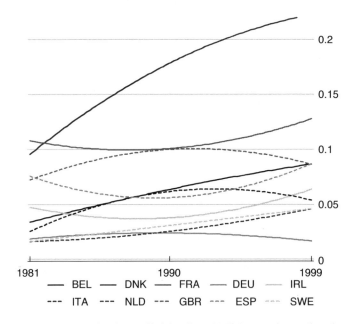

Figure 4.13 Joining in unofficial strikes, EVS (proportion saying 'have done'), over time.

Note
Best fit quadratic smoothed lines.

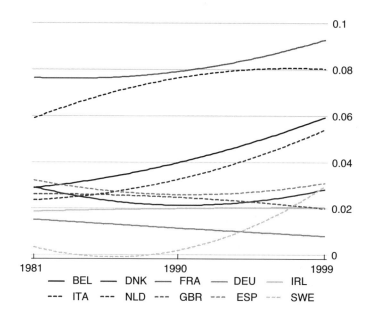

Figure 4.14 Occupying buildings or factories, EVS (proportion saying 'have done'), over time.

Note
Best fit quadratic smoothed lines.

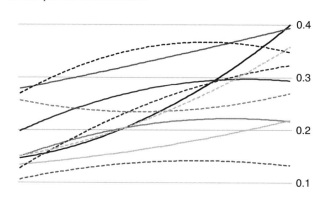

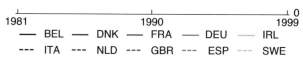

Figure 4.15 Attending lawful demonstrations, EVS (proportion saying 'have done'), over time.

Note
Best fit quadratic smoothed lines.

respondents participating in demonstrations, though Belgium and the Netherlands catch up with them by the third wave. However, Figure 4.16 for the period
2002–2006 shows a decline in Germany, Ireland and Sweden. Spain here is the
clear outlier – with almost 35 per cent of respondents saying they participated in
a public demonstration in 2004. This is in part explained by the growing number
of Spanish demonstrations against terrorism that took place from the late 1990s,
and culminating in 2004, which involved large sections of the population
(Jiménez 2007: 404). While attending a demonstration rises in all countries
except Spain in the period 1981–1999, this pattern is reversed in three nations
and positive in none in 2002–2006. Moreover, with the exception of Spain, and
as with signing a petition (below) the proportion of respondents saying they took
part in this activity is noticeably higher in 1999 than 2002. Most interestingly,
Table 4.1 shows that while demonstrating rose in eight out of ten countries in
1981–1990, it only continued to rise in four out of ten countries in 1990–1999
and *fell* in three countries in 2002–2006. This evidence goes counter to the modernisation thesis that elite-challenging participation is rising.

Joining a boycott

Figure 4.17 shows rising trends in boycotting 1981–1999 in all nations except
France, Ireland and Spain; it rose steeply in Sweden, Denmark and the Netherlands. Figure 4.18 for 2002–2006 and Table 4.1, however, show negative

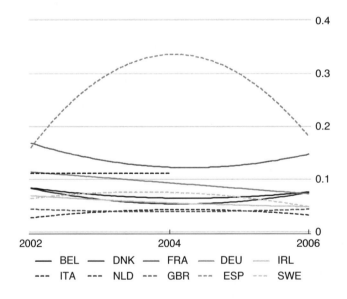

Figure 4.16 Demonstrated in last twelve months, ESS (proportion saying 'yes'), over
time.

Note
Best fit quadratic smoothed lines.

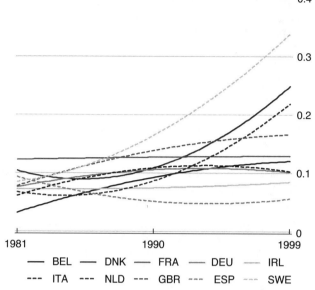

Figure 4.17 Joining in boycotts, EVS (proportion saying 'have done'), over time.

Note
Best fit quadratic smoothed lines.

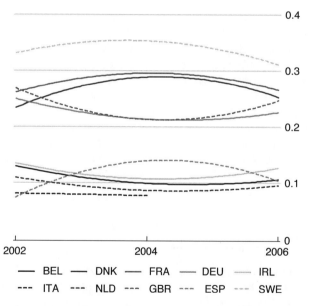

Figure 4.18 Boycotted in last twelve months, ESS (proportion saying 'yes'), over time.

Note
Best fit quadratic smoothed lines.

pattern in Belgium and Germany. Unlike with petition-signing and demonstrating, the percentage of respondents saying that they joined a boycott is similar in the EVS and ESS surveys. This piece of evidence, together with the fact that levels for petitioning and demonstrating from the EVS and ESS are relatively similar for Spain, a relatively new democracy, suggests that perhaps the 'have you ever' question in the EVS overestimates actual levels of participation in the population in a specified time period. Since Spain is a new democracy, where demonstrating and petitioning only became real possibilities for citizens post-1975, and since boycotting is a relatively new activity, which only rose to prominence in the 1980s, particularly in relation to the anti-apartheid campaigns, here the EVS comes closer to actual levels of participation in the population at the time of the survey rather than including participation in previous time periods. The evidence presented here, in comparing EVS- and ESS-estimated levels of participation, would suggest that the ESS provides a more accurate estimate of the proportion of individuals actually engaging in specific activities at a given time, whereas the EVS estimates how many individuals in the population have, at some point in their lives, engaged in a certain activity. As such, while at most 10–15 per cent of individuals say they have demonstrated in the ESS surveys, this is a far cry from the 30–40 per cent levels estimated from the EVS 1999.

Signing a petition

Figure 4.19 shows that signing a petition in 1981–1999 rises in all ten countries. The rise is particularly steep in Belgium, Sweden, Ireland and the Netherlands. Great Britain and Sweden stand out. With levels at about 80 per cent in the third wave, more individuals 'have done' this activity than voted in Britain, and about as many have done it in Sweden. However, Figure 4.20 for 2002–2006 shows declining trends in Belgium, Germany and Italy. Table 4.1 shows that the regression coefficients for signing a petition in all three countries are negative and significant. While signing a petition rises in all nations except Germany in the period 1981–1999, this trend is reversed in three nations and positive only in Denmark and Sweden in 2002–2006. Again, comparing Figure 4.19 and Figure 4.20 shows that, probably due to wording, the proportion of respondents saying they signed a petition is noticeably lower in 2002 than in 1999.

Participation in social movement organisations (SMOs)

Figure 4.21 shows that ecology, environmental or animal rights group membership (EEAR) 1981–1999 is rising in eight out of ten countries in 1981–1990. However, this pattern is reversed in four countries in 1990–1999 and only continues to rise in the Netherlands. Not only is the slope very steep, but membership in EEAR groups is atypically high in the Netherlands, with over 40 per cent of respondents saying they are members of EEAR by 1999.

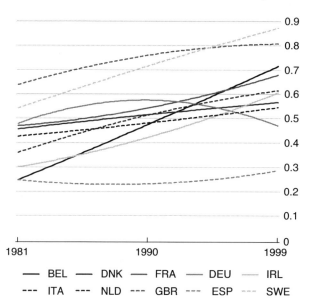

Figure 4.19 Signing petitions, EVS (proportion saying 'have done'), over time.

Note
Best fit quadratic smoothed lines.

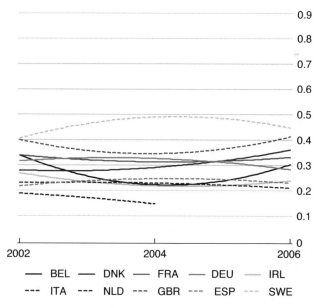

Figure 4.20 Signed petition in last twelve months, ESS (proportion saying 'yes'), over time.

Note
Best fit quadratic smoothed lines.

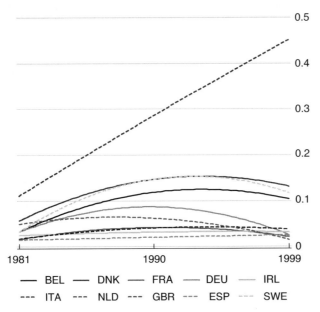

Figure 4.21 Environment, animal rights group membership, EVS (proportion saying 'yes'), over time.

Note
Best fit quadratic smoothed lines.

Dalton (2005: 443) argues that this pattern "reflects both the political traditions of the nation and membership in conservation groups as a by-product of the nation's park and nature preserve system". Van Der Heijden (1997) reports that membership in four environmental organisations rose from 412,000 in 1980 to 2,036,000 in 1995 in the Netherlands and in a more recent study (Van Der Heijden 2002) that between 1991 and 2001 their total constituency further increased from 2,158,600 to 3,744,850 – a nine-fold rise in the period 1980–2001. By contrast, the EVS data only register a four-fold rise. However, with a population of sixteen million, 40 per cent would still be equivalent to about 6.4 million people according to survey estimates, compared to about 3.7 million according to Van Der Heijden's (2002) membership count. From the Dutch national EVS documentation files it appears that the wording of the question has varied considerably through the years, possibly contributing to the relatively high numbers.

Figure 4.22 shows that membership in third world and human rights (TWHR) organisations rose in Belgium, the Netherlands and Sweden throughout the period under study. Again, the Netherlands registers the steepest rise. This pattern is fairly similar to that for EEAR group membership, which points to the overlap in the constituencies of new movements. In France, this pattern is reversed in 1990–1999. In Germany TWHR participation declines in 1990–1999.

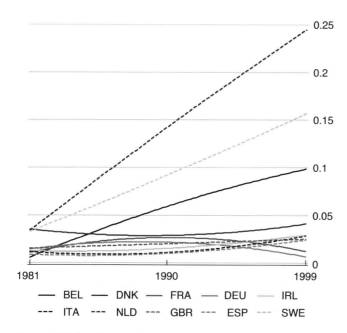

Figure 4.22 Development, human rights group membership, EVS (proportion saying 'yes'), over time.

Note
Best fit quadratic smoothed lines.

In Italy and Spain it rises in the second period only, suggesting that these organisations have become more popular in recent times. Figures 4.23 and 4.24 show over-time patterns for voluntary work for new groups: this goes up in Britain for both groups. Again, in Germany and France, the rising pattern is reversed in 1989–1999, and Italy and Spain come to these activities later. Finally, it is worth pointing out that the number of individuals engaging in these activities is quite small.

Conclusions

Studies of voter turnout and party membership often suggest that Western publics are becoming increasingly disengaged from politics. Meanwhile, scholars studying 'unconventional' participation claim that a significantly new type of participation is becoming influential. The results of this chapter suggest that political contexts matter. There is considerable diversity between countries and time periods in terms of over-time patterns in participation. As such, it is unlikely that societal modernisation alone is affecting trends in political participation across Western Europe. In subsequent time periods and within the same countries, participation in 'elite-challenging' activities initially goes up, but then goes down again. This suggests that unconventional political participation is not

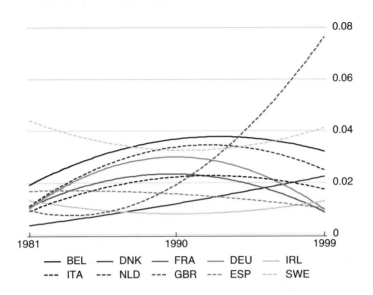

Figure 4.23 Environment, animal rights group unpaid work, EVS (proportion saying 'yes'), over time.

Note
Best fit quadratic smoothed lines.

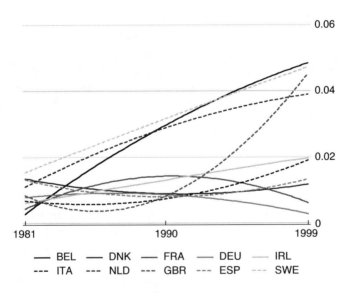

Figure 4.24 Development, human rights group unpaid work, EVS (proportion saying 'yes'), over time.

Note
Best fit quadratic smoothed lines.

continuing to rise across countries and across the various indicators. We conclude that nation-specific contexts, the actions of parties and the dynamic interaction between political actors and social groups have an important explanatory role to play concerning the divergent trajectories of different nations.

Note

1 Lowess (locally weighted scatterplot smoothing) curves are an ideal way to plot smooth curves that can be easily eye-balled without having to specify a potentially restrictive global function to fit the data.

References

Blais, A., E. Gidengil and N. Nevitte (2004). "Where Does Turnout Decline Come from?" *European Journal of Political Research* 43: 221–36.

Dalton, R. and M. Wattenberg (2000). *Parties without Partisans: Political Change in Advanced Industrial Democracies*. Oxford, Oxford University Press.

Dalton, R. J. (2005). "The Greening of the Globe? Cross-national Levels of Environmental Group Membership". *Environmental Politics* 14(4): 441–59.

EIRO (1997, 27 March). "European Industrial Relations Observatory: Denmark". www.eurofound.europa.eu/eiro/1997/03/inbrief/dk9703105n.htm (accessed 16 November 2015).

Franklin, M. N. (2004). *Voter Turnout and the Dynamics of Electoral Competition in Established Democracies since 1945*. Cambridge, Cambridge University Press.

Gill, C., H. Kundsen and J. Lind (1998). "Are There Cracks in the Danish Model of Industrial Relations?" *Industrial Relations Journal* 29(1): 30–41.

Gratschew, M. (2004). Compulsory Voting in Western Europe. *Voter Turnout in Western Europe Since 1945: A Regional Report*. IDEA. Stockholm, IDEA.

Gray, M. and M. Caul (2000). "Declining Voter Turnout in Advanced Industrial Democracies, 1950–1997. The Effects of Declining Group Mobilisation". *Comparative Political Studies* 33: 1091–1122.

Inglehart, R. (1977). *The Silent Revolution: Changing Values and Political Styles among Western Publics*. Princeton, Princeton University Press.

Inglehart, R. (1990). *Culture Shift in Advanced Industrial Society*. Princeton, Princeton University Press.

Inglehart, R. and G. Catterberg (2002). "Trends in Political Action: The Developmental Trend and the Post-Honeymoon Decline". *International Journal of Comparative Sociology* 43: 300–16.

Inglehart, R. and C. Welzel (2005). *Modernization, Cultural Change and Democracy: The Human Development Sequence*. Cambridge, Cambridge University Press.

Jiménez, M. (2007). "Mobilizations against the Iraq War in Spain: Background, Participants and Electoral Implications". *South European Society and Politics* 12(3): 399–420.

Mair, P. (2006). "Ruling the Void? The Hollowing of Western Democracy". *New Left Review* 42: 25–51.

Mair, P. and I. Van Biezen (2001). "Party Membership in Twenty European Democracies, 1980–2000". *Party Politics* 7(1): 5–21.

Manin, B. (1997). *The Principles of Representative Government*. Cambridge, Cambridge University Press.

Norris, P., Ed. (1999). *Critical Citizens: Global Support for Democratic Governance*. Oxford, Oxford University Press.

Norris, P. (2002). *Democratic Phoenix: Reinventing Political Activism*. Cambridge, Cambridge University Press.

Norris, P. (2004). Young People and Political Activism: From the Politics of Loyalties to the Politics of Choice? *Civic Engagement in the 21st Century: Toward a Scholarly and Practical Agenda*. University of Southern California.

Norris, P. (2011). *Democratic Deficit: Critical Citizens Revisited*. New York, Cambridge University Press.

Norris, P., S. Walgrave and P. Van Aelst (2005). "Who Demonstrates? Anti-State Rebels, Conventional Participants, or Everyone?" *Comparative Politics* 37(2): 189–205.

Scarrow, S. (2000). Parties Without Members? *Parties without Partisans: Political Change in Advanced Industrial Democracies*. R. J. Dalton and M. P. Wattenberg. Oxford, Oxford University Press: xiv, 314p.

Van Biezen, I., P. Mair and T. Poguntke (2012). "Going, Going, … Gone? The Decline of Party Membership in Contemporary Europe". *European Journal of Political Research* 51(1): 24–56.

Van Der Heijden, H.-A. (1997). "Political Opportunity Structure and the Institutionalisation of the Environmental Movement". *Environmental Politics* 6(4): 25–50.

Van Der Heijden, H.-A. (2002). "Dutch Environmentalism at the Turn of the Century". *Environmental Politics* 11(4): 120–30.

Whiteley, P. and P. Seyd (2002). *High-Intensity Participation: The Dynamics of Party Activism in Britain*. Ann Arbor, University of Michigan Press.

5   Generations and formal political participation in Western Europe

Chapter 4 showed that in general, the patterns of political participation in Western European publics have changed over the last thirty years or so in significant ways. Certain forms of participation, generally associated with what has traditionally been considered the 'conventional' repertoire, are becoming less popular. Meanwhile, participation associated with the 'unconventional' repertoire, emerging since the 1960s, has become more popular. However, this rise seems to have halted since 1990.

Given these changes in political participation patterns across Western Europe, it should be unsurprising that generational replacement and cohort differences in political participation have become increasingly prominent features in studies of political behaviour. These factors promise to explain the observed changes:

> a remarkable consensus has grown over the observation that in most Western societies the political orientations of younger age cohorts differ in fundamental ways from those embodied by their predecessors ... current opinion research tends to show marked differences between generations.
>
> (Hooghe 2004: 331)

However, the fact that there are differences between the political behaviour of older and younger cohorts does not in and of itself tell us anything about the processes of social change at play. Unless cohort differences are sustained over time, observed differences between older and younger age cohorts could simply be the reflection of the fact that individuals are situated in different stages of the life-cycle at the time of study.

Given that the direction of age effects for different forms of participation is normally understood to vary, with middle and old age generally seen as the peak point of conventional participation and youth generally seen as the key moment of unconventional participation, we examine cohort differences on each mode of political participation in turn. This chapter focuses on cohort differences in conventional participation; the next (Chapter 6) looks at cohort differences for unconventional engagement. More specifically, this chapter aims to analyse whether cohort – and therefore, generational – effects are more important than age effects for explaining observed differences in conventional political participation. This part of the investigation is aimed at understanding whether the observed differences between young and old are durable and likely to lead to social change in participation patterns through intergenerational replacement or whether, instead, they are simply temporary age-related differences, destined to subside as younger cohorts enter adulthood (Grasso 2011, Grasso 2013, Grasso 2014). This chapter begins its investigation by examining whether the patterns of participation analysed at the level of the nation in Chapter 4 are replicated when analysed by cohort. In turn, this chapter considers whether there are discernible over-time patterns in participation by cohort where none were found at the level of the nation. We also examine whether different types of conventional participation exhibit similar cohort participation patterns, or whether age effects are more important for explaining participation in certain types of activities than others. Moreover, we investigate whether cohort differences in different countries present themselves in the patterns suggested in the literature. The conventional pattern is that the youngest cohorts participate the least in these activities, whereas the oldest participate the most. The key question is thus whether there are significant differences between cohorts in their patterns of conventional participation.

The results presented in this chapter show that observed cohort differences in party membership are genuine generational differences and not simply attributable to age effects. The results show that education plays a mediating role for these cohort differences. In turn, this suggests that in the absence of rising levels of education amongst younger cohorts, cohort differences in conventional participation would have likely been much more marked. For voting, cohort effects are significant in eight out of ten countries, with the younger cohorts being significantly more likely than the post-WWII cohort to vote. However, age effects are also at play in France, Germany, Ireland and Great Britain. This is because younger people in these countries are significantly less likely than middle age people to vote. On the other hand, younger cohorts are significantly more likely than older cohorts to contact politicians. However, whereas in the case of the '80s and '90s cohort this is accounted for by higher education levels, this is generally not true of the baby-boomers. This suggests that whereas the pre- and post-WWII cohorts tend to be more involved in activities pertaining to parties and elections than younger cohorts, younger cohorts tend to be more involved in more 'consultative' types of conventional political participation which can be seen to have gained prominence as a result of the trends towards more managerial-style politics in many Western European countries (Mair 2006).

This chapter also investigates whether a gender bias remains in conventional participation. It asks whether individuals with lower education levels participate less, as has traditionally been found. More generally, the chapter examines whether there is still inequality in participation, whether more politicised individuals participate more than others and whether people with different sets of political values exhibit different levels of engagement. The chapter therefore reflects on key cross-national differences in this respect, and considers if there are salient differences in these patterns across types of indicators. These two topics of reflection lead onto a discussion of two different types of implications of this research for prominent theories of generational replacement.

Mair (2006) argues that politicians are increasingly open to consultation and other procedural mechanisms in a bid to 'engage' the citizenry. At the same time, parties become less important. Turnout and party membership fall since politicians refrain from ideological discourse and therefore downplay the 'popular' component of democracy. In turn, this leads individuals to perceive party politics and election outcomes as irrelevant to their lives, since no "issues of vital concern [are] presented" (Boechel 1928: 517). Therefore, theories that suggest the nature of democratic politics is changing are not necessarily in conflict with empirical results that show younger cohorts participate in certain conventional activities more than older cohorts.

Key themes and previous research

Analyses of conventional political participation in the literature tend to contrast the present state of politics to a time when politics "was seen to belong to the citizen and something in which the citizen could, and often did, participate in" (Mair 2006: 44). Some suggest that we are witnessing the transformation of party democracy into 'audience democracy' (Manin 1997). Turnout is falling and parties are 'haemorrhaging members' (Franklin 2004; Mair and Van Biezen 2001; Van Biezen *et al.* 2012). Young people are the least likely age group to register to vote. Some authors argue that for this generation politics has become a dirty word (Wilkinson and Mulgan 1995). Young people are described as an age group who are mainly distinctive in their lack of interest in traditional politics (Park 1995).

Worries about young people and conventional participation are by no means restricted to Britain. Research from across Western countries shows that younger cohorts vote less than older cohorts (Franklin 2004). Younger cohorts, who learn the habit of voting in less politically combative contexts, turn out at lower rates relative to older cohorts, who learned the habit of voting when elections were perceived as more important.

While Franklin's (2004) account emphasises the importance of institutional arrangements (and primarily the lowering of the voting age) as having a negative impact on young people's electoral participation, other explanations for these observed differences have also been offered (Blais *et al.* 2004; Fieldhouse *et al.* 2007; Plutzer 2002). The lack of ideological debate between parties (Bara and Budge 2001), the absence of meaningful alternatives in the sphere of party choice and the rise of more managerial-style politics (Mair 2006), lower levels of political interest (Blais *et al.* 2004) and a number of other factors could explain why people in general, and young people in particular, turn out to vote at lower rates. As Hooghe (2004: 332) points out: "turnout figures are not the only indicators corroborating the observation that the relation between young people and institutionalised party politics is under serious stress". Younger cohorts are also less likely to be party members, or to closely identify with parties. However, these observations could be the result of age effects, since people in middle or older age have more stable social networks and life arrangements.

However, if participation is changing, explanations for this process are to be found either in period effects, which affect the population as a whole, or in cohort effects. The latter would mean that younger generations have distinctive experiences which lead them to shun certain types of political participation and engage in others. As result of population replacement, this leads to changes in patterns of participation across societies. Of course, both these processes might be at play to some extent. Age effects, on the other hand, are unlikely to explain changing patterns of behaviour since they tend to be stable over time. Hence, by examining whether observed generational differences in conventional participation are based in real cohort effects or rather simply the reflection of age effects, this study will be able to assess whether the effects of these observed differences between younger and older people could have implications for the patterns of conventional political participation in Western Europe in the future.

Findings

Party membership

The primary aim of this analysis is to investigate whether the patterns of participation analysed at the level of the nation in Chapter 4 are replicated when analysed by cohort. The analysis therefore seeks to ascertain whether there are discernible over-time patterns in participation by cohort where there were none found at the level of the nation. This will return preliminary information concerning whether there are cohort differences in conventional participation within countries. Figure 5.1 shows the levels of party membership by cohort for each country over the 1981–1999 period.[1] The lines plot the overall proportion of party membership in the population; the levels of party membership for the pre-WWII generation; the levels of party membership for the post-WWII generation; the levels of party membership for the baby-boom generation; the levels of party membership of the '80s generation; the levels of party membership for the '90s generation. This cohort only enters the sample in 1990 and as such the levels are plotted over just two time points. Figure 5.1 shows that party members are generally drawn from older cohorts but there is quite a high degree of variation between countries in terms of which of the older cohorts is the most participatory, and in some cases the curves for different cohorts overlap, suggesting the presence of age effects. Figure 5.2 for party membership in the 2002–2006 period shows a similar pattern, with the exception of Spain, where the '90s generation, and younger cohorts more generally, are particularly participatory. A further point to note from Figure 5.1 and Figure 5.2 is that in some countries, there are large cohort differences in party membership (i.e. the vertical gap between the curves is wider), whereas in other countries the different cohorts exhibit relatively similar levels of party membership. Additionally, Figures 5.1 and 5.2 show that in some countries, such as Belgium (where party membership

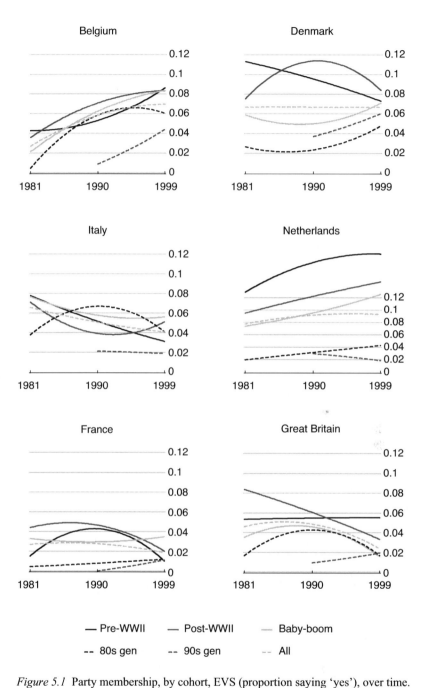

Figure 5.1 Party membership, by cohort, EVS (proportion saying 'yes'), over time.

Note

Best fit quadratic smoothed lines.

continued

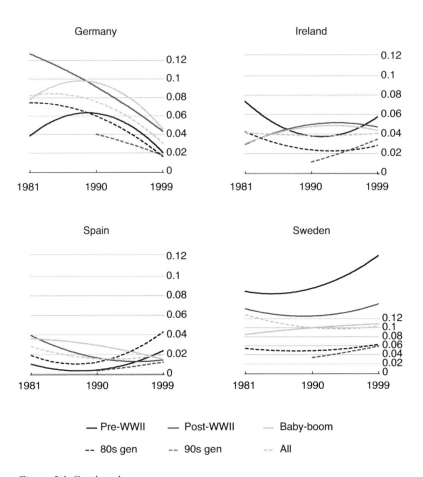

Figure 5.1 Continued

is rising) and Germany (where party membership is falling) the over-time patterns are relatively similar across cohorts (in other words, the curves slope in the same direction).

In other countries, over-time patterns vary between cohorts to a greater degree. In Denmark, for example, party membership is rising amongst the youngest cohorts whereas it is falling amongst the older cohorts.[2] In Italy, where party membership is generally decreasing, it reaches a peak in 1990 for the '80s generation. This is probably as a result of the popularity of the Socialist party amongst young voters in that period.[3] Moreover, Figure 5.1 shows that where party membership is decreasing, cohorts tend to converge in their levels of party membership, whereas where party membership rises it tends to do so more for older cohorts. Taken together, these results show that while older cohorts tend to be more involved in parties than younger cohorts, the magnitude of these cohort

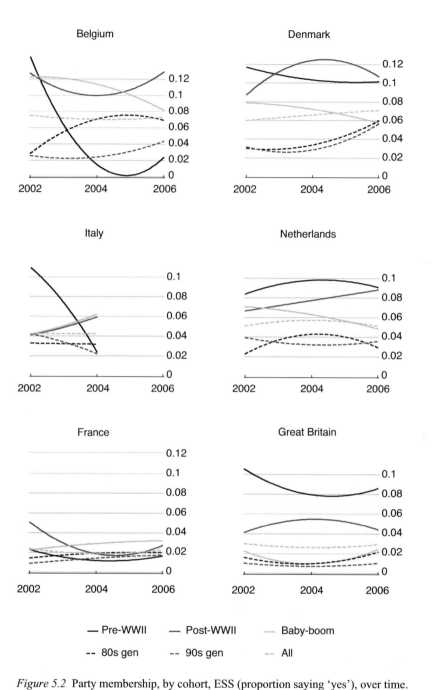

Figure 5.2 Party membership, by cohort, ESS (proportion saying 'yes'), over time.

Note

Best fit quadratic smoothed lines.   *continued*

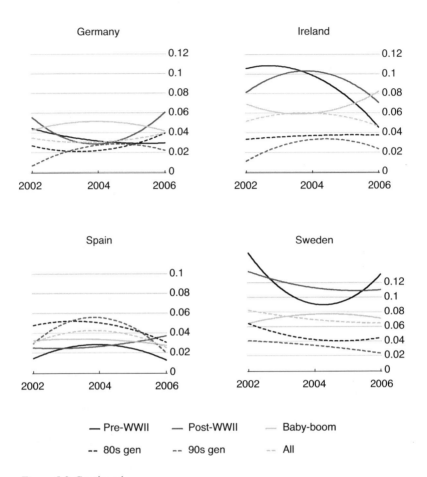

Figure 5.2 Continued

differences varies by country. With few exceptions, the over-time patterns in party membership tend to be similar across cohorts. As such, there is at least some evidence presented for period effects affecting all cohorts in the same way, though as discussed in Chapter 4, these period effects are by no means all pointing to increasing levels of disengagement amongst Western European publics. Indeed, Germany, Italy and Great Britain stand out as the three countries where party membership is falling most sharply.

The analysis has now described cohort differences in party membership in the different countries. In the next section, the aim is to provide a more robust empirical analysis of age, period and cohort effects and their implications for social change. The percentages in the cells in columns 2–6 of Table 5.1 report the levels of party membership, by cohort, for each country. The significance levels for the percentages in these cells are based on logistic regression, where the post-WWII cohort is the reference category. Thus, the significance-level stars capture whether

Table 5.1 Party membership, by cohort and country (%) EVS

Country	Pre-WWII	Post-WWII	Baby-boomers	80s gen.	90s gen.	Δ 80-BB	Δ 90-BB	Δ 90–80	N
Belgium	6	7	5	5	3***	0	−2*	−2	5,681
Denmark	10	9	6*	3***	5*	−3*	−1	+2	3,130
France	2	3	3	1**	1**	−2**	−2**	0	3,710
Germany, W.	5***	9	8	5***	3***	−3**	−5**	−2	4,364
Ireland	6	4	4	3	3	−1	−1	0	3,103
Italy	6	5	6	6	2***	0	−4***	−4***	5,323
Netherlands	15	12	10	3***	3***	−7***	−7**	0	3,149
Great Britain	6	6	4	3*	2**	−1	−2*	−1	3,468
Spain	1**	2	3	2	1*	−1	−2**	−1	6,001
Sweden	19*	14	10*	6***	5***	−4**	−5**	−1	2,907

Notes
Significance levels:
* $p \le 0.05$.
** $p \le 0.01$.
*** $p \le 0.001$.
The significance levels in columns 2–6 are based on logistic regression, where the post-WWII cohort is the reference category. Therefore, the significance-level stars capture whether there are significant differences in party membership between the post-WWII cohort and each of the other four cohorts in turn. The Δ columns on the right-hand side report the differences in percentages. The significance levels in the Δ columns on the right-hand side are derived by testing for coefficient differences between the two relevant cohort dummy variables post-regression.

there are significant differences in levels of party membership between the post-WWII cohort and each of the other four cohorts in turn. The Δ columns 7–9 on the right-hand side of the table, on the other hand, show the percentage point differences, between the levels of party membership amongst pairs of cohorts. The first Δ column (7), for example, reports the percentage difference in party membership levels between the '80s generation and the baby-boom generation. Significance levels here are derived by testing for coefficient differences between the two relevant cohort dummy-variables post-regression via the Wald test.

The results presented in Table 5.1 show that, across Western European countries, and as expected, the lowest levels of party membership can be found amongst the youngest cohorts: the '80s and '90s generations, and more so amongst the latter. There are only very small differences between the three oldest generations (pre-WWII, post-WWII and the baby-boomers). Moreover, the Δ columns 7–9 show that there are significant differences in party membership also between the baby-boomers and the '80s and '90s generations. These are largest between the '90s generation and the baby-boomers. Differences between the '90s and '80s generation are negligible. There appear to be clear generational differences in levels of party membership across Western Europe between the oldest three generations, up to and including the baby-boomers, and those coming of age in later periods: the '80s and '90s generations.

The figures reported above provide some initial support for generational differences in party membership based in socialisation experiences. This is insofar as the three older cohorts are significantly more involved with parties than the two youngest cohorts across countries. These differences do not decrease smoothly as one would expect from a straightforward age gradient. Rather, they show a break after the baby-boomers, suggesting that something may have changed in the political socialisation process of cohorts coming of age since the 1980s. However, it remains unclear, from this analysis alone, whether age effects – rather than, or in combination with, cohort effects – are at play here. It may simply be the case that older people tend to be more involved with parties and younger people tend to be less likely to join them due life-cycle effects rather than socialisation. Indeed, as the Appendix shows, all of the members of the pre-WWII cohort are in the oldest age group (51–90 years); and the majority of the post-WWII cohort is also part of this age group. The majority of baby-boomers belong to the middle age group (34–50 years) and the majority of the '80s generation and all of the '90s generation belong to the youngest age group (18–30 years).

Therefore, it is important to examine age group differences in party membership to examine if these overlap with cohort differences. Are people in the oldest age group more likely to be involved with parties? Are young people less likely to be party members? Table 5.2 shows that there are indeed age group differences in participation. People in the young age group are significantly less likely than both middle and older people to be party members. In some countries, differences are greater between young and old people. In others, they are greater

Table 5.2 Party membership, by age group and country (%) EVS

	18–33 yrs	34–50 yrs	51–90 yrs	Δ Young-middle	Δ Middle-old	Δ Young-old	N
Belgium	4*	6	7	−2*	−1	−3*	5,681
Denmark	4*	7	10**	−3*	−3**	−6***	3,130
France	1***	4	2	−3***	+2	−1*	3,710
Germany, W.	5***	9	6**	−4***	+3**	−1	4,364
Ireland	3	4	6	−1	−2	−3*	3,103
Italy	5	6	5	−1	+1	0	5,323
Netherlands	4***	10	14**	−6***	−4**	−10***	3,149
Great Britain	3*	5	5	−2*	0	−2**	3,468
Spain	2**	3	1***	−1**	+2***	+1*	6,001
Sweden	6***	11	16**	−5***	−5**	−10***	2,907

Notes
Significance levels:
* $p \leq 0.05$.
** $p \leq 0.01$.
*** $p \leq 0.001$.
The significance levels in columns 2–4 are based on logistic regression, where the 34–50 age group is the reference category. Therefore, the significance-level stars capture whether there are significant differences in party membership between the 34–50 age group and each of the other two age groups in turn. The Δ columns on the right-hand side report the differences in percentages. The significance levels in the Δ columns are derived as above and by testing for coefficient differences between the old and young age group dummies post-regression.

between young and middle aged people. This suggests that if there are age effects, these are linear in some countries but curvilinear in others. However, in and of itself, this does not exclude socialisation effects. Perhaps in some countries, party politics became more central to political life from the mid-1960s and 1970s, whereas in other countries parties were more important in the previous period. If this is true, then the differences between old and middle age people might still reflect differing socialisation experiences in the respective national contexts.

Given this consideration, age and cohort effects cannot be separated based on the information in these tables. It may be the case that age effects are at play explaining cohort differences in party membership. Therefore, this chapter turns to regression analyses controlling for each of cohorts, age and period to separate these effects. As shown and discussed in more detail in the Appendix, age and cohort effects can be separated in regression models by controlling for survey year. This is because each age group is spread over at least two cohorts in each survey year and the model is thus 'identifiable'. As also discussed in the Appendix and Chapter 3, the categorisations applied to cohort and age group variables in this study are helpful for the purpose of identification, and are also theoretically meaningful in the analysis of the results. As Mason *et al.* (1973: 242) argued, the identification of these effects only makes sense if "the researcher entertains relatively strong hypotheses about the nature of the life-cycle, period and generation effects" and their expected direction. In this case, the analysis examines two alternatives: (1) whether observed cohort differences in party membership are the result of life-cycle effects, so that older people tend to be members of parties more than younger people because they are more socially embedded. Or, (2) whether these observed differences are the result of generation effects, so that older cohorts are more likely than younger cohorts to be involved in parties because they were socialised at a time when parties mattered and were key to political life and political mobilisation. As discussed above, this investigation has implications for what can be said about the future of political participation. The primacy of generational effects would suggest that this type of activity in society will decline as older, more participatory, cohorts are replaced by younger, less participatory, cohorts, as argued by Franklin (2004) with respect to voter turnout in Western democracies.

Table 5.3 presents the results of logistic regression for party membership, for each of the ten countries analyses here, controlling for cohort, age group and survey year (Model(s) 1). The results for Model 1 across the ten countries show that with the exception of Spain, there are no significant age effects. On the other hand, there are significant cohort effects in seven out of ten countries analysed here, and (except for Germany) they all show that the youngest cohorts are significantly less likely to be party members relative to the post-WWII cohort (in Italy and Spain, this is only true of the '90s generation). This analysis gives us evidence to support the claim that cohort effects are more important than age effects for explaining generational differences in party membership. It appears that in at least some of the countries, the experiences of different generations

Table 5.3 Logistic regression on party membership, EVS, by country (APC and education)

	BEL		DNK		FRA		DEU		IRL	
	Model 1	Model 2	Model 1	Model 2	Model 1	Model 2	Model 1	Model 2	Model 1	Model 2
Pre-WWII	0.14	0.23	-0.08	-0.05	-0.46	-0.37	-0.74**	-0.68**	0.22	0.23
Baby-boom	-0.42	-0.47	-0.05	-0.13	-0.25	-0.38	-0.12	-0.20	0.37	0.36
80s gen.	-0.67*	-0.80*	-0.45	-0.58	-1.34*	-1.50*	-0.40	-0.60	0.18	0.15
90s gen.	-1.63***	-1.81***	0.25	0.08	-1.05	-1.18	-0.74	-1.05*	0.31	0.27
18–33	0.17	0.14	-0.46	-0.43	-0.54	-0.72	-0.29	-0.27	-0.22	-0.23
51+	-0.27	-0.16	0.43	0.47	-0.68	-0.57	-0.09	-0.04	0.48	0.49
1981	-0.84***	-0.78***	0.12	0.10	-0.15	-0.03	0.17	-0.25	0.23	0.23
1999	0.36*	0.32*	-0.07	0.05	-0.20	-0.25	-1.06***	-1.02***	0.08	0.09
Edu (low)		-0.82***		-0.45*		-1.18***		-0.91***		-0.10
Intercept	-2.44***	-2.18***	-2.58***	-2.44***	-2.81***	-2.36***	-2.15***	-1.61***	-3.54***	-3.48***
Pseudo-RSq	0.02	0.03	0.02	0.03	0.03	0.06	0.04	0.05	0.01	0.01
LogLike	-1,151.39	-11.11	-753.38	-749.62	-391.55	-380.48	-1014.2	-994.72	-528.56	-528.42
N	5,411	5,411	3,035	3,035	3,595	3,595	4,313	4,313	3,058	3,058

	ITA		NLD		GBR		ESP		SWE	
	Model 1	Model 2	Model 1	Model 2	Model 1	Model 2	Model 1	Model 2	Model 1	Model 2
Pre-WWII	0.14	0.19	0.20	0.27	0.08	0.18	-0.46	-0.37	0.42*	0.45*
Baby-boom	0.11	-0.05	-0.08	-0.17	-0.53	-0.66	-0.31	-0.42	-0.40	-0.41
80s gen.	-0.05	-0.29	-1.06**	-1.22***	-0.86	-1.06*	-0.67	-0.92	-1.01**	-1.03**
90s gen.	-1.09*	-1.37**	-1.17	-1.33*	-1.59*	-1.73*	-1.62*	-1.94*	-1.24*	-1.26**
18–33	0.20	0.14	-0.41	-0.48	-0.04	-0.20	0.01	-0.14	-0.03	-0.07
51+	-0.10	-0.02	0.09	0.16	-0.21	-0.10	-1.01**	-0.86*	-0.04	0.00
1981	0.19	0.35	-0.20	-0.18	-0.44	-0.37	0.51	0.44	0.03	0.11
1999	-0.19	-0.17	0.05	-0.01	-0.99***	-1.01***	0.66*	0.67*	0.17	0.17
Edu (low)		-0.87***		-0.75***		-1.52***		-1.18***		-0.28
Intercept	-2.89***	-2.45***	-1.97***	-1.66***	-2.36***	-1.45***	-3.55***	-2.84***	-1.88***	-1.82***
Pseudo-RSq	0.01	0.03	0.04	0.06	0.03	0.09	0.03	0.06	0.03	0.03
LogLike	-1,035.14	-1,016.58	-891.88	-877.78	-570.35	-536.11	-566.03	-548.61	-861.68	-859.92
N	5,215	5,215	3,048	3,048	3,327	3,327	5,767	5,767	2,584	2,584

Notes

Model 1: age, period and cohort; Model 2: age, period, cohort and education.

Significance levels:

* $p \leq 0.05$.

** $p \leq 0.01$.

*** $p \leq 0.001$.

Reference categories: Post-WWII cohort (2); 34–50 age group (2); 1990 (2), therefore, 1981 is the inverse of the period effect 1981–1990; Edu (low) is a dummy variable where 1 means the respondent left school before the age of 17.

have an impact on whether they join parties or not. The models in Table 5.3 compare the coefficients for each cohort with that of the reference category, namely the post-WWII cohort.

This analysis justifies the claim that party membership is significantly lower in the '80s and '90s cohorts than in the post-WWII cohort (conditional on the other variables in the model). However, it is also important to check whether the '90s cohort are significantly different from the '80s cohort, the baby-boomers, and so on. This cannot be directly inferred from Table 5.3. This study therefore conducted further analyses to facilitate the relevant comparisons. Table 5.4 shows the significance levels for coefficient differences (estimated post-regression via the Wald test), which are not captured in the regression analyses presented in Model(s) 1. The results reported here provide further evidence for the primacy of cohort over age effects. Even when controlling for age and period, there are significant generational differences in party membership. The baby-boomers are significantly more likely to be members of a party relative at least to one of the two younger cohorts (Δ 80-BB and Δ 90-BB) in six out of ten countries analysed.

Given the massive expansion of education since the 1960s in Western Europe, and the well-established association between education and political participation at the individual level, one would have expected that the '80s and '90s cohorts should be more, not less, active in political parties than the previous generations. Figures A.1 and A.2 in the Appendix clearly show that there are large cohort differences in the percentages of respondents leaving school at or before the age of sixteen (or completing less than ten years of formal education). In the whole sample, 72 per cent of the pre-WWII cohort did not complete secondary education, compared to 61 per cent of the post-WWII cohort. This falls to 42 per cent with the baby-boom cohort. Amongst the '80s and '90s generations, on the other hand, only 29 and 21 per cent respectively did not complete secondary education. Given these differences, it is important to control for education to ascertain whether the expansion of education has attenuated generational differences in

Table 5.4 Wald tests for Model(s) 1

	BEL	DNK	FRA	DEU	IRL	ITA	NLD	GBR	ESP	SWE
Δ 80-BB	ns	ns	*	ns	ns	ns	***	ns	ns	*
Δ 90-BB	**	ns	ns	ns	ns	***	*	ns	*	*
Δ 90-80	*	ns	ns	ns	ns	***	ns	ns	ns	ns
Δ Young-old	ns	ns	ns	ns	ns	ns	ns	ns	ns	ns
Δ 1981-1999	***	ns	ns	***	ns	ns	ns	ns	ns	ns

Notes
Significance levels:
* $p \leq 0.05$.
** $p \leq 0.01$.
*** $p \leq 0.001$.
Δ significance levels are calculated post-regression model by testing for coefficient differences; ns means no significant differences.

party membership. If this is the case, it would mean that, without the expansion of education, younger cohorts' socialisation experiences would have driven them to be even less participatory. Due to the mediating influences of rising education levels, cohort effects based in socialisation may appear weaker than they actually are.

Model(s) 2 in Table 5.3 present the results of logistic regression models on party membership, including education level as a predictor.[4] The results for Model(s) 2 relative to those for Model(s) 1, all reported in Table 5.3, show that including education emphasises generational differences in party membership. In every country, except for Ireland and Sweden, receiving a lower-level education has a significant negative effect on party membership. These results show that, once again, with the exception of Spain, there are no significant age effects when controlling for cohort, period and education level. On the other hand, there are significant cohort effects in eight out of ten countries analysed here, and they all show that the youngest cohorts are significantly less likely to be party members relative to the post-WWII cohort. This analysis provides us with more evidence to support the claim that cohort effects are more important than age effects for explaining generational differences in party membership.

Moreover, these results also suggest that given the well-established association between education and participation at the individual level, without the expansion of education, cohort differences in party membership could have possibly been more marked. As such, the results show that cohort membership has an impact on whether individuals join parties or not. While rising education levels attenuate cohort differences in party membership, these still remain. However, if there are ceiling effects to rising education levels, then education may not continue to mediate generational differences. This would mean in turn that cohort differences in conventional participation, with younger cohorts being less likely to participate than older ones, may further exacerbate in the future. Table 5.5 reports the significance levels for cohort coefficient differences (Wald tests) (e.g. differences between the baby-boom and '80s generations). The results

Table 5.5 Wald tests for Model(s) 2

	BEL	DNK	FRA	DEU	IRL	ITA	NLD	GBR	ESP	SWE
Δ 80-BB	ns	ns	*	*	ns	ns	***	ns	ns	*
Δ 90-BB	***	ns	ns	ns	ns	***	*	ns	**	*
Δ 90-80	**	ns	ns	ns	ns	**	ns	ns	*	ns
Δ Young-old	ns	*	ns	ns	ns	ns	ns	ns	ns	ns
Δ 1981-1999	***	ns	ns	**	ns	ns	ns	ns	ns	ns

Notes
Significance levels:
* $p \leq 0.05$.
** $p \leq 0.01$
*** $p \leq 0.001$.
Δ significance levels are calculated post-regression model by testing for coefficient differences; ns means no significant differences.

reported here provide further evidence for the primacy of cohort over age effects. When controlling for education, age and period, there are significant generational differences in party membership, with the baby-boomers, significantly more likely to be members of a party relative at least to one of the two younger cohorts in seven out of ten countries analysed here. It is also important to note that there are significant age differences here for Denmark. This suggests that perhaps in this country (Denmark), age rather than cohort effects have a more salient role in explaining the observed cohort differences in membership of political parties.

The results presented in Table 5.6 replicate the models in Table 5.3 above for the European Social Surveys data (ESS 2002, 2004, 2006) and show similar patterns. The youngest cohorts are in five countries significantly less likely than the post-WWII cohort to be party members. The fact that so many coefficients are significant given the small number of cases suggests that these cohort differences are important. Where results are not significant, the coefficients are negative. Given a larger sample size, we might expect these results to be significant in the direction expected since the size of the coefficient is of a relatively similar magnitude to those for cohort effects which are significant (for cohorts from which we have a larger sample size). With the exception of Germany, there are no significant age effects. Again, including education as a predictor shows that the coefficient for negative cohort effects increases, suggesting that education plays a mediating role in attenuating cohort differences in party membership. As such, the evidence presented here shows that cohort effects are more important than age effects for explaining cohort differences in party membership. It also shows that while cohort effects are not significant in some countries, there are reasons to believe that this is due to the small sample size judging on coefficient magnitudes.

Tables 5.7 and 5.8 present the results of logistic regression on party membership (both for the EVS and the ESS data) for the fully specified model discussed above for each country in the sample. Here, cohort differences, with the youngest cohorts participating in parties significantly less than the post-WWII cohort, persist when controlling for all the other predictor variables. In seven out of ten countries the coefficients for either or both of the '80s and '90s generation are significant and negative. This means that members of these cohorts are significantly less likely, relative to the post-WWII cohort, to be members of a party. In Belgium, Sweden and Great Britain, there are persistent and significant negative cohort effects for both of the two most recent generations. In all these cases, the coefficients for the '90s generation are of greater magnitude. This indicates that, relative to the post-WWII cohort, the '90s generation is significantly less likely than the '80s generation to join a party. Moreover, in Britain, the baby-boomer cohort is also significantly less likely than the post-WWII cohort to be party members. On the other hand, in Sweden, members of the pre-WWII cohort are significantly more likely, relative to members of the post-WWII one, to be members of a party. In Germany, however, contrary to expectations, the post-WWII is significantly more likely than the pre-WWII cohort to join parties.

Unlike cohort effects, age effects are only present in Spain for 1981–1999, where older people are significantly less likely than middle aged people to be party members. This is probably due to the fact that in Spain at least, the 'old' age group is more right-wing than the 'young' and 'middle' age groups (with 42 per cent of 'old' versus, 30 and 28 per cent of respectively, 'middle' and 'young' respondents placing themselves on points 6 to 10 of the left 1-right 10 scale), but that party members in Spain are disproportionately from the left. This is probably due to the popularity of the PSOE (respectively, 18, 16 and 24 per cent of party members place themselves on points 1, 2 and 3 of the left 1-right 10 scale) in Spain in the period under study.

In terms of over-time change in party membership, only Germany and Great Britain exhibit significant negative period effects, and only for the period 1989–1990. The only other significant negative period effects are to be found in Spain for 1981–1990, though the coefficient for 1981 is only significant in the full model. In Belgium, on the other hand, there are positive period effects in 1981–1990. Controlling for class in the full model in Table 5.7 accounts for this period effect. This could be explained in part by the split of the Christian Democrats (1968) and Socialists (1978) along linguistic lines. The creation of new parties along linguistic lines, thus providing novel incentives for membership, in this period would therefore explain why party membership rises in Belgium in the 1981–1990 period. There are significant and positive period effects for party membership in Spain for the 1990–1999 period. This may be a result of the expanding popular base of the PSOE, following the re-election of Felipe Gonzalez and the post-Marxist consensus in the party. This was a key factor in the Socialists' victory in 1982, increasing their popular vote from 5.5 million in 1979 to ten million. Overall then, in terms of period effects for party membership, they are negative in Germany (West) and Great Britain only, and for the 1990–1999 period alone. In Spain and Belgium, on the other hand, party membership rises. There are no significant period effects in any of the other countries, which is to be expected given the tiny number of cases for party membership in cross-national survey data and the fact that we have split the period into two separate segments. Due to, on the one hand, the rise of political freedom and left-wing joining incentives, and on the other, the splitting of the major parties along linguistic lines, distinctive national-context factors are probably what explain why Spain and Belgium experience positive period effects.

As expected, men are more likely than women to join parties in every country, although this effect is no longer significant in France for the period 2002–2006. Being male significantly increases the chances of joining a party and more so in the more traditional Southern European and strongly Catholic countries: Spain, Ireland and Italy. Furthermore, being male also (oddly) has a comparable magnitude of effect in (West) Germany. The magnitude of the effect of male gender is the smallest in the more liberal Northern-European and Scandinavian countries: Denmark, the Netherlands and Sweden; and at mid-level in weaker Catholic/part-Catholic North European countries: Belgium and France. Having completed formal education earlier (at or before the age of sixteen, or

Table 5.6 Logistic regression on party membership, ESS, by country (APC and education)

	BEL		DNK		FRA		DEU		IRL	
	Model 1	Model 2	Model 1	Model 2	Model 1	Model 2	Model 1	Model 2	Model 1	Model 2
Pre-WWII	-0.44	-0.41	0.05	0.06	-0.58	-0.55	-0.29	-0.06	0.16	0.11
Baby-boom	-0.05	-0.12	-0.58**	-0.60**	0.02	-0.03	0.09	-0.04	-0.11	-0.08
80s gen.	-0.61*	-0.72**	-1.35***	-1.37***	-0.38	-0.45	-0.04	-0.17	-0.72*	-0.68
90s gen.	-1.21*	-1.35**	-1.01*	-1.04*	-1.08	-1.17	-0.12	-0.26	-1.84**	-1.79**
18–33	-0.04	-0.04	-0.50	-0.50	0.50	0.48	-0.49	-0.48	0.69	0.70
51+	0.21	0.23	-0.31	-.30	0.19	0.23	0.53	0.56*	0.15	0.11
2002	0.10	0.10	-0.12	-0.12	0.23	0.22	0.20	0.22	-0.20	-0.18
2006	0.07	0.07	0.07	0.08	0.22	0.18	0.32*	0.31	-0.10	-0.09
Edu (low)		-0.39**		-0.11		-0.30		-1.00***		0.25
Intercept	-2.27***	-2.09***	-1.78***	-1.75***	-3.78***	-3.62***	-3.63***	-3.42***	-2.46***	-2.55***
Pseudo-RSq	0.03	0.04	0.03	0.03	0.01	0.02	0.02	0.03	0.03	0.03
LogLike	-1,231.63	-1,226.62	-982.05	-981.78	-515.47	-514.51	-1,198.3	-1,182.49	-1,066.97	-1,065.35
N	4,636	4,636	4,026	4,026	4,765	4,765	7,515	7,515	5,227	5,227

	ITA		NLD		GBR		ESP		SWE	
	Model 1	Model 2	Model 1	Model 2	Model 1	Model 2	Model 1	Model 2	Model 1	Model 2
Pre-WWII	0.58	0.66	0.12	0.22	0.77**	0.91***	-0.64	-0.59	0.12	0.17
Baby-boom	0.25	0.12	-0.28	-0.36	-0.77**	-0.93**	0.03	-0.08	-0.53***	-0.59***
80s gen.	-0.48	-0.67	-0.99**	-1.12***	-0.77	-1.01	0.27	0.10	-0.83**	-0.91**
90s gen.	-0.49	-0.77	-1.25*	-1.40**	-0.96	-1.19	0.43	0.21	-1.61**	-1.70**
18–33	0.05	-0.02	0.55	0.53	-0.26	-0.28	-0.46	-0.47	0.39	0.38
51+	0.01	0.06	0.00	0.05	0.56	0.64	-0.08	-0.01	0.10	0.14
2002	-0.13	-0.09	-0.13	-0.16	0.09	0.05	-0.17	-0.15	0.21	0.21
2006			0.01	-0.03	0.07	-0.01	-0.46*	-0.47*	-0.04	-0.06
Edu (low)		-0.77***		-0.54***		-0.95***		-0.53*		-0.25
Intercept	-2.93***	-2.51***	-2.37***	-2.13***	-3.59***	-3.26***	-3.16***	-2.81***	-2.17***	-2.07***
Pseudo-RSq	0.01	0.03	0.02	0.03	0.07	0.08	0.01	0.01	0.04	0.04
LogLike	-427.57	-421.28	-1,208.63	-1,200.46	-679.71	-667.27	-652.42	-648.46	-1,311.2	-1,309.35
N	2,409	2,409	5,699	5,699	5,730	5,730	4,355	4,355	5,170	5,170

Notes

Model 1: age, period and cohort; Model 2: age, period, cohort and education.

Significance levels:

* $p \leq 0.05$.

** $p \leq 0.01$.

*** $p \leq 0.001$.

Reference categories: Post-WWII cohort (2); 34–50 age group (2); 2004 (2), therefore, 2002 is the inverse of the period effect 2002–2004; Edu (low) is a dummy variable where 1 means the respondent left school before the age of 17.

Table 5.7 Logistic regression on party membership, EVS, by country (APC and all controls)

	BEL	DNK	FRA	DEU	IRL	ITA	NLD	GBR	ESP	SWE
Pre-WWII	0.18	-0.14	-0.35	-0.61*	0.27	0.24	0.17	0.14	-0.32	0.45*
Baby-boom	-0.41	-0.09	-0.49	-0.24	0.35	-0.09	-0.19	-0.75*	-0.53	-0.39
80s gen.	-0.75*	-0.44	-1.43*	-0.51	0.10	-0.23	-1.12**	-1.06*	-1.01	-1.04**
90s gen.	-1.74***	0.23	-0.90	-0.95	0.13	-1.28**	-1.18	-1.67*	-1.87*	-1.25*
18-33	0.18	-0.49	-0.81	-0.34	-0.13	0.10	-0.51	-0.19	-0.28	-0.11
51+	-0.19	0.50	-0.5	-0.03	0.48	-0.06	0.15	-0.24	-0.81*	0.00
1981	-0.78***	0.26	-0.16	-0.29	0.26	0.18	-0.24	-0.38	0.57	0.01
1999	0.32	-0.04	-0.53	-1.11***	0.11	-0.13	-0.03	-1.03***	0.67	0.19
Edu (low)	-0.56**	-0.27	-1.03**	-0.66***	-0.12	-0.64***	-0.59***	-1.16***	-1.06***	-0.34*
Male	0.66***	0.39*	0.58*	0.99***	0.94***	1.21***	0.38**	0.40*	0.77***	0.56***
Working cl.	-0.65***	-0.42*	-0.55	-0.70***	-0.16	-0.26	-0.47*	-1.12***	0.06	0.08
Left	0.93***	1.29***	1.77***	1.12***	0.95	0.83***	1.04***	1.58***	1.59***	0.33
Right	0.45	0.77**	1.35**	1.18***	-0.19	0.23	0.87**	0.76*	1.22*	0.75**
Left-auth.	0.19	-0.53	-0.57	-0.56*	0.83**	-0.06	-0.09	-0.13	-0.57	-0.48*
Right-lib.	0.17	0.13	-0.24	-0.68**	0.89**	-0.43	-0.19	-0.29	-0.51	-0.59**
Right-auth.	0.28	0.41	-0.99*	-0.55*	0.58	-0.15	0.08	-0.05	-0.31	-0.29
Intercept	-2.71***	-2.85***	-2.62***	-1.76***	-4.63***	-3.21***	-1.87***	-1.50***	-3.49***	-1.89***
Pseudo-RSq	0.06	0.06	0.15	0.11	0.05	0.08	0.09	0.14	0.14	0.06
LogLike	-1,100.38	-722	-343.57	-935.18	-508.35	-960.83	-852.8	-505.5	-504.57	-836.34
N	5,408	3,035	3,595	4,313	3,053	5,215	3,047	3,326	5,767	2,570

Notes
Models with age, period, cohort, education, gender, class, ideology and values.
Significance levels:
* $p \leq 0.05$.
** $p \leq 0.01$.
*** $p \leq 0.001$.
Reference categories: Post-WWII cohort (2); 34–50 age group (2); 1990 (2), therefore, 1981 is the inverse of the period effect 1981–1990; Left-libertarian (1); Edu (low) is a dummy variable where 1 means the respondent left school before the age of 17; Working class is a dummy variable where 1 means the respondent is an unskilled, semi-skilled or skilled manual worker; Left and right are dummy variables derived from the left-right scale where left (1) means values 0/1 and right (1) means values 9/10.

Table 5.8 Logistic regression on party membership, ESS, by country (APC and all controls)

	BEL	DNK	FRA	DEU	IRL	ITA	NLD	GBR	ESP	SWE
Pre-WWII	-0.38	0.10	-0.53	0.00	0.15	0.80	0.19	0.78***	-0.51	0.16
Baby-boom	-0.08	-0.52**	0.01	0.01	-0.05	0.07	-0.29	-0.96**	-0.14	-0.57***
80s gen.	-0.68*	-1.27***	-0.35	-0.08	-0.63	-0.67	-1.07**	-1.05	-0.01	-0.87***
90s gen.	-1.33**	-0.91*	-1.03	-0.22	-1.73**	-0.78	-1.34**	-1.33	0.19	-1.72**
18–33	-0.03	-0.50	0.47	-0.42	0.68	-0.17	0.50	-0.17	-0.52	0.39
51+	0.24	-0.27	0.21	0.53	0.10	-0.02	-0.01	0.58	-0.07	0.15
2002	0.09	-0.14	0.20	0.21	-0.22	0.03	-0.18	0.03	-0.06	0.22
2006	0.08	0.03	0.18	0.33*	-0.16		-0.02	0.02	-0.38	-0.06
Edu (low)	-0.34*	0.20	-0.25	-0.61***	0.21	-0.72**	-0.31*	-0.70**	-0.43*	-0.19
Male	0.42***	0.83***	0.34	0.86***	0.70***	1.43***	0.45***	0.57***	0.69***	0.23*
Working cl.	-0.22	-0.61***	-0.16	-0.74***	-0.14	0.04	-0.92***	-0.77***	-0.30	-0.22
Left	0.92***	0.98***	1.28***	1.00***	0.66	1.42***	0.91***	0.28	1.33***	0.67***
Right	0.75**	0.50*	1.28***	1.48***	0.95***	1.12**	1.17***	0.91**	1.78***	0.55***
Left-auth.	-0.17	-0.17	0.08	-0.26	-0.33	-0.40	-0.09	-0.42	-0.46*	-0.01
Right-lib.	-0.16	-0.22	0.08	-0.04	-0.77*	-0.57	-0.22	-0.42	0.07	0.28
Right-auth.	-0.17	0.01	0.55	0.03	-0.28	-0.96**	0.25	-0.23	-0.56	-0.07
Intercept	-2.28***	-2.18***	-4.24***	-3.87***	-2.67***	-3.33***	-2.42***	-3.13***	-3.08***	-2.26***
Pseudo-RSq	0.05	0.06	0.06	0.07	0.06	0.12	0.06	0.11	0.07	0.05
LogLike	-1,202.38	-948.78	-493.51	-1,132.43	-1,030.87	-380.62	-1,158.85	-649.86	-610.2	-1,295.96
N	4,625	4,026	4,765	7,515	5,204	2,409	5,699	5,730	4,355	5,170

Notes
Models with age, period, cohort, education, gender, class, ideology and values.
Significance levels:
* $p \leq 0.05$.
** $p \leq 0.01$.
*** $p \leq 0.001$.
Reference categories: Post-WWII cohort (2); 34–50 age group (2); 2004 (2), therefore, 2002 is the inverse of the period effect 2002–2004; Left-libertarian (1); Edu (low) is a dummy variable where 1 means the respondent left school before the age of 17; Working class is a dummy variable where 1 means the respondent is an unskilled, semi-skilled or skilled manual worker; Left and right are dummy variables derived from the left-right scale where left (1) means values 0/1 and right (1) means values 9/10.

having had ten or fewer years of formal education in the ESS) has a negative effect on party membership almost everywhere (except for Denmark and Ireland in 1981–1999 and Denmark, France, Ireland and Sweden in 2002–2006).

This is perhaps due to the fact that countries such as Denmark and Sweden have very strong and popular social-democratic parties, which attract large numbers of working class members with lower education levels. Indeed, having a manual occupation does not have a negative effect on party membership in France (1981–1999 and 2002–2006), Ireland (1981–1999 and 2002–2006), Italy (1981–1999 and 2002–2006), Spain (1981–1999 and 2002–2006) and Sweden (1981–1999 and 2002–2006), all countries with relatively strong left-wing traditions. For Ireland, it could be true that because of the religious political cleavage structure, parties attract members regardless of their level of resources. Moreover, except for gender and left-right ideology, none of the other indicators are significant for party membership in Ireland, pointing to the fact that ideological reasons probably play a stronger role than socio-economic factors.

In terms of politicisation, ideology and political values, in every country except for Ireland (1981–1999 and 2002–2006), Great Britain (2002–2006) and Sweden (1981–1999), being strongly left wing has a positive effect on party membership; this effect is not however significant for being strongly right wing in Belgium (1981–1999) and Italy (1981–1999). In general, high levels of politicisation on either the left or the right of the political spectrum have strong positive effects on party membership. Moreover, political values do not appear to be particularly important for explaining party membership. In any case, the effects are quite different between countries: in Germany, left-authoritarians, right-libertarians and right-authoritarians are all less likely relative to left-libertarians to join a party. A similar pattern can be seen in Sweden, though not for right-authoritarians; in Spain, only left-authoritarians are less likely than left-libertarians to join parties; in Ireland on the other hand, both left-wing authoritarians and right-libertarians are more likely than left-libertarians to join parties.

Overall then, contrary to the literature that emphasises generalised and negative period effects on conventional participation across Europe, this research only finds evidence of negative period effects on party membership in (West) Germany and Great Britain and solely for the 1990–1999 period. It finds evidence of age effects (older people significantly less likely than middle aged people to be party members) in Spain alone – and explains this by reference to proportional left-right ideology. On the other hand, the present study finds evidence of generational effects for party membership across countries with the '80s and '90s cohorts generally being significantly less likely, relative to the post-WWII generation, to join a party (despite the relatively small number of cases). Based on these results, the current findings stress the primacy of cohort membership over age effects when explaining generational differences in party membership. The next two sections of the analysis turn to examining whether similar age, period and cohort effects are at play for explaining other types of conventional political participation: voting and contacting a politician. If modernisation is driving the decline in conventional participation and the concomitant rise in unconventional participation, then one should expect cohort effects to be significant and in the same direction as those found for party membership for these other two modes of conventional action.

Voting at national elections

First, this section turns to examining self-reported turnout levels by cohort over time. It is worth pointing out that turnout levels tend to be overestimated in survey responses (Fieldhouse *et al.* 2007). However, this limitation of survey turnout data is not particularly problematic for this analysis since we are mainly interested in relative levels.[5] To deal with the social desirability bias of reporting turnout even when one has not voted, the ESS adopts a question wording so that abstention is 'normalised':

> *Some people don't vote nowadays for one reason or another. Did you vote in the last [country] national election in [month/year]?*

Figure 5.3 shows that in most countries, the oldest cohorts tend to say that they voted more than younger cohorts. However, it is generally the post-WWII and the baby-boom cohort that vote at higher levels. This suggests that there might be life-cycle effects at play, since these cohorts tend to fall in the middle age group in 2002–2006. With the exception of Italy and Belgium, the '90s generation reports the lowest turnout levels. This is not because of a lack of opportunity to vote, since individuals in this cohort are aged 21–33 in 2002. Even the small proportion of individuals aged twenty-one in 2002 should have had a chance to vote in the preceding three years of their lives in at least some countries. Assuming that elections are held every four to five years, this alone cannot explain lower turnout levels for this cohort. Moreover, Figure 5.3 shows that in some countries, the differences between older and younger cohorts are much larger than in others. In France, Ireland and Britain (which, from Chapter 4, also had some of the larger falls in turnout in the 1970–2008 period), the differences between the '90s generation and the other cohorts is reasonably large. In France, 50 per cent of respondents from the '90s generation said they voted, whereas almost 90 per cent of respondents from the post-WWII generation said they voted. In those countries where the proportion reporting voting fell, levels fell across the whole sample for the period 2002–2006 (from Figure 4.1 in Ch. 4: France, Germany, Ireland, Italy and the Netherlands). It seems that with the exception of Italy, the curve is steeper for the youngest cohorts. In Italy, the low turnout levels for the pre-WWII generation (aged 79–95 by 2004) probably denote age effects due to lower mobility. It appears that turnout is not falling for the other cohorts in Italy, and hence that the pre-WWII cohort is driving the decline.

In order to control for age effects and to identify the model, Table 5.9 presents the results of logistic regression on voting for each of the ten countries, including cohort, age and period variables (Model(s) 1); Model(s) 2 include education. The results show that in eight out of ten countries, at least one of the youngest

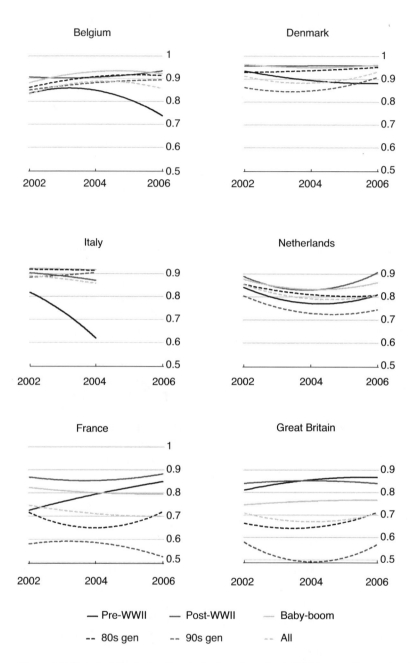

Figure 5.3 Voted at the last national election, by cohort, ESS (proportion saying 'yes'), over time.

Note
Best fit quadratic smoothed lines. *continued*

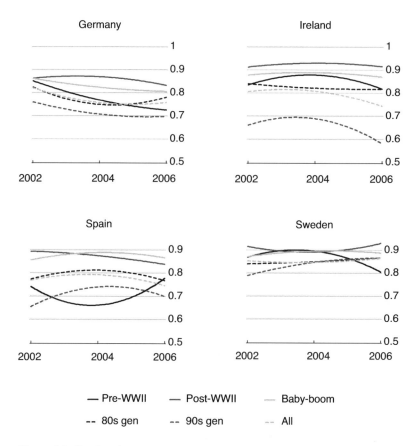

Figure 5.3 Continued

three cohorts is significantly less likely than the post-WWII cohort to turn out. In Britain and France this is true of all three of the youngest cohorts, including the baby-boomers. In Ireland and Spain this is true of the '80s and '90s cohorts. In Germany, including education in the model exacerbates cohort differences in voting. This suggests that had the youngest cohorts not been more educated, cohort differences here would have been more marked. In Italy, the baby-boomers are actually significantly more likely than older cohorts to vote. In every country, having a lower level of education has a strong negative effect on voting. While there is some evidence to support cohort differences in voting, the results in Table 5.9 also provide evidence for age effects on voting. In France, Germany, Ireland and Great Britain, young people are significantly less likely than people in the middle age group to vote. In Belgium, in Britain and in the Netherlands, people in the 51+ age group are significantly more likely than people in the 34–50 age group to vote. Both effects could be at play in France, Germany, Ireland and Great Britain. However, since the cohort variable is

Table 5.9 Logistic regression on voting, ESS, by country (APC and education)

	BEL		DNK		FRA		DEU		IRL	
	Model 1	Model 2	Model 1	Model 2	Model 1	Model 2	Model 1	Model 2	Model 1	Model 2
Pre-WWII	-0.79***	-0.74***	-0.89**	-0.81**	-0.62**	-0.56**	-0.40*	-0.12	-0.75**	-0.66**
Baby-boom	0.18	0.05	-0.1	-0.26	-0.35***	-0.45***	-0.11	-0.35**	-0.21	-0.29
80s gen.	0.33	0.13	-0.61	-0.80	-0.80***	-1.02***	-0.28	-0.54**	-0.58*	-0.67**
90s gen.	0.56	0.29	-1.11*	-1.36**	-1.20***	-1.47***	-0.29	-0.56**	-1.17***	-1.29***
18-33	-0.49	-0.50	-0.39	-0.36	-0.33*	-0.41**	-0.49**	-0.48**	-0.47**	-0.49**
51+	0.57**	0.61**	-0.20	-0.13	0.23	0.33	0.18	0.24	0.23	0.31
2002	-0.27*	-0.28*	0.10	0.12	0.12	0.10	0.26***	0.30***	-0.11	-0.13
2006	0.02	0.01	0.27	0.31	0.05	-0.02	-0.07	-0.09	-0.38***	-0.39***
Edu (low)		-0.70***		-0.86***		-0.77***		-1.15***		-0.51***
Intercept	1.89***	2.28***	3.28***	3.60***	1.62***	2.09***	1.57***	1.99***	2.35***	2.54***
Pseudo-RSq	0.01	0.03	0.04	0.05	0.07	0.08	0.02	0.05	0.08	0.09
LogLike	-1,532.48	-1,512.22	-923.23	-908.31	-2,445	-2,403.19	-3,605.5	-3,483.6	-2,246.24	-2,232.6
N	4,624	4,624	3,999	3,999	4,588	4,588	7,508	7,508	5,259	5,259

	ITA		NLD		GBR		ESP		SWE	
	Model 1	*Model 2*	*Model 1*	*Model 2*	*Model 1*	*Model 2*	*Model 1*	*Model 2*	*Model 1*	*Model 2*
Pre-WWII	-0.94**	-0.89**	-0.47**	-0.34	0.02	0.08	-0.88***	-0.86***	-0.44*	-0.31
Baby-boom	0.73*	0.63*	0.06	-0.06	-0.36**	-0.45***	-0.02	-0.09	-0.35*	-0.55***
80s gen.	0.87*	0.71	-0.11	-0.37	-0.58**	-0.74***	-0.75***	-0.86***	-0.79**	-1.04***
90s gen.	0.53	0.25	-0.53*	-0.83**	-0.71**	-0.86***	-1.15***	-1.30***	-0.67*	-0.97***
18–33	0.15	0.06	0.12	0.09	-0.58***	-0.59***	-0.13	-0.14	-0.31	-0.33
51+	0.63	0.69*	0.36*	0.45*	0.36*	0.42*	-0.15	-0.10	-0.22	-0.11
2002	-0.04	0.00	0.36***	0.32***	0.11	0.08	-0.15	-0.14	-0.14	-0.15
2006			0.20*	0.16	0.13	0.09	-0.21*	-0.22*	0.09	0.07
Edu (low)		-0.75***		-0.86***		-0.50***		-0.36***		-0.71***
Intercept	1.59***	2.10***	1.47***	1.94***	1.27***	1.51***	2.22***	2.48***	2.57***	2.93***
Pseudo-RSq	0.02	0.03	0.02	0.04	0.06	0.06	0.04	0.04	0.01	0.02
LogLike	-724.35	-713.09	-2,436.25	-2,386.48	-3,157.69	-3,139.23	-2,092.13	-2,083.67	-1,956.71	-1,935.49
N	2,398	2,398	5,690	5,690	5,713	5,713	4,340	4,340	5,165	5,165

Notes

Model 1: age, period and cohort; Model 2: age, period, cohort and education.

Significance levels:

* $p \leq 0.05$.

** $p \leq 0.01$.

*** $p \leq 0.001$.

Reference categories: Post-WWII cohort (2); 34–50 age group (2); 2004 (2); therefore, 2002 is the inverse of the period effect 2002–2004; Edu (low) is a dummy variable where 1 means the respondent left school before the age of 17.

significant, this would suggest that this is a pattern that will continue in time (see also Chapter 4 for aggregate turnout) if it reflects different socialisation experiences of this cohort.

Table 5.10 presents the results of the full model for voting. It shows that cohort differences remain significant even when controlling for the other variables. The age effects from the Models in Table 5.10 are also still significant. The negative effect of having a lower education is still significant. Unlike with party membership, there is no gender bias to voting (except for Germany and Italy). However, being working class has a strong negative effect on voting in every country, with the exception of Italy and Belgium where the effect is not significant. This is interesting, since Belgium and Italy (along with Denmark) also have the highest levels of turnout.[6] It suggests that in countries where turnout is lower, the people who do not vote tend to be disproportionately drawn from the working class. Therefore, lower voter turnout is potentially linked to greater inequalities in representation, not just by age, but also by socio-economic status. Indeed this has generally been an important concern in research on participation and a key focus of Verba *et al.*'s (1995) seminal work. Simple cross-tabulations show that the gap in turnout between people in the working class and others is about 1 percentage point in Italy and Belgium (88 versus 87 per cent and 85 versus 86 per cent, respectively); in other countries this ranges from a high of 14 percentage points in Germany and 13 in France to a low of 5 percentage points in Spain and 6 in Denmark and Ireland. This gap is 10 points in the Netherlands, 7 Britain and 8 in Sweden.

As might be expected, politicisation and ideology have a weaker effect on voting than on party membership. Interestingly, being strongly left wing has a strong negative effect on turnout in Britain. This is not surprising, given New Labour's move to the centre and the first-past-the-post system. Somebody who is very left wing in Britain has no reason to vote, since the main left-wing party is not particularly left wing and the first-past-the-post makes voting for small left-wing parties a purely symbolic affair. Turnout for very left-wing individuals is on average just 63 per cent, 7 points lower than that for those selecting other values on the left-right scale, including the moderates, in other words people who are not politicised. On the other hand, being very right-wing has a strong positive effect on voting in five out ten countries. Political values do not have particularly interesting effects on voting.

Contacting a politician

The final indicator of conventional political participation that this chapter examines is contacting a politician. The ESS asks whether individuals contacted a politician in the last twelve months. Figure 5.4 presents an interesting picture. Given that theory suggests that older cohorts should be more likely than younger cohorts to engage in conventional political participation, it is surprising that in almost every country examined here, individuals from the pre-WWII generation tend to be the ones engaging the least in this type of activity. On the other hand,

Table 5.10 Logistic regression on voting, ESS, by country (APC and all controls)

	BEL	DNK	FRA	DEU	IRL	ITA	NLD	GBR	ESP	SWE
Pre-WWII	-0.73***	-0.84**	-0.56**	-0.13	-0.70**	-0.79**	-0.34	0.05	-0.88***	-0.35
Baby-boom	0.03	-0.26	-0.45**	-0.36**	-0.26	0.66*	-0.06	-0.49***	-0.10	-0.53***
80s gen.	0.10	-0.82	-1.00***	-0.54***	-0.65*	0.75	-0.39	-0.76***	-0.87**	-0.99***
90s gen.	0.24	-1.39**	-1.44***	-0.56*	-1.26***	0.30	-0.87***	-0.92***	-1.31***	-0.95***
18–33	-0.49	-0.37	-0.41*	-0.51**	-0.48*	0.02	0.12	-0.58***	-0.13	-0.32
51+	0.60**	-0.14	0.30	0.26	0.28	0.70*	0.44*	0.42*	-0.14	-0.12
2002	-0.26*	0.12	0.09	0.30***	-0.14	0.04	0.34***	0.08	-0.10	-0.13
2006	0.02	0.26	-0.01	-0.08	-0.42***		0.21*	0.08	-0.16	0.04
Edu (low)	-0.65***	-0.62***	-0.65***	-0.89***	-0.39***	-0.78***	-0.70***	-0.37***	-0.28***	-0.57***
Male	-0.12	0.16	0.06	0.22**	0.06	0.51**	0.11	0.06	0.05	-0.02
Working cl.	-0.14	-0.66***	-0.44***	-0.81***	-0.41***	0.16	-0.56***	-0.41***	-0.34***	-0.45***
Left	-0.25	-0.25	0.19	0.20	-0.30	-0.02	0.11	-0.54**	0.61***	0.18
Right	0.25	0.54	0.44*	-0.01	0.75***	0.89***	0.98***	0.31	0.49	0.51*
Left-auth.	-0.34**	-0.26	-0.07	-0.02	0.01	-0.09	-0.28**	-0.06	0.04	0.03
Right-lib.	-0.26	-0.05	-0.15	0.55***	-0.02	-0.33	0.04	0.19	0.09	0.24
Right-auth.	-0.27	-0.45*	-0.09	0.01	-0.02	-0.38	-0.01	-0.16	0.01	-0.14
Intercept	2.61***	3.96***	2.14***	2.02***	2.58***	1.91***	2.01***	1.67***	2.44***	3.00***
Pseudo-RSq	0.03	0.07	0.09	0.08	0.09	0.05	0.05	0.07	0.05	0.03
LogLike	-1,502.69	-892.48	-2,383.44	-3,390.86	-2,208.53	-701.77	-2,350.35	-3,111.58	-2,068.76	-1,916.5
N	4,613	3,999	4,588	7,508	5,235	2,398	5,690	5,713	4,340	5,165

Notes

Models with age, period, cohort, education, gender, class, ideology and values.

Significance levels:

* $p \leq 0.05$.
** $p \leq 0.01$.
*** $p \leq 0.001$.

Reference categories: Post-WWII cohort (2); 34–50 age group (2); 2004 (2), therefore, 2002 is the inverse of the period effect 2002–2004; Left-libertarian (1); Edu (low) is a dummy variable where 1 means the respondent left school before the age of 17; Working class is a dummy variable where 1 means the respondent is an unskilled, semi-skilled or skilled manual worker; Left and right are dummy variables derived from the left-right scale where left (1) and right (1) means values 9/10.

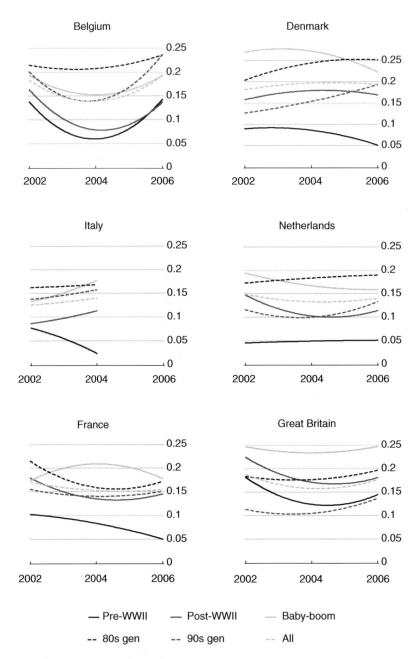

Belgium

Denmark

Italy

Netherlands

France

Great Britain

— Pre-WWII   — Post-WWII   — Baby-boom

-- 80s gen   -- 90s gen   -- All

Figure 5.4 Contacted a politician in the last twelve months, by cohort, ESS (proportion saying 'yes'), over time.

Note
Best fit quadratic smoothed lines.   *continued*

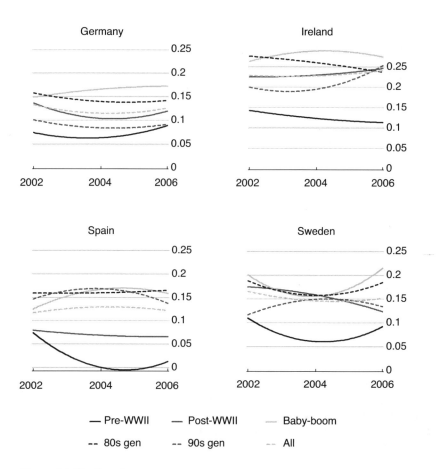

Figure 5.4 Continued

the baby-boom generation and the '80s generation tend to be the cohorts report-ing the highest levels of contacting politicians. This suggests that while younger cohorts might be voting and joining parties less than older cohorts, this is not the case for other types of conventional activities. This finding contradicts modern-isation theory's (Inglehart 1990) argument that younger cohorts are less likely than older cohorts to engage in all the various types of 'elite-directed', or con-ventional, political actions. However, it does not conflict with Mair's (2006) argument that politicians are becoming more open to consultation and other pro-cedural mechanisms to 'engage' the citizenry. At the same time, on this argu-ment, parties decline in importance and turnout and party membership falls since politicians refrain from ideological discourse and therefore downplay the 'popular' component of democracy. In turn, this leads individuals to perceive party politics as irrelevant to their lives, since no "issues of vital concern [are] presented" (Boechel 1928: 517).

In Ulrich Beck's terms, the dynamic moves from Politics, with a capital 'P', linked to parties, the ideological struggle between left and right, and democratic antagonism between opposing visions of how to organise society, to politics with a lower-case 'p', or what he calls 'sub-politics'. This is characterised by the professionalisation of politicians and the abandonment of grand ideological visions in favour of a more managerial take on politics and the role of the politicians in society (Mair 2006). In this sense then, it is not surprising that younger cohorts are less likely than older ones to vote and to join parties. This is because parties, whose role was traditionally to articulate collective interests, are becoming less important to Western publics. On the other hand, however, younger cohorts are more likely than older cohorts to engage in other types of conventional participation, which have potentially gained more centrality in an increasingly managerial context. Alternatively, given the higher levels of deference to various authorities in society in the past, this type of activity might have only become widespread in the public since the period of socialisation of the baby-boomers – i.e. the 1960s. This could also explain why this cohort would be more likely to engage in this activity than older cohorts, who were not introduced to this type of political action in their youth.

However, it might simply be the case that the baby-boomers and '80s generation contact politicians more than other cohorts due to age effects, with people in the middle age group being more likely to conduct this activity, since the baby-boomers and '80s generation are aged 34–60 in 2002–2006. This would follow from evidence showing that people in their middle age tend to be more likely to be involved in conventional political activities than older and younger age groups. In order to control for age effects and to identify the model, Table 5.11 presents the results of logistic regression on contacting a politician for each of the ten countries, including cohort, age and period variables (Model(s) 1); Model(s) 2 includes education. The results presented in Table 5.11 show that the baby-boomers are significantly more likely than the post-WWII cohort to contact a politician in nine out of ten countries. In Germany and Spain, the '80s generation is also significantly more likely than the post-WWII cohort to engage in this activity. In Belgium and Italy, the '80s and '90s generations are also significantly more likely than the post-WWII cohort to contact a politician. There are also some significant age effects with young people being significantly less likely than people in the middle age group to contact a politician in four out of ten countries. The results for Model(s) 2 show that controlling for education accounts for the cohort differences between the '80s and '90s cohorts and the post-WWII generation in engaging in this activity whereas the cohort differences between the baby-boomers and the post-WWII generation persist in most countries. This shows that where the '80s and '90s generations contact politicians more than the post-WWII generation, this is due to their higher education levels. In Italy and France this is also true of the baby-boomers. Indeed, being less educated has a strong and significant depressing effect on this type of activity in every country, and more so in Germany and in Italy (respectively, 14 versus 5 per cent, and 19 versus 7 per cent, for those with higher versus those with lower education levels). Taken together, these results show that younger cohorts are actually significantly more likely than older cohorts to engage in this type of conventional political activity. However, whereas in the case of the '80s and '90s cohorts this tendency is accounted for by their higher education levels, this is generally not true of the baby-boomers.

Table 5.12 presents the results of the full logistic regression model for contacting a politician. It shows that cohort effects, with the baby-boomers being significantly more likely than the post-WWII cohort to contact a politician, are still significant. Interestingly, in Britain, the '90s generation is significantly less likely than the post-WWII cohort to contact a politician. This effect becomes significant when including political values in the model: left-libertarians in the '90s cohort contact politicians at higher levels than those with other types of political preferences. Moreover, the results presented in Table 5.12 show that being male has a strong positive effect on contacting a politician in most countries except Belgium. Being working class has a depressing effect in most countries. Politicisation on the left-right spectrum increases the chances that someone will contact a politician in Belgium and France, whereas contacting a politician is practiced more by left-wing individuals in Denmark and Germany. In Denmark and Sweden being left or right-authoritarian relative to being left-libertarian has a negative effect on whether an individual performs this activity. In the Netherlands, Great Britain and Spain, left-authoritarians are significantly less likely than left-libertarians to contact a politician, whereas in Italy right-authoritarians are significantly less likely to contact a politician than left-libertarians.

Conclusions

The results presented in this chapter show that younger cohorts are in most countries significantly less likely than older cohorts to join a party and to vote at national elections. For party membership, generational effects are more important than age effects in explaining the observed differences between generations in the levels of party adherents. In France, Germany, Ireland and Great Britain young people are also significantly less likely than people in the middle age group to vote. Therefore, it is not possible to adjudicate between age and cohort effects in these countries. However, the presence of cohort effects suggests that turnout will probably continue to fall in these countries in the future, as older cohorts which vote at higher levels are replaced by younger cohorts which vote at lower levels.

However, the results outlined in this chapter show that younger cohorts are not significantly less likely than older cohorts to engage in all types of conventional political activities. Indeed, (with the exception of Britain) younger cohorts are actually significantly more likely than older cohorts to contact politicians. The results also show that education plays a mediating role for conventional participation. For party membership, this means that in the absence of rising levels of education, cohort differences between younger and older cohorts for

Table 5.11 Logistic regression on contacting a politician, ESS, by country (APC and education)

	BEL		DNK		FRA		DEU		IRL	
	Model 1	Model 2	Model 1	Model 2	Model 1	Model 2	Model 1	Model 2	Model 1	Model 2
Pre-WWII	-0.17	-0.13	-0.85**	-0.79**	-0.66*	-0.61*	-0.56*	-0.28	-0.72**	-0.70**
Baby-boom	0.37**	0.28*	0.40**	0.31*	0.31*	0.24	0.38***	0.23*	0.32***	0.30***
80s gen.	0.53**	0.40	0.02	-0.09	0.31	0.19	0.39*	0.23	0.11	0.09
90s gen.	0.52*	0.35	-0.05	-0.18	0.35	0.21	0.02	-0.15	0.16	0.14
18–33	-0.20	-0.21	-0.53*	-0.51*	-0.30	-0.34	-0.22	-0.21	-0.35	-0.36
51+	-0.13	-0.12	-0.39*	-0.35*	0.14	0.19	0.18	0.22	-0.01	0.01
2002	0.37***	0.37***	-0.14	-0.13	0.18	0.16	0.13	0.16	-0.04	-0.05
2006	0.40***	0.40***	-0.04	-0.02	-0.01	-0.06	0.07	0.06	0.02	0.01
Edu (low)		-0.51***		-0.63***		-0.48***		-1.29***		-0.12
Intercept	-2.07***	-1.84***	-1.14***	-0.98***	-1.90***	-1.65***	-2.23***	-1.98***	-1.19***	-1.15***
Pseudo-RSq	0.02	0.02	0.02	0.03	0.01	0.01	0.01	0.03	0.01	0.01
LogLike	-2,127.2	-2,112.99	-1,967.06	-1,950.57	-2,112.45	-2,098.82	-2,857.3	-2,790.91	-2,870.64	-2,869.58
N	4,638	4,638	4,021	4,021	4,767	4,767	7,524	7,524	5,213	5,213

	ITA		NLD		GBR		ESP		SWE	
	Model 1	Model 2	Model 1	Model 2	Model 1	Model 2	Model 1	Model 2	Model 1	Model 2
Pre-WWII	-0.72	-0.60	-1.02***	-0.87**	-0.19	-0.09	-0.91*	-0.84*	-0.60**	-0.42*
Baby-boom	0.59**	0.41	0.26*	0.15	0.29**	0.17	0.65***	0.48**	0.19	-0.02
80s gen.	0.74*	0.46	0.10	-0.10	0.15	-0.05	0.62*	0.36	-0.07	-0.30
90s gen.	0.84**	0.43	-0.01	-0.23	-0.25	-0.44	0.61	0.28	0.04	-0.23
18–33	-0.72*	-0.84*	-0.52*	-0.55*	-0.19	-0.21	-0.10	-0.13	-0.53*	-0.56*
51+	0.31	0.40	-0.23	-0.16	0.21	0.28	-0.27	-0.16	-0.23	-0.14
2002	-0.16	-0.11	0.14	0.10	0.20*	0.17	0.04	0.07	0.14	0.14
2006			0.10	0.05	0.14	0.07	-0.07	-0.08	0.07	0.04
Edu (low)		-1.23***		-0.83***		-0.74***		-0.81***		-0.80***
Intercept	-2.35***	-1.71***	-1.73***	-1.38***	-1.73***	-1.44***	-2.20***	-1.68***	-1.55***	-1.22***
Pseudo-RSq	0.01	0.06	0.01	0.03	0.01	0.03	0.02	0.04	0.01	0.02
LogLike	-975.74	-932.53	-2,383.88	-2,343.88	-2,705.87	-2,671.37	-1,661.6	-1,630.65	-2,250.74	-2,220.57
N	2,411	2,411	5,705	5,705	5,732	5,732	4,367	4,367	5,176	5,176

Notes

Model 1: age, period and cohort; Model 2: age, period, cohort and education.

Significance levels:

* $p \leq 0.05$.

** $p \leq 0.01$.

*** $p \leq 0.001$.

Reference categories: Post-WWII cohort (2); 34–50 age group (2); 2004 (2), therefore, 2002 is the inverse of the period effect 2002–2004; Edu (low) is a dummy variable where 1 means the respondent left school before the age of 17.

Table 5.12 Logistic regression on contacting a politician, ESS, by country (APC and all controls)

	BEL	DNK	FRA	DEU	IRL	ITA	NLD	GBR	ESP	SWE
Pre-WWII	-0.13	-0.79**	-0.61*	-0.25	-0.68**	-0.59	-0.85**	-0.14	-0.83*	-0.44*
Baby-boom	0.28*	0.33**	0.28*	0.26*	0.30**	0.42	0.20	0.12	0.47*	0.01
80s gen.	0.40	-0.06	0.29	0.29	0.10	0.50	-0.06	-0.09	0.37	-0.26
90s gen.	0.34	-0.13	0.33	-0.11	0.15	0.49	-0.23	-0.53*	0.28	-0.27
18-33	-0.19	-0.54*	-0.35	-0.2	-0.37	-0.86**	-0.53*	-0.17	-0.14	-0.54*
51+	-0.12	-0.34*	0.19	0.24	-0.01	0.36	-0.19	0.27	-0.14	-0.12
2002	0.38***	-0.13	0.16	0.17	-0.06	-0.09	0.12	0.19	0.12	0.18
2006	0.41***	-0.08	-0.06	0.07	-0.01		0.07	0.07	-0.05	0.00
Edu (low)	-0.47***	-0.42***	-0.38***	-1.02***	-0.10	-1.03***	-0.63***	-0.61***	-0.70***	-0.58***
Male	0.13	0.42***	0.39***	0.42***	0.27***	0.85***	0.40***	0.21**	0.64***	0.40***
Working cl.	-0.15	-0.52***	-0.37***	-0.72***	-0.10	-0.49**	-0.61***	-0.36***	-0.31*	-0.61***
Left	0.36*	0.52*	0.34*	0.76***	0.29	0.35	0.21	0.14	0.22	0.25
Right	0.46*	0.09	0.42*	-0.09	0.39*	0.49	0.05	-0.01	0.09	0.16
Left-auth.	-0.09	-0.36**	0.08	-0.14	-0.17	-0.29	-0.28*	-0.27*	-0.30*	-0.52***
Right-lib.	-0.06	-0.17	0.13	0.07	-0.16	0.22	0.00	0.12	0.23	-0.02
Right-auth.	-0.02	-0.31**	0.15	-0.03	-0.21	-0.62**	0.14	0.00	-0.26	-0.43***
Intercept	-1.86***	-0.91***	-1.97***	-2.11***	-1.10***	-1.97***	-1.53***	-1.34***	-1.86***	-1.06***
Pseudo-RSq	0.03	0.04	0.02	0.05	0.01	0.09	0.05	0.03	0.06	0.04
LogLike	-2,102.36	-1,919.72	-2,072.67	-2,735.11	-2,840.59	-898.69	-2,306.9	-2,648.6	-1,598.57	-2,172.72
N	4,627	4,021	4,767	7,524	5,191	2,411	5,705	5,732	4,367	5,176

Notes

Models with age, period, cohort, education, gender, class, ideology and values.

Significance levels:

* $p \leq 0.05$.
** $p \leq 0.01$.
*** $p \leq 0.001$.

Reference categories: Post-WWII cohort (2); 34–50 age group (2); 2004 (2), therefore, 2002 is the inverse of the period effect 2002–2004; Left-libertarian (1); Edu (low) is a dummy variable where 1 means the respondent left school before the age of 17; Working class is a dummy variable where 1 means the respondent is an unskilled, semi-skilled or skilled manual worker; Left and right are dummy variables derived from the left-right scale where left (1) means values 0/1 and right (1) means values 9/10.

this activity could have possibly been more marked. For contacting a politician, whereas for the '80s and '90s cohort, higher levels of participation relative to older cohorts are accounted for by higher education levels, this is generally not true of the baby-boomers. This suggests that whereas the pre- and post-WWII cohorts tend to be more involved in activities pertaining to parties and elections than younger cohorts, younger cohorts tend to be more involved in more 'consultative' types of conventional political participation. These may have gained prominence as a result of the trends towards more managerial-style politics in many Western European countries as suggested by some authors.

Therefore, these results suggest that cohort effects have a role to play for explaining why party membership and turnout are falling in many Western countries. This confirms findings in previous research on the subject. On the other hand, they also suggest that other conventional activities such as contacting politicians should not be falling in the future based on the fact that younger cohorts tend to be more active than older cohorts in this respect. Moreover, this chapter showed that there is still a gender bias for party membership and contacting a politician, but that men and women tend to vote at about the same levels. In most countries there are class inequalities in conventional participation: working class individuals participating less than others. However, these effects are somewhat weaker for party membership in countries with traditionally strong left-wing subcultures. The results also showed that high levels of politicisation on the left-right spectrum increase the chances of joining a party as might be expected, but that the effect of ideological politicisation is somewhat weaker for contacting a politician and almost negligible for voting across countries. This is consistent with the fact that smaller numbers of individuals join parties, or only the very ideologically polarised do so, whereas voting is something which almost everyone does, including individuals with more moderate political views. Finally, the results showed that the effect of having different types of political values varies idiosyncratically across countries and for different types of conventional political activities. Therefore, voting, joining a party and contacting a politician do not seem to be practiced disproportionately by individuals with specific sets of political values.

In terms of the wider implications, following modernisation theory (Inglehart 1977, 1990; Inglehart and Catterberg 2002; Inglehart and Welzel 2005), similar processes, affecting all Western European democracies in roughly the same way, should be driving younger cohorts to participate less in conventional or 'elite-directed' actions. The implication of this is that cohort effects should be roughly similar across different types of 'conventional' indicators, and relatively similar across countries. However, the evidence presented here shows that this is not found across the different types of conventional activities. Therefore, the idea that modernisation leads younger cohorts to disengage from 'elite-directed' political activities is not supported by this evidence. On the other hand, the evidence presented here is not inconsistent with Mair's (2006) argument that politicians are increasingly more open to consultation and other procedural mechanisms to 'engage' the citizenry. At the same time, parties decline in importance and turnout and party membership falls since politicians refrain from ideological discourse and therefore downplay the 'popular' component of democracy, leading individuals to perceive party politics as irrelevant. Political context theories highlight the interaction between the supply and demand aspects of political participation as an explanatory factor governing why different patterns should be observed. Therefore, theories that suggest the nature of democratic politics is transforming, giving way to a context where parties and elections are less important but procedural, consultative aspects of democracy are emphasised, would not be in conflict with these results. This is because the results show that the '80s and '90s cohorts participate in certain conventional activities more than older cohorts, regardless of the depressing effect of their young age.

In conclusion, the results from this chapter suggest that cohort effects have a role to play for explaining why turnout and party membership are falling in Western Europe. The results suggest no such claims can be made for other conventional activities, such as contacting a politician. This would seem to support the idea that the seeds for these changes are not to be found in universal processes of societal modernisation, but rather require a more fine-tuned analysis of the changing nature of the political context and party competition, since younger cohorts participate significantly more than older cohorts in certain types of conventional activities. Given these results, the next chapter critically examines whether younger cohorts are significantly more likely than older cohorts to engage in various types of unconventional or 'elite-directing' participation. It therefore seeks to ascertain whether cohort effects, rooted in modernisation and post-materialist value change, could play a role for explaining the rising prominence of these types of activities in Western Europe.

Notes

1 The plotted curves are best fit quadratic smoothed lines.
2 This probably reflects age effects with middle age being the key moment of participation: the curves show that as older cohorts age, they participate less and as younger cohorts age, they participate more.
3 The subsequent decline in party membership amongst the '80s generation in Italy could be linked to the demise of the Socialists as a result of the corruption-fed scandals of Tangentopoli in the early 1990s.
4 Details in the Appendix.
5 The assumption here is that different cohorts overestimate turnout at about the same rate, which seems reasonable.
6 This is unsurprising since both have compulsory voting. However, while it is strictly enforced in Belgium, the rules were relaxed in the 1970s in Italy so that in practice voting is no longer compulsory.

References

Bara, J. and I. Budge (2001). "Party Policy and Ideology: Still New Labour?" *Parliamentary Affairs* 54: 590–606.

Blais, A., E. Gidengil and N. Nevitte (2004). "Where Does Turnout Decline Come from?" *European Journal of Political Research* 43: 221–36.

Boechel, R. (1928). *Voting and Non-Voting in Elections*. Washington, DC, Editorial Research Reports.

Fieldhouse, E., M. Tranmer and A. Russell (2007). "Something about Young People or Something about Elections? Electoral Participation of Young People in Europe: Evidence from a Multilevel Analysis of the European Social Survey". *European Journal of Political Research* 46: 797–822.

Franklin, M. N. (2004). *Voter Turnout and the Dynamics of Electoral Competition in Established Democracies since 1945*. Cambridge, Cambridge University Press.

Grasso, M. T. (2011). *Political Participation in Western Europe*. Nuffield College, University of Oxford. D. Phil. Thesis.

Grasso, M. T. (2013). "The Differential Impact of Education on Young People's Political Activism: Comparing Italy and the United Kingdom". *Comparative Sociology* 12: 1–30.

Grasso, M. T. (2014). "Age-Period-Cohort Analysis in a Comparative Context: Political Generations and Political Participation Repertoires". *Electoral Studies* 33: 63–76.

Hooghe, M. (2004). "Political Socialisation and the Future of Politics". *Acta Politica* 39: 331–41.

Inglehart, R. (1977). *The Silent Revolution: Changing Values and Political Styles among Western Publics*. Princeton, Princeton University Press.

Inglehart, R. (1990). *Culture Shift in Advanced Industrial Society*. Princeton, Princeton University Press.

Inglehart, R. and G. Catterberg (2002). "Trends in Political Action: The Developmental Trend and the Post-Honeymoon Decline". *International Journal of Comparative Sociology* 43: 300–16.

Inglehart, R. and C. Welzel (2005). *Modernization, Cultural Change and Democracy: The Human Development Sequence*. Cambridge, Cambridge University Press.

Mair, P. (2006). "Ruling the Void? The Hollowing of Western Democracy". *New Left Review* 42: 25–51.

Mair, P. and I. Van Biezen (2001). "Party Membership in Twenty European Democracies, 1980–2000". *Party Politics* 7(1): 5–21.

Manin, B. (1997). *The Principles of Representative Government*. Cambridge, Cambridge University Press.

Mason, K. O., W. M. Mason, H. H. Winsborough and W. K. Poole (1973). "Some Methodological Issues in Cohort Analysis of Archival Data". *American Sociological Review* 38(2): 242–58.

Park, A. (1995). Teenagers and their Politics. *British Social Attitudes: The 12th Report*. R. Jowell. Dartmouth, Aldershot.

Plutzer, E. (2002). "Becoming a Habitual Voter: Inertia, Resources, and Growth in Young Adulthood". *American Political Science Review* 96: 41–56.

Van Biezen, I., P. Mair and T. Poguntke (2012). "Going, Going, … Gone? The Decline of Party Membership in Contemporary Europe". *European Journal of Political Research* 51(1): 24–56.

Verba, S., K. Schlozman and H. Brady (1995). *Voice and Equality: Civic Voluntarism in American Politics*. Cambridge, MA, Harvard University Press.

Wilkinson, H. M. and G. Mulgan (1995). *Freedom's Children*. London, Demos.

6 Generations and informal political participation in Western Europe

Chapter 4 showed that the patterns of political participation amongst Western European publics have changed over the last thirty years or so in salient ways. Certain forms of participation, generally associated with what has traditionally been considered the 'conventional' repertoire, are becoming less popular, while those associated with the 'unconventional' repertoire, emerging since the 1960s, have become more popular in most countries. However, this rise seems to have halted or slowed down since 1990. In Chapter 5, it was pointed out that given these changes in the patterns of political participation in Western Europe, it was not surprising that generational replacement and cohort differences in political participation have become increasingly prominent features in studies of political behaviour. This is because they hold the promise of explaining, or at least contributing in part to an explanation, of the changes observed. However, it was argued that differences between young and old people in their patterns of participation do not in and of themselves tell us anything about the potential process of social change at play. Unless these cohort differences are sustained throughout time, the observed differences between older and younger age cohorts could simply be the reflection of the fact that individuals are situated in different life-cycle stages (Grasso 2011, Grasso 2013, Grasso 2014). Moreover, given that the direction of age effects postulated for different forms of participation varies, with middle and old age generally being seen as the peak point of conventional participation, and youth generally being seen as the key moment of unconventional participation, Chapter 5 focused on conventional participation. This chapter, on the other hand, focuses on analysing cohort effects in unconventional political participation and in establishing whether these are more salient than age effects for accounting for generational differences in participation. The investigation begins by examining whether the patterns of participation, analysed at the level of the nation in Chapter 4, are replicated when analysed by cohort. The analysis also considers whether different types of unconventional participation exhibit similar cohort participation patterns or whether age effects are more important for explaining participation in certain types of activities than others. Moreover, the analysis investigates whether cohort differences in different countries present themselves in the patterns suggested in the literature: that the youngest cohorts participate the most in these activities, whereas the oldest participate the least. In other words, it considers whether there are significant differences between cohorts in their patterns of unconventional participation. Another area for research in this chapter is to examine, if, as was found for conventional participation, there is a gender bias for unconventional participation, if individuals with lower education participate less, whether there is still inequality in participation, whether more politicised individuals participate more than others, and whether people with different sets of political values and different ideologies exhibit different patterns of participation. Finally, the chapter reflects on key cross-national differences and analyses whether there are salient differences in these effects by type of indicator.

This chapter shows that not one of the three younger cohorts is significantly more likely than the older cohorts to engage in certain types of 'elite-challenging' activism: participation in/unpaid work for social movement organisations (SMOs). Moreover, the results presented in this chapter show that the baby-boomers are in most countries significantly more likely than the post-WWII cohort to demonstrate and sign a petition and, to a lesser extent, to join boycotts.

Differences between each of the '80s and '90s generations and the post-WWII cohort are much less marked than those between the baby-boomers and the post-WWII cohort for these activities. Where differences between the '80s/'90s cohort and the post-WWII generation are significant, they are generally accounted for by higher education levels. The same is not generally true of the baby-boomers. Therefore, the argument that all the younger cohorts should be engaging in elite-challenging activities more than older cohorts is not universally supported with respect to protest activism based on the evidence presented here, and more so for demonstrating. This suggests that rather than modernisation, which should affect all cohorts, and more so young ones, it is formative experiences which set the baby-boomers apart from later cohorts, and is therefore likely to be what explains their higher participatory patterns as suggested by Della Porta and Diani (2006). Moreover, it appears that the fact that "subsequent political contexts differed greatly" (Della Porta and Diani 2006) has had a depressing impact on the likelihood of cohorts coming of age in later periods to demonstrate and participate in other protest activities. This suggests that formative experiences matter. Based on this evidence, the baby-boomers, coming of age in the radicalising period of the late 1960s and 1970s, stand out as 'the protest generation'. The baby-boomers are distinctive in being significantly more likely than the post-WWII generation to engage in the various types of protest activities; and more so, since their higher levels of participation are not accounted for simply by their higher levels of education, as is the case with the '80s and '90s generations.

Key themes and previous research

One of the most common explanations for changing patterns of political participation in the literature is that of intergenerational change by population replacement. Whether it is scholars explaining the decline in conventional participation or others arguing for the rise of new repertoires of engagement relating to social movement organisations (SMOs) and protest activism, the argument is that older cohorts are being replaced by younger cohorts, who exhibit different patterns of participation due to their divergent socialisation experiences. Franklin (2004: 210) shows that declining turnout is explained by a cohort replacement mechanism, since new cohorts of voters are more impressionable to changes in the character of electoral competition. In their seminal study on 'unconventional' political participation, Barnes and Kaase (1979: 524) saw the "potential for protest to be a lasting characteristic of democratic mass publics and not just a sudden surge in political involvement bound to fade away as time goes by". Inglehart (1977, 1990; Inglehart and Catterberg 2002; Inglehart and Welzel 2005) has argued that declining 'elite-directed political mobilisation' and rising 'elite-challenging political behaviour' were due to an intergenerational shift to post-materialist values, since younger birth cohorts, with higher levels of political skills and 'cognitive mobilisation', placed increasing value on self-expression and shaping political decisions rather than trusting those in authority to make these for them. Inglehart and Catterberg (2002: 301–3) argue that:

> It is not a trend toward civic inertness, but an intergenerational shift from elite-directed participation toward increasing rates of elite-challenging participation.... As younger, better-educated, and more post-materialist cohorts replace older ones in the adult population, intergenerational population replacement will tend to bring a shift toward increasingly participant publics.

New social movement theorists, such as Della Porta and Diani (2006), link the rise in protest activism and SMOs to the rise of a 'new middle class'. This is seen to emerge in the 1960s, and was "as a result of their technical and cultural competence and of their economic-function position ... more likely to mobilise in conflicts", for example, fighting against "technocrats, public and private agencies engaged in the dissemination of information and the construction of consensus, the military, and the apparatus responsible for social control" (Della Porta and Diani 2006: 47–8).

Given these arguments in the literature, this chapter focuses on examining whether more recent cohorts are more likely than older cohorts to engage in 'elite-challenging participation', in terms of protest activism and participation in new social movements or social movements organisations (SMOs). If participation in elite-challenging activism is rising as a result of older cohorts being replaced by younger, more participatory ones, then it would be expected that the baby-boomers, '80s and '90s generation should demonstrate at higher rates than the pre- and post-WWII cohorts. This should not be due to age effects. However, given that the political context has changed a great deal in the last thirty years, as suggested by Della Porta and Diani (2006), it might be expected that the decline of ideological competition between the Left and the Right as a result of the end of the Cold War, alongside rising levels of political apathy in society, might have halted or slowed down this process of rising unconventional participation amongst the younger generations. Instead, the baby-boomer generation of the 1960s might stand out as the exception to the rule, rather than as the initiators of a rising trend in demonstration activity.

Findings

Demonstrating

The primary focus of the analysis in this chapter is to investigate whether the patterns of participation analysed at the level of the nation in Chapter 4 are replicated when analysed by cohort. This will return preliminary information regarding whether there are cohort differences in unconventional participation within countries. Figure 6.1 shows the levels of demonstration activity by cohort for each country over the 1981–1999 period.[1] The lines plot the overall proportion of demonstrating in the population; the levels of demonstrating for the pre-WWII generation; the levels for the post-WWII generation; the levels of demonstrating for the baby-boom generation; the levels of demonstrating of the '80s generation and the levels of demonstrating for the '90s generation. This cohort only enters the sample in 1990 and as such the levels are plotted over just two time points. The graphs in Figure 6.1 show that the younger cohorts tend to demonstrate at higher levels than the older cohorts, and that, in most countries, period effects impact on the different cohorts in similar ways. However, in Denmark, Ireland and Britain, the '90s cohorts demonstrate at lower levels in 1999 than in 1990 whereas most other cohorts demonstrate more as time goes by. Perhaps more interesting is the fact that in several countries the curve for the baby-boomer is above those for both the '80s and '90s generation. Following the modernisation account, it would be expected that the curve for the '90s generation should sit at the top, followed, in descending order, by the one for the '80s generation, and then the one for the baby-boomers. However, this pattern is only true in Germany, and to an extent in Italy. In some countries, like Britain, cohort differences in demonstrating are narrow; in other countries, such as Denmark and the Netherlands, they are very large (interestingly, this was also the case for party membership in these countries). For example, in Britain and Denmark, the pre-WWII cohort tend to demonstrate at about the same level, but about 35 per cent of the baby-boomers said they had demonstrated in Denmark, whereas only about 20 per cent amongst this cohort said so for Britain. Moreover, Figure 6.1 shows that in some countries the curves slope upwards for both 1981–1990 and 1990–1999 but that in some other countries period effects are different and curves slope downwards or are flat in either period. Thus, while period effects tend to be similar within countries, they vary across countries, even for this activity which is generally rising. As such, these results show that demonstration activity generally went up within birth cohorts over time.

However, demonstrating went down by 3 points amongst the '90s generation in Denmark; by 6 points amongst the '80s generation and by 8 points amongst

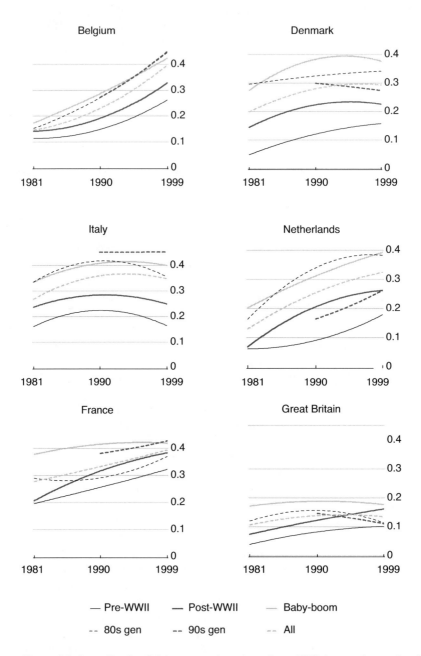

Belgium

Denmark

Italy

Netherlands

France

Great Britain

— Pre-WWII   — Post-WWII   — Baby-boom

-- 80s gen   -- 90s gen   -- All

Figure 6.1 Attending lawful demonstrations, by cohort, EVS (proportion saying 'have done'), over time.

Note
Best fit quadratic smoothed lines.

continued

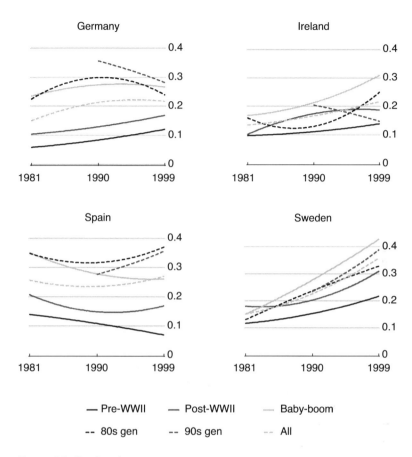

Figure 6.1 Continued

the '90s generation in Germany; by 5 points amongst the '90s generation in Ireland; by 6 points amongst the '80s generation in Italy; and by 3 points amongst the '80s generation and 2 points amongst the '90s generation in Britain. Figure 6.2 shows demonstration levels by cohort for the period 2002–2006. Again, older cohorts generally demonstrate at lower levels than younger cohorts but these differences are much smaller in some countries than others. Again, as in 1981–1999 the '90s generation demonstrates at the highest levels only in a couple of countries, unlike what one would expect based on modernisation theories. Moreover, even in the Noughties, aged between forty-five and sixty in the period 2002–2006, the baby-boomers demonstrated at about the same level as the '90s and '80s generation, or at higher levels (the Netherlands and Sweden). These results provide some preliminary evidence that the baby-boomers are quite active in protest activities relative to other cohorts and that even as they age, they maintain these higher levels of participation. This would suggest at

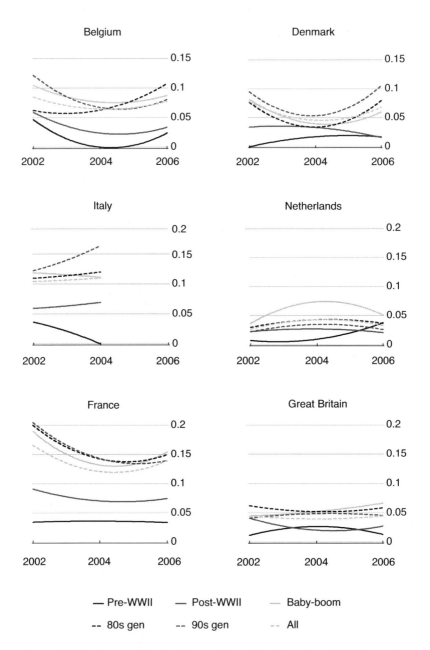

Figure 6.2 Demonstrated in the last twelve months, by cohort, ESS (proportion saying 'yes'), over time.

Note
Best fit quadratic smoothed lines.

continued

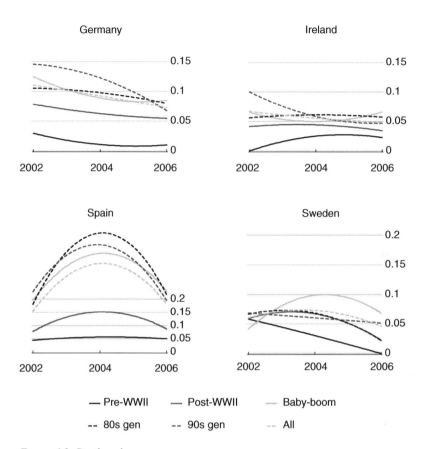

Figure 6.2 Continued

least some role for formative experiences in the radicalising late 1960s and 1970s, since the literature has traditionally shown that young people tend to be much more likely than middle aged people to demonstrate.

Having described cohort differences in demonstration levels in the different countries, the aim of the analysis is now to provide a more robust empirical basis for these patterns: to quantify these differences and to test for whether they are statistically significant. The percentages in the cells in columns 2–6 of Table 6.1 report the levels of demonstration activity, by cohort, for each country. The significance levels for the percentages in these cells are based on logistic regression, where the post-WWII cohort is the reference category. Thus, the significance level stars capture whether there are significant differences in levels of demonstration activity between the post-WWII cohort and each of the other four cohorts in turn. The Δ columns seven to nine on the right-hand side of the table, on the other hand, show the percentage point differences, between the levels of party membership amongst pairs of cohorts. The first Δ column (7), for example, reports the

Table 6.1 Demonstrating by cohort and country (%) EVS

Country	Pre-WWII	Post-WWII	Baby-boomers	80s gen.	90s gen.	Δ 80-BB	Δ 90-BB	Δ 90–80	N
Belgium	16***	22	32***	32***	36***	+0	+4	+4	5,333
Denmark	9***	19	34***	33***	28**	−1	−6*	−5	3,020
France	23**	31	41***	33	42***	−8**	+1	+9**	3,584
Germany, W.	8***	13	26***	27***	32***	+1	+6	+5	4,069
Ireland	11**	16	22**	19	17	−3	−5	−2	2,993
Italy	18***	26	38***	38***	45***	+0	+7*	+7**	5,020
Netherlands	9***	17	30***	32***	24*	+2	−6	−8*	3,077
Great Britain	6***	11	18***	13	14	−5**	−4	+1	3,366
Spain	11***	18	30***	33***	32***	+3	+2	−1	5,284
Sweden	13***	23	28**	25	34***	−3	+6	+9**	2,846

Notes
Significance levels:
* $p \leq 0.05$.
** $p \leq 0.01$.
*** $p \leq 0.001$.
The significance levels in columns 2–6 are based on logistic regression, where the post-WWII cohort is the reference category. Therefore, the significance-level stars capture whether there are significant differences in demonstrating between the post-WWII cohort and each of the other four cohorts in turn. The Δ columns on the right-hand side report the differences in percentages. The significance levels in the Δ columns on the right-hand side are derived by testing for coefficient differences between the two relevant cohort dummy variables post-regression.

percentage difference in demonstration levels between the 1980s generation and the baby-boom generation. Significance levels here are derived by testing for coefficient differences (post-regression via the Wald test) between the two relevant cohort dummy variables. Table 6.1 shows that, across Western European countries, and as expected, the pre-WWII cohort demonstrates less than the post-WWII cohort and that in general, the baby-boom, '80s and '90s generations demonstrate more than the older cohorts. However, in Ireland and Britain, the '80s and '90s cohorts are *not* significantly more likely to demonstrate than the post-WWII cohort. The same is true of the '80s generation in France and Sweden. This evidence runs counter to what would be expected from an intergenerational shift. Moreover, it would be expected that the '80s generation should demonstrate more than the baby-boomers and that the '90s generation should demonstrate more than both the baby-boom and '80s generations. However, nowhere does the '80s generation demonstrate significantly more than the baby-boomers; and in France and Britain, the baby-boomers actually demonstrate significantly more than the '80s generation. The '90s generation only demonstrates more than the baby-boom generation in Italy. In Denmark, the baby-boomers demonstrate more than the '90s generation. Only in France, Italy and Sweden, does the '90s generation demonstrate at higher levels than the '80s cohort; in the Netherlands, the baby-boomers demonstrate *more* than the '90s generation.

However, it may be that age effects are at play here. For example, since the majority of the baby-boomers are drawn from the middle age group in those countries where the baby-boomers are more active, perhaps being in the middle age group makes one more likely to demonstrate than the other two age groups. On the other hand, age effects might explain why the '90s generation exhibits higher levels of participation in some countries, since it has been generally been shown that young people demonstrate more than older people given they are less risk averse and have more time.

Table 6.3 shows that there are indeed age group differences in participation, with people in the middle and young age group being significantly more likely than older people to attend demonstrations. However, the differences between middle aged and young people are weaker: only in Germany, Italy and Spain are young people significantly more likely than people in the middle age group to attend demonstrations. Note that these are the same three countries where differences between all three of the baby-boomers, '80s and '90s cohorts and the post-WWII cohort are significant. More generally, the results presented here mean that separate age and cohort effects cannot be separated based on the information in these tables. It may be the case that age effects are at play explaining cohort differences in demonstration activity. Therefore, the analysis turns to regression analyses controlling for each of cohorts, age and period to separate these effects. As discussed in detail in the Appendix, age and cohort effects can be separated in regression models by controlling for survey year, because each age group is spread over at least two cohorts in each survey year and the model is thus identifiable. Also as discussed in Chapter 3, the categorisations applied to cohort and age group variables in this study are not only helpful for the purposes of identification, but are also theoretically meaningful in the analysis of the results. As Mason *et al.* (1973: 243) argued, the identification of these effects only makes sense if "the researcher entertains relatively strong hypotheses about the nature of the life-cycle, period and generation effects" and their expected direction. As Rodgers (1982: 774) points out: "the specification and measurement of the theoretical variables for which age, period and generation effects are indirect indicators" is required for solving the identification problem. In this case, we are focusing on whether observed cohort differences in demonstrating activity are the result of life-cycle effects (e.g. younger people tend to demonstrate more than older people) or generation effects (e.g. younger cohorts are more likely to demonstrate than older cohorts because they were socialised at time where demonstrations became more popular). As discussed above, this has significant implications for what can be said about the future of political participation. The primacy of generational effects would suggest that this type of activity in society will rise further as older, less demonstrative, cohorts are replaced by younger, more participatory, cohorts, as suggested by the modernisation account. Therefore, identifying the models to assess the relative impact of these variables controlling for period effects is key if one is to say anything meaningful about what differences in the political behaviour of younger and older cohorts could spell out in terms of their implications for democratic practice. Table 6.2 presents the results of logistic regression for demonstrating 1981–1999, for each of the ten countries analysed here, controlling for cohort, age group and survey year (Model(s) 1). The results

Table 6.2 Logistic regression on demonstrating, EVS, by country (APC and education)

	BEL		DNK		FRA		DEU		IRL	
	Model 1	Model 2	Model 1	Model 2	Model 1	Model 2	Model 1	Model 2	Model 1	Model 2
Pre-WWII	-0.18	-0.11	-0.73***	-0.70**	-0.33*	-0.24	-0.53***	-0.49**	-0.40*	-0.38
Baby-boom	0.35*	0.31*	0.58***	0.51**	0.38***	0.23	0.77***	0.72***	0.44*	0.39*
80s gen.	0.40*	0.26	0.46*	0.34	-0.01	-0.21	0.67**	0.54*	0.23	0.13
90s gen.	0.55*	0.34	0.11	-0.04	0.19	-0.04	0.78**	0.55	-0.03	-0.17
18–33	-0.36*	-0.38**	-0.01	0.01	0.01	-0.11	0.20	0.19	-0.09	-0.14
51+	-0.40**	-0.32*	-0.28	-0.22	-0.04	0.02	-0.05	0.01	-0.03	0.00
1981	-0.60***	-0.56***	-0.48***	-0.49***	-0.23*	-0.19	-0.36**	-0.73***	-0.19	-0.16
1999	0.39***	0.37***	0.08	0.2	0.29**	0.26*	0.02	0.03	0.26	0.28*
Edu (low)		-0.73***		-0.51***		-0.99***		-0.79***		-0.41***
Intercept	-1.02***	-0.77***	-1.11***	-0.96***	-0.81***	-0.32*	-1.78***	-1.30***	-1.68***	-1.43***
Pseudo-RSq	0.04	0.06	0.05	0.06	0.02	0.05	0.05	0.07	0.02	0.02
LogLike	-2,838.35	-2,796.01	-1,559.65	-1,547.91	-2,177.26	-2,105.44	-1,860.39	-1,824.16	-1,325.68	-1,318.3
N	5,087	5,087	2,928	2,928	3,473	3,473	4,022	4,022	2,950	2,950

	ITA		NLD		GBR		ESP		SWE	
	Model 1	Model 2	Model 1	Model 2	Model 1	Model 2	Model 1	Model 2	Model 1	Model 2
Pre-WWII	-0.32*	-0.29	-0.41	-0.35	-0.63**	-0.59*	-0.34*	-0.27	-0.18	-0.15
Baby-boom	0.34**	0.18	0.61***	0.51**	0.52**	0.46*	0.35**	0.27*	0.01	-0.01
80s gen.	0.23	-0.02	0.32	0.10	-0.17	-0.31	0.36*	0.16	-0.11	-0.13
90s gen.	0.43*	0.14	-0.44	-0.67*	-0.45	-0.55	0.22	-0.04	0.01	-0.02
18–33	0.08	0.01	0.34*	0.25	0.40	0.29	0.31*	0.22	-0.14	-0.17
51+	-0.38**	-0.30*	-0.21	-0.12	0.01	0.09	-0.36*	-0.26	-0.39*	-0.35*
1981	-0.37***	-0.21*	-0.84***	-0.84***	-0.51**	-0.47**	0.20*	0.14	-0.50***	-0.44***
1999	-0.06	-0.05	0.43***	0.36**	-0.06	-0.09	0.21*	0.23*	0.52***	0.51***
Edu (low)		-0.91***		-1.03***		-1.04***		-0.88***		-0.29*
Intercept	-0.69***	-0.19	-1.39***	-0.97***	-1.97***	-1.29***	-1.45***	-0.86***	-1.02***	-0.95***
Pseudo-RSq	0.03	0.06	0.06	0.09	0.03	0.06	0.04	0.06	0.03	0.04
LogLike	-2,986.46	-2,902.93	-1,478.42	-1,437.88	-1,143.52	-1,103.65	-2,702.56	-2,629.63	-1,324.74	-1321.98
N	4,923	4,923	2,981	2,981	3,228	3,228	5,095	5,095	2,527	2,527

Notes

Model 1: age, period and cohort; Model 2: age, period, cohort and education.

Significance levels:

* $p \leq 0.05$.

** $p \leq 0.01$.

*** $p \leq 0.001$.

Reference categories: Post-WWII cohort (2); 34–50 age group (2); 1990 (2), therefore, 1981 is the inverse of the period effect 1981–1990; Edu (low) is a dummy variable where 1 means the respondent left school before the age of 17.

Table 6.3 Demonstrating, by age group and country (%) EVS

	18–33 yrs	34–50 yrs	51–90 yrs	Δ Young-middle	Δ Middle-old	Δ Young-old	N
Belgium	29*	32	21***	–3*	+11***	+8***	5,333
Denmark	29	32	15***	–3	+17***	+14***	3,020
France	35	36	31**	–1	+5**	+4**	3,584
Germany, W.	28***	20	12***	+8***	+8***	+16***	4,069
Ireland	17	20	15***	–3	+5***	+2	2,993
Italy	40**	36	23***	+4**	+13***	+17***	5,020
Netherlands	25	26	17***	–1	+9***	+8***	3,077
Great Britain	14	14	10**	+0	+4**	+4***	3,366
Spain	34***	25	14***	+9***	+11***	+20***	5,284
Sweden	25	29	21***	–4	+8***	+4*	2,846

Notes
Significance levels:
* $p \leq 0.05$.
** $p \leq 0.01$.
*** $p \leq 0.001$.
The significance levels in columns 2–4 are based on logistic regression, where the 34–50 age group is the reference category. Therefore, the significance-level stars capture whether there are significant differences in demonstrating between the 34–50 age group and each of the other two age groups in turn. The Δ columns on the right-hand side report the differences in percentages. The significance levels in the Δ columns are derived as above and by testing for coefficient differences between the old and young age group dummies post-regression.

for Model 1 across the ten countries show that the baby-boomers are significantly more likely to demonstrate than the post-WWII cohort in almost every country (except Sweden); the '80s generation is only significantly more likely than the post-WWII cohort to demonstrate in Belgium, Denmark, Germany and Spain and the '90s generation is only significantly more likely than the post-WWII cohort to demonstrate in Belgium, Germany and Italy. Older people are significantly less likely than middle aged people to demonstrate in Belgium, Italy and Sweden. Including education in Model(s) 2, shows that in six out of ten countries only the baby-boomers are significantly more likely than the post-WWII cohort to demonstrate. Only in Germany do significant differences between the '80s generation and the post-WWII cohort persist when controlling for education; in the Netherlands, controlling for education means that the '90s generation is significantly less likely than the post-WWII generation to demonstrate.

These results suggest that higher education levels play an important role in explaining the higher participatory levels of the younger cohorts. In France and Italy, higher education levels are also important in explaining differences between the baby-boomers and the post-WWII cohort. However, in all the other six countries where these differences persist, this evidence suggests that something else about the baby-boomers makes them more likely to demonstrate than the other cohorts. Since there are no confounding age effects, it is likely that their formative experiences in the late 1960s and 1970s left an imprint on their political behaviour. This is similar to conventional participation; having a lower education has a strong negative effect on demonstrating. Table 6.4 reports the results of the equivalent models for the ESS 2002–2006 data and the results here are remarkably similar to those from Table 6.2. In every country except Sweden, the baby-boomers are significantly more likely than the post-WWII cohort to demonstrate. Including education in Model(s) 2 mitigates cohort differences in demonstration activity. In Denmark and Spain, all three of the younger cohorts are significantly more likely than the post-WWII generation to demonstrate. However, in all the other countries, there is again very little evidence for modernisation theories suggesting that each younger cohort should be significantly more likely relative to the post-WWII cohort to demonstrate. Instead, the results presented here show that the most marked differences are those between the baby-boomers and the post-WWII cohort, whereas the '80s and '90s cohorts are in most countries about as likely as older cohorts to demonstrate. Moreover, where there are significant differences these are generally attributable to higher education levels amongst the youngest cohorts, whereas education does not appear to be able to account for why the baby-boomers demonstrate more than older cohorts in most countries.

Tables 6.5 and 6.6 present the results of logistic regression on demonstrating (both for the EVS and the ESS data) for the fully specified model, discussed in Chapter 5 above, for each country. They show that across countries having a lower education has a strong negative effect on demonstrating, that men are significantly more likely than women to demonstrate, that being strongly left wing has a strong positive effect on demonstrating, and that left-libertarians are significantly more likely than both right-libertarians and also left-authoritarians and right-authoritarians to demonstrate. This suggests that post-materialism may well be a poor proxy for progressive liberalism as some authors have suggested. Since right-libertarians are not as likely as those on the left to demonstrate, it therefore appears that 'old' cleavages have not been overcome, nor that values alone predict elite-challenging activism. However, it should be noted that for 2002–2006 right-libertarians are about as likely as left-libertarians to demonstrate in Ireland, Italy, the Netherlands, Great Britain and Spain. This suggests that perhaps in these countries the social value cleavage dimension is becoming more important relative to the redistributive one.

Being strongly right wing has a negative effect on demonstrating in Italy and Sweden. Moreover, in Denmark, Italy and Spain (and for 2002–2006 also in the Netherlands) individuals in manual occupations are just as likely to everyone else to demonstrate suggesting that in these countries at least demonstrating has been 'democratised' (Van Aelst and Walgrave 2001). Additionally, for 2002–2006 gender differences for this activity disappear in Denmark, Great Britain, Spain and Sweden suggesting that, at least in some countries, the advances of gender egalitarianism may have impacted on participatory propensities. Similarly, having a lower education no longer has a negative effect in Denmark, Ireland and Sweden. Taken together, the results from the EVS 1981–1999 and ESS 2002–2006 suggest that the profile of demonstrators has become more representative of the wider population. This is not surprising given

Table 6.4 Logistic regression on demonstrating, ESS, by country (APC and education)

	BEL		DNK		FRA		DEU		IRL	
	Model 1	Model 2	Model 1	Model 2	Model 1	Model 2	Model 1	Model 2	Model 1	Model 2
Pre-WWII	-0.31	-0.28	-0.95	-0.92	-0.81*	-0.73	-1.23**	-1.02*	-1.20	-1.13
Baby-boom	0.94***	0.86***	0.89***	0.84***	0.70***	0.60***	0.40**	0.28	0.49*	0.45
80s gen.	0.79**	0.69*	0.93*	0.87*	0.51*	0.32	0.10	-0.02	0.26	0.20
90s gen.	0.60	0.46	1.50**	1.42**	-0.10	-0.32	-0.29	-0.41	-0.26	-0.32
18–33	0.44	0.43	-0.34	-0.32	0.67***	0.61*	0.65**	0.66*	0.80*	0.78*
51+	0.03	0.05	0.00	0.02	-0.32	-0.24	-0.40*	-0.37*	-0.27	-0.22
2002	0.46**	0.45**	0.63***	0.63***	0.36**	0.34**	0.22*	0.23*	0.16	0.15
2006	0.37*	0.37*	0.45*	0.47*	0.11	0.04	-0.14	-0.15	-0.01	-0.02
Edu (low)		-0.39*		-0.34		-0.80***		-0.91***		-0.34
Intercept	-3.56***	-3.38***	-4.01***	-3.92***	-2.29***	-1.91***	-2.46***	-2.27***	-3.06***	-2.96***
Pseudo-RSq	0.02	0.03	0.03	0.04	0.03	0.04	0.02	0.03	0.02	0.02
LogLike	-1,169.72	-1,165.98	-829.54	-828.13	-1,831.28	-1,802.24	-2,072.93	-2,050.73	-1,106.14	-1,103.92
N	4,636	4,636	4,028	4,028	4,767	4,767	7,527	7,527	5,149	5,149

	ITA		NLD		GBR		ESP		SWE	
	Model 1	Model 2	Model 1	Model 2	Model 1	Model 2	Model 1	Model 2	Model 1	Model 2
Pre-WWII	-0.97	-0.86	-0.77	-0.65	-0.59	-0.50	-0.74*	-0.66*	-0.38	-0.31
Baby-boom	0.55*	0.39	0.53*	0.44	0.61**	0.50*	1.18***	1.03***	0.36	0.27
80s gen.	0.32	0.08	-0.13	-0.29	0.40	0.22	1.22***	0.96***	0.07	-0.03
90s gen.	0.57	0.21	-0.43	-0.61	0.24	0.07	1.02***	0.67*	0.12	0.01
18–33	0.24	0.16	0.19	0.18	0.12	0.11	0.18	0.16	0.10	0.09
51+	-0.17	-0.11	-0.28	-0.23	-0.17	-0.11	-0.06	0.06	0.01	0.05
2002	-0.22	-0.18	-0.52**	-0.55**	0.13	0.11	-0.90***	-0.90***	-0.19	-0.20
2006			-0.30	-0.35	0.19	0.13	-0.94***	-0.99***	-0.63***	-0.64***
Edu (low)		-1.02***		-0.65**		-0.65**		-0.88***		-0.32
Intercept	-2.36***	-1.81***	-3.02***	-2.74***	-3.46***	-3.22***	-1.54***	-0.96***	-2.70***	-2.57***
Pseudo-RSq	0.02	0.05	0.02	0.02	0.01	0.02	0.08	0.10	0.01	0.01
LogLike	-800.34	-777.54	-838.39	-831.88	-1,003.9	-997.9	-2,160.01	-2,106.19	-1,121.82	-1,119.84
N	2,415	2,415	5,702	5,702	5,734	5,734	4,372	4,372	5,176	5,176

Notes

Model 1: age, period and cohort; Model 2: age, period, cohort and education.

Significance levels:

* $p \leq 0.05$.

** $p \leq 0.01$.

*** $p \leq 0.001$.

Reference categories: Post-WWII cohort (2); 34–50 age group (2); 2004 (2), therefore, 2002 is the inverse of the period effect 2002–2004; Edu (low) is a dummy variable where 1 means the respondent left school before the age of 17.

Table 6.5 Logistic regression on demonstrating, EVS, by country (APC and all controls)

	BEL	DNK	FRA	DEU	IRL	ITA	NLD	GBR	ESP	SWE
Pre-WWII	-0.09	-0.63**	-0.23	-0.38*	-0.29	-0.25	-0.20	-0.53*	-0.21	-0.14
Baby-boom	0.31*	0.36*	0.16	0.65***	0.36	0.11	0.40*	0.40	0.19	-0.03
80s gen.	0.23	0.26	-0.28	0.51*	0.04	-0.02	0.11	-0.39	0.06	-0.12
90s gen.	0.42	-0.08	0.00	0.53	-0.31	0.21	-0.59	-0.63	-0.10	0.08
18–33	-0.40**	0.00	-0.11	0.15	-0.14	-0.06	0.19	0.28	0.12	-0.21
51+	-0.27	-0.18	0.03	0.05	0.02	-0.29*	-0.13	0.13	-0.18	-0.34
1981	-0.68***	-0.92***	-0.44***	-0.94***	-0.23	-0.43***	-1.02***	-0.64***	0.12	-0.91***
1999	0.22*	0.07	0.14	-0.01	0.17	-0.03	0.20	-0.16	0.22*	0.37**
Edu (low)	-0.61***	-0.46***	-0.94***	-0.65***	-0.43***	-0.90***	-0.87***	-0.96***	-0.93***	-0.39**
Male	0.63***	0.33***	0.75***	0.60***	0.94***	0.76***	0.30**	0.80***	0.47***	0.20*
Working cl.	-0.30***	0.04	-0.41***	-0.29***	-0.34**	0.06	-0.55***	-0.53***	0.10	-0.44**
Left	1.14***	1.53***	1.07***	1.16***	0.89***	0.98***	1.53***	0.96***	1.08***	0.91***
Right	-0.16	-0.54	0.29	0.19	-0.43	-0.46*	-0.55	-0.59	0.11	-0.69**
Left-auth.	-0.48***	-0.95***	-0.66***	-0.84***	-0.52***	-0.59***	-0.83***	-0.77***	-0.62***	-0.46*
Right-lib.	-0.38***	-0.91***	-0.58***	-0.74***	-0.16	-0.43***	-0.59***	-0.79***	-0.74***	-0.71***
Right-auth.	-0.66***	-1.10***	-0.91***	-1.01***	-0.40**	-0.60***	-1.41***	-1.06***	-0.71***	-0.95***
Intercept	-0.67***	-0.46**	-0.17	-0.91***	-1.45***	-0.23	-0.54**	-1.05***	-0.83***	-0.33
Pseudo-RSq	0.09	0.12	0.11	0.11	0.07	0.11	0.16	0.12	0.12	0.08
LogLike	-2,680.04	-1,449.18	-1,965.96	-1,738.64	-1,256.97	-2,735	-1,320.66	-1,036.27	-2,477.2	-1,257.82
N	5,084	2,928	3,473	4,022	2,945	4,923	2,980	3,227	5,095	2,513

Notes
Models with age, period, cohort, education, gender, class, ideology and values.
Significance levels:
* $p \leq 0.05$.
** $p \leq 0.01$.
*** $p \leq 0.001$.
Reference categories: Post-WWII cohort (2); 34–50 age group (2); 1990 (2), therefore, 1981 is the inverse of the period effect 1981–1990; Left-libertarian (1); Edu (low) is a dummy variable where 1 means the respondent left school before the age of 17; Working class is a dummy variable where 1 means the respondent is an unskilled, semi-skilled or skilled manual worker; Left and right are dummy variables derived from the left-right scale where left (1) means values 0/1 and right (1) means values 9/10.

Table 6.6 Logistic regression on demonstrating, ESS, by country (APC and all controls)

	BEL	DNK	FRA	DEU	IRL	ITA	NLD	GBR	ESP	SWE
Pre-WWII	-0.21	-0.94	-0.64	-0.93*	-1.02	-0.88	-0.54	-0.56	-0.62	-0.25
Baby-boom	0.87***	0.65*	0.53***	0.29	0.39	0.30	0.45	0.43	0.97***	0.25
80s gen.	0.72*	0.80*	0.30	-0.01	0.17	-0.01	-0.20	0.15	0.86***	-0.01
90s gen.	0.49	1.44**	-0.29	-0.42	-0.35	0.12	-0.48	-0.06	0.60*	-0.03
18–33	0.42	-0.40	0.55*	0.63*	0.73	0.08	0.11	0.15	0.13	0.02
51+	0.07	0.04	-0.25	-0.30	-0.24	-0.19	-0.22	-0.12	0.06	0.13
2002	0.48**	0.60**	0.33*	0.26*	0.12	-0.13	-0.56**	0.13	-0.91***	-0.20
2006	0.37*	0.32	0.09	-0.17	-0.02		-0.40*	0.16	-1.00***	-0.73***
Edu (low)	-0.35*	-0.26	-0.71***	-0.73***	-0.34	-1.05***	-0.63***	-0.53**	-0.81***	-0.36
Male	0.47***	-0.20	0.51***	0.28**	0.44**	0.79***	0.56***	-0.06	0.12	0.15
Working cl.	-0.40*	-0.36*	-0.41***	-0.38***	-0.08	-0.02	0.12	-0.52**	-0.23*	-0.02
Left	1.11***	1.65***	1.13***	1.09***	1.21***	1.43***	1.18***	0.31	0.75***	1.16***
Right	0.40	-1.26	-0.25	-0.06	-0.18	0.60	-1.03	0.51	-0.01	-0.05
Left-auth.	-0.37**	-0.53**	-0.45***	-0.56***	-0.56***	-0.55**	-0.35	-0.45*	-0.46***	-0.84***
Right-lib.	-0.40*	-1.04***	-0.40*	-0.51***	-0.60	-0.45	-0.36	-0.45	-0.10	-0.89***
Right-auth.	-0.68***	-1.21***	-0.85***	-1.20***	-0.76***	-0.98***	-1.06***	-0.69***	-0.76***	-1.18***
Intercept	-3.37***	-3.01***	-1.94***	-1.83***	-2.64***	-1.88***	-2.77***	-2.63***	-0.62***	-2.06***
Pseudo-RSq	0.05	0.10	0.09	0.07	0.04	0.11	0.06	0.03	0.12	0.06
LogLike	-1,131.28	-770.06	-1,717.57	-1,971.86	-1,076.75	-724.13	-801.34	-985.44	-2,062.82	-1,070.56
N	4,625	4,028	4,767	7,527	5,127	2,415	5,702	5734	4,372	5,176

Notes

Models with age, period, cohort, education, gender, class, ideology and values.

Significance levels:

* $p \leq 0.05$.

** $p \leq 0.01$.

*** $p \leq 0.001$.

Reference categories: Post-WWII cohort (2); 34–50 age group (2); 2004 (2), therefore, 2002 is the inverse of the period effect 2002–2004; Left-libertarian (1); Edu (low) is a dummy variable where 1 means the respondent left school before the age of 17; Working class is a dummy variable where 1 means the respondent is an unskilled, semi-skilled or skilled manual worker; Left and right are dummy variables derived from the left-right scale where left (1) means values 0/1 and right (1) means values 9/10.

that this activity has entered the mainstream political sphere, and has become a regular, institutionalised and media-choreographed occurrence in most advanced Western democracies (Van Aelst and Walgrave 2001).

Therefore, the key results for demonstrating with respect to cohort differences are that, while the baby-boomers are generally more likely than the post-WWII cohort to demonstrate, there are hardly any significant differences between the post-WWII cohort and the '80s and '90s generation. Where these differences are significant, they are generally accounted for by their higher education levels. The same is not generally true of the baby-boomers. Therefore, the argument that younger cohorts should be engaging in elite-challenging activities more than older cohorts is not supported with respect to this activity. Rather, this is only true of the baby-boomers, which suggests that rather than modernising influences, formative experiences which set them apart from later cohorts have a role to play for explaining their higher participatory patterns, as suggested by Della Porta and Diani (2006). It also appears that the fact that 'subsequent political contexts differed greatly' has had a depressing impact on the likelihood of cohorts coming of age in later periods to demonstrate. Therefore, the results for demonstrating presented in this section would suggest that the context of formative years matters and that the baby-boomers are still the 'protest generation'. However, this may only be true for demonstrating. Therefore, the next sections examine cohort differences for other kinds of protest activism, or 'elite-challenging' participation to ascertain whether this holds true at least for some of the other indicators.

Boycotting

The next indicator of unconventional or 'elite-challenging' participation this chapter examines is joining boycotts. Boycotting is a relatively new activity compared to demonstrating. It rose to prominence in the early '80s in Western Europe, particularly with the anti-apartheid campaigns. As such, it might be expected that the '80s and '90s cohorts, coming of age precisely in the period when this activity was rising to prominence, might participate in this activity more than the other generations. Figure 6.3 shows the proportion of respondents saying they had boycotted by cohort for each country over the 1981–1999 period. As with demonstrating and the activities examined in Chapter 5, period effects vary across countries. However, they tend to be similar within countries. The older cohorts are generally those reporting the lowest levels of participation in this activity. In most countries, the baby-boomers and the '80s generations tend to say that they have joined a boycott the most; however, in most countries cohort differences for this activity are very slight. The '90s generation boycott more than any other cohorts in Denmark and Ireland, but in other countries such as France, Italy, the Netherlands and Britain they boycott less, or as little, as the pre-WWII generation. Figure 6.4 reports levels for 2002–2006. Again, the baby-boomers and the '80s generation tend to boycott the most, though in Spain and Sweden the '90s generation catches up with their predecessors. The greatest

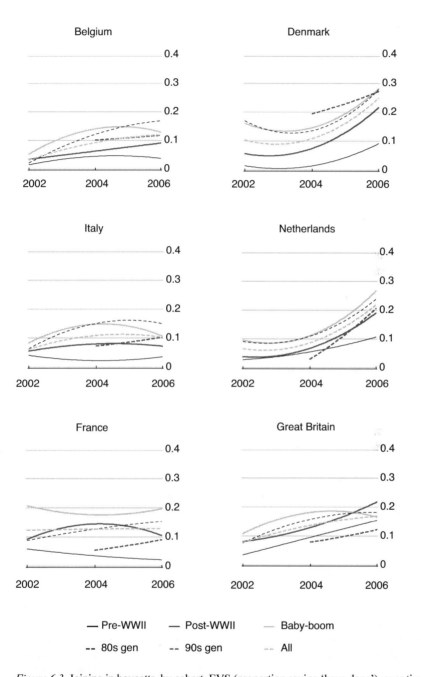

Figure 6.3 Joining in boycotts, by cohort, EVS (proportion saying 'have done'), over time.

Note

Best fit quadratic smoothed lines.

continued

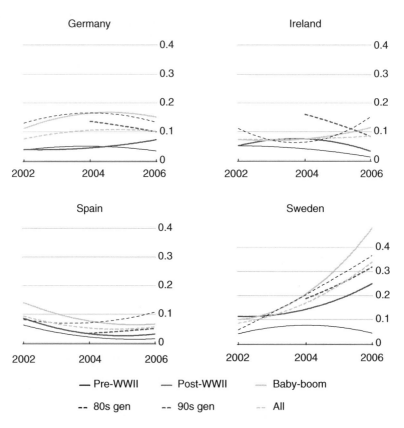

Figure 6.3 Continued

differences for this activity are those between the pre-WWII generation and the others, but in Denmark, Ireland and Spain, the post-WWII generation also tend to join boycotts quite a lot less than the youngest (three) cohorts. However, the differences observed in Figures 6.3 and 6.4 could be due solely to age effects, with middle age individuals being more likely to boycott than young people in those countries where the baby-boomers are more active in boycotts, and young people preferring this repertoire in those countries where the '90s generation is the more participatory. Therefore, the analysis turns to examining the results of logistic regression for the identified model, presented in Table 6.7.

The results show that the baby-boomers are significantly more likely than the post-WWII cohort to boycott in Belgium, Denmark, France, Germany and in the Netherlands. The '80s generation is significantly more likely to boycott than the post-WWII generation in Belgium, Germany and Ireland. The '90s generation is, on the other hand, only significantly more likely than the post-WWII cohort to boycott in Germany. In France and Italy (controlling for education), and in Great Britain, across Models 1 and 2, the '90s generation is significantly less likely

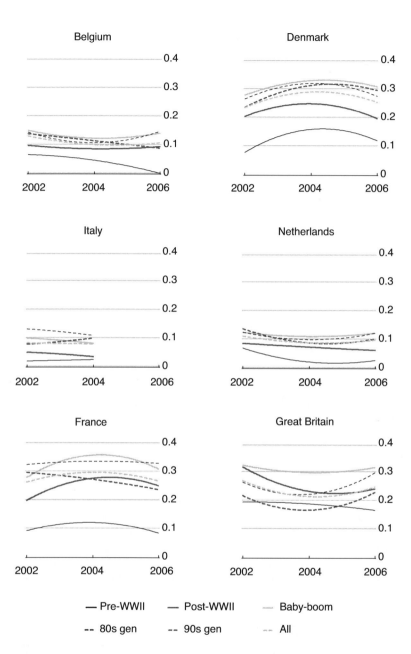

Figure 6.4 Boycotted in the last twelve months, by cohort, ESS (proportion saying 'yes'), over time.

Note
Best fit quadratic smoothed lines.

continued

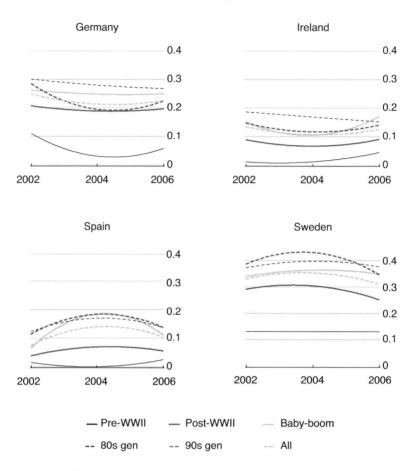

Figure 6.4 Continued

than the post-WWII cohort to join a boycott. Model(s) 2 in Table 6.7 show that having a lower education has a strong negative effect on boycotting and that education mediates cohort differences in participation: where younger cohorts are significantly more likely than the post-WWII cohort to boycott, including education in the model reduces the coefficient size: where differences are insignificant, including education turns negative coefficients significant. Again, the evidence presented here shows that education levels play an important role for explaining why younger cohorts participate more or as much as the post-WWII cohort in this activity. Moreover, the results for 2002–2006 presented in Table 6.8 confirm this pattern: in every case, including education in Model(s) 2 decreases the size of the significant cohort coefficients. The only pieces of evidence supporting the idea of a cohort replacement hypothesis for boycotting are Ireland and Spain in this period. All three of the younger cohorts participate more than the post-WWII cohort in this activity.

The results from this section thus suggest that, with the exception of the baby-boomers, there is very little evidence that younger cohorts are significantly more likely than older ones to engage in this activity across Europe. Differences between the '80s generation and the post-WWII cohort are more marked in the 2002–2006 period. Again, education plays a mediating role for participation in this activity. The results for the full model presented in Tables 6.9 and 6.10 show that the effects of the predictors are remarkably similar to those for demonstrating. Again, working class people are not less likely to boycott than others in Denmark, Italy (also in 2002–2006), Spain (also in 2002–2006) and Sweden, adding further evidence to suggest that in these countries protest activism is a means for those individuals which participate less in so-called 'conventional' activities to get a say in the political affairs of the nation. Again, being strongly left wing has a positive effect on boycotting, and being strongly right wing has a negative effect in three countries. Therefore, while with conventional activities both left- and right-wing politicisation contributed to participation, unsurprisingly, it is just left-wing politicisation which contributes to boycotting. Again, left-libertarians are significantly more likely than the others to boycott in 1981–1999 though in 2002–2006 there are no significant differences between left- and right-libertarians in most countries suggesting that for boycotting at least, values might have begun to take precedence over the 'old' left-right divide in terms of motivating people to this action. Indeed, given the fact that this activity generally falls within the scope of 'consumer politics' and 'ethical shopping' this is not surprising. Interestingly, while being male has a strong positive effect on boycotting for 1981–1999, this effect is no longer significant for 2002–2006 and indeed women are significantly more likely than men to boycott in Denmark and Sweden suggesting that the gender divide has been overcome and sometimes reversed at least for one type of participation. Therefore, it is less a sign of the transcendence of 'public man/private woman' than a result of the institutionalisation of this type of action into the mainstream domain of daily life.

Petitioning

The next indicator of 'elite-challenging' participation to which the analysis of this chapter turns is petitioning. It is possible to question whether this activity should be classed as 'elite-challenging', given the fact that so many individuals engage in it. Moreover, it is problematic to suggest that this activity is part of a new repertoire emerging in the 1960s. This is because it has been a common practice in many Western European countries dating back much further in time. However, given that the literature on unconventional participation since Barnes and Kaase (1979) has included this indicator this chapter first turns to examining levels of participation in this activity as presented in Figures 6.5 and 6.6 before turning to the identified models. Again, the evidence presented in Figure 6.5 shows that in most countries the baby-boomers and '80s generation engage in elite-challenging activities the most; in Figure 6.6 for petitioning in the Noughties, the '90s generation petitions at higher levels than the other cohorts only in Belgium and Denmark.

Table 6.7 Logistic regression on boycotting, EVS, by country (APC and education)

	BEL		DNK		FRA		DEU		IRL	
	Model 1	Model 2	Model 1	Model 2	Model 1	Model 2	Model 1	Model 2	Model 1	Model 2
Pre-WWII	-0.44	-0.38	-1.29***	-1.28***	-1.04***	-0.94**	-0.12	-0.08	-0.18	-0.17
Baby-boom	0.51*	0.46*	0.46*	0.39	0.54*	0.38	1.29***	1.23***	0.38	0.36
80s gen.	0.75**	0.60*	0.39	0.29	0.02	-0.20	1.23***	1.09***	0.82*	0.76*
90s gen.	0.56	0.35	0.28	0.16	-0.59	-0.86*	0.91*	0.67	0.74	0.66
18–33	-0.32	-0.33	0.16	0.17	0.15	0.03	0.12	0.10	-0.25	-0.28
51+	-0.23	-0.13	-0.21	-0.14	-0.19	-0.14	0.19	0.25	-0.28	-0.26
1981	-1.08***	-1.03***	-0.08	-0.08	-0.12	-0.07	-0.33*	-0.67***	0.04	0.06
1999	-0.11	-0.14	0.99***	1.09***	0.14	0.11	0.03	0.05	-0.04	-0.03
Edu (low)		-0.80***		-0.44***		-1.14***		-0.80***		-0.25
Intercept	-2.31***	-2.06***	-2.32***	-2.18***	-2.01***	-1.50***	-3.02***	-2.54***	-2.70***	-2.55***
Pseudo-RSq	0.04	0.05	0.08	0.09	0.03	0.07	0.05	0.06	0.02	0.02
LogLike	-1,427.44	-1,408.81	-1,087.48	-1,081.93	-1,195.99	-1,156.3	-1,154.79	-1,134.47	-769.24	-767.89
N	4,918	4,918	2,799	2,799	3,304	3,304	3,885	3,885	2,904	2,904

	ITA		NLD		GBR		ESP		SWE	
	Model 1	Model 2	Model 1	Model 2	Model 1	Model 2	Model 1	Model 2	Model 1	Model 2
Pre-WWII	-0.52	-0.46	-0.40	-0.33	-0.32	-0.30	0.03	0.06	-0.75*	-0.67*
Baby-boom	0.12	-0.09	0.58**	0.49*	-0.11	-0.15	0.29	0.25	0.26	0.21
80s gen.	0.19	-0.12	0.41	0.20	-0.48	-0.57	0.02	-0.11	0.18	0.13
90s gen.	-0.40	-0.76*	-0.04	-0.23	-1.09**	-1.16**	-0.67	-0.84	0.02	-0.06
18–33	0.06	-0.02	0.12	0.04	0.40	0.32	0.20	0.12	-0.15	-0.22
51+	-0.69***	-0.60**	-0.11	-0.02	-0.39	-0.34	-0.62*	-0.54*	-0.38	-0.28
1981	-0.48**	-0.29	-0.29	-0.26	-0.96***	-0.94***	0.60***	0.56***	-0.71***	-0.56***
1999	0.12	0.14	1.10***	1.04***	0.31*	0.30	0.25	0.26	0.80***	0.80***
Edu (low)		-1.11***		-0.99***		-0.72***		-0.62***		-0.80***
Intercept	-2.08***	-1.52***	-2.66***	-2.29***	-1.50***	-1.00***	-2.90***	-2.50***	-1.52***	-1.36***
Pseudo-RSq	0.03	0.06	0.07	0.09	0.03	0.05	0.03	0.04	0.08	0.09
LogLike	-1,398.51	-1,355.93	-983.79	-963.41	-1,176.13	-1,156.57	-1,147.21	-1,135.23	-1,087.97	-1,073.72
N	4,803	4,803	2,953	2,953	3,187	3,187	4,848	4,848	2,480	2,480

Notes

Model 1: age, period and cohort; Model 2: age, period, cohort and education.

Significance levels:

* $p \leq 0.05$.

** $p \leq 0.01$.

*** $p \leq 0.001$.

Reference categories: Post-WWII cohort (2); 34–50 age group (2); 1990 (2), therefore, 1981 is the inverse of the period effect 1981–1990; Edu (low) is a dummy variable where 1 means the respondent left school before the age of 17.

Table 6.8 Logistic regression on boycotting, ESS, by country (APC and education)

	BEL		DNK		FRA		DEU		IRL	
	Model 1	Model 2	Model 1	Model 2	Model 1	Model 2	Model 1	Model 2	Model 1	Model 2
Pre-WWII	-0.73*	-0.67*	-0.71**	-0.63**	-1.00***	-0.94***	-1.27***	-1.08***	-1.62**	-1.44**
Baby-boom	0.53***	0.40**	0.40***	0.29**	0.41***	0.29**	0.24*	0.12	0.68***	0.57***
80s gen.	0.61**	0.42	0.17	0.05	0.55**	0.34	0.25	0.13	0.69**	0.55*
90s gen.	-0.01	-0.25	0.35	0.20	0.06	-0.20	-0.07	-0.20	0.74*	0.59*
18–33	0.52	0.52	-0.25	-0.23	0.21	0.14	0.02	0.03	-0.36	-0.40
51+	0.20	0.22	-0.22	-0.18	0.13	0.24	-0.21	-0.17	-0.28	-0.17
2002	0.24*	0.24*	-0.30***	-0.29**	-0.16	-0.19*	0.19**	0.21**	0.28*	0.25*
2006	0.11	0.11	-0.18*	-0.16	-0.17*	-0.27**	0.05	0.04	0.17	0.14
Edu (low)		-0.75***		-0.71***		-0.92***		-0.86***		-1.02***
Intercept	-2.61***	-2.29***	-0.92***	-0.74***	-1.16***	-0.70***	-1.18***	-0.98***	-2.43***	-2.16***
Pseudo-RSq	0.01	0.02	0.01	0.03	0.01	0.04	0.01	0.03	0.03	0.04
LogLike	-1,641.37	-1,620.52	-2,278.95	-2,253.44	-2,774.39	-2,703.61	-4,151.23	-4,091.57	-1,913.46	-1,880.13
N	4,633	4,633	4,015	4,015	4,759	4,759	7,514	7,514	5,147	5,147

	ITA		NLD		GBR		ESP		SWE	
	Model 1	Model 2	Model 1	Model 2	Model 1	Model 2	Model 1	Model 2	Model 1	Model 2
Pre-WWII	-0.87	-0.77	-0.71*	-0.57	-0.44**	-0.35*	-1.56***	-1.47*	-0.95***	-0.86***
Baby-boom	0.60	0.45	0.42**	0.33*	0.24*	0.12	0.91***	0.71***	0.28**	0.16
80s gen.	0.68	0.44	0.48*	0.30	0.05	-0.17	1.21***	0.90**	0.35*	0.21
90s gen.	0.39	0.04	0.69*	0.49	-0.15	-0.35	1.19***	0.79*	0.33	0.17
18–33	-0.68	-0.76	-0.39	-0.42	-0.09	-0.1	0.06	0.03	0.05	0.03
51+	-0.45	-0.41	0.10	0.17	0.09	0.17	0.13	0.28	-0.09	-0.03
2002	0.20	0.24	0.30*	0.27*	0.29***	0.26**	-0.59***	-0.57***	-0.12	-0.12
2006			0.09	0.05	0.18*	0.11	-0.36**	-0.39***	-0.18*	-0.20**
Edu (low)		-0.94***		-0.77***		-0.76***		-0.99***		-0.44***
Intercept	-2.84***	-2.32***	-2.73***	-2.42***	-1.27***	-0.96***	-2.67***	-2.06***	-0.73***	-0.54***
Pseudo-RSq	0.03	0.05	0.01	0.02	0.01	0.02	0.04	0.07	0.02	0.02
LogLike	-632.08	-617.29	-1,800.6	-1,778	-3,233.64	-3,188.66	-1,478.31	-1,439.27	-3,240.94	-3,225.27
N	2,414	2,414	5,693	5,693	5,721	5,721	4,360	4,360	5,164	5,164

Notes

Model 1: age, period and cohort; Model 2: age, period, cohort and education.

Significance levels:

* $p \leq 0.05$.

** $p \leq 0.01$.

*** $p \leq 0.001$.

Reference categories: Post-WWII cohort (2); 34–50 age group (2); 2004 (2), therefore, 2002 is the inverse of the period effect 2002–2004; Edu (low) is a dummy variable where 1 means the respondent left school before the age of 17.

Table 6.9 Logistic regression on boycotting, EVS, by country (APC and all controls)

	BEL	DNK	FRA	DEU	IRL	ITA	NLD	GBR	ESP	SWE
Pre-WWII	-0.36	-1.21***	-0.95**	0.03	-0.02	-0.42	-0.15	-0.27	0.26	-0.63*
Baby-boom	0.46*	0.22	0.32	1.13***	0.28	-0.21	0.34	-0.22	0.03	0.19
80s gen.	0.57	0.19	-0.19	1.08***	0.66	-0.14	0.23	-0.62*	-0.36	0.15
90s gen.	0.42	0.08	-0.76	0.65	0.54	-0.75*	-0.08	-1.21**	-1.03*	-0.01
18–33	-0.34	0.17	0.01	0.06	-0.37	-0.04	-0.07	0.3	-0.04	-0.25
51+	-0.06	-0.12	-0.11	0.27	-0.25	-0.54*	-0.03	-0.39	-0.40	-0.26
1981	-1.24***	-0.37*	-0.22	-0.88***	-0.1	-0.57*	-0.33	-1.06***	0.64***	-0.86***
1999	-0.41**	1.06***	-0.03	-0.01	-0.12	0.16	0.92***	0.29	0.23	0.65***
Edu (low)	-0.65***	-0.39**	-0.98***	-0.59***	-0.38*	-0.99***	-0.74***	-0.59***	-0.57***	-0.87***
Male	0.64***	0.25*	0.62***	0.49***	0.53***	0.38***	0.33*	0.48***	1.01***	-0.12
Working cl.	-0.41**	0.13	-0.66***	-0.49***	-0.03	-0.19	-0.58***	-0.47***	-0.03	-0.28
Left	1.26***	1.36***	1.04***	1.35***	1.32***	0.70***	1.31***	0.96***	1.48***	0.54**
Right	0.11	-0.69	-0.09	0.55	-0.88**	-0.70*	-1.39	0.27	-0.79***	-0.79***
Left-auth.	-0.55**	-1.08***	-0.78***	-0.63***	-0.71***	-1.08***	-1.38***	-0.47**	-1.17***	-0.49*
Right-lib.	-0.69***	-0.69***	-0.47*	-0.73***	-0.70**	-0.52**	-0.67***	-0.59***	-0.63***	-0.38**
Right-auth.	-1.11***	-0.57**	-0.72***	-1.01***	-0.67***	-0.92***	-1.41***	-0.46*	-1.63***	-0.92***
Intercept	-1.81***	-1.89***	-1.43***	-2.16***	-2.12***	-1.14***	-1.90***	-0.83***	-2.77***	-0.76***
Pseudo-RSq	0.11	0.13	0.12	0.11	0.06	0.11	0.16	0.08	0.18	0.11
LogLike	-1,323.41	-1,026.68	-1,085.31	-1,078.77	-738.02	-1,289.21	-882.3	-1,119.42	-970.78	-1,038.78
N	4,916	2,799	3,304	3,885	2,900	4,803	2,952	3,186	4,689	2,466

Notes

Models with age, period, cohort, education, gender, class, ideology and values.

Significance levels:

* $p \leq 0.05$.

** $p \leq 0.01$.

*** $p \leq 0.001$.

Reference categories: Post-WWII cohort (2); 34–50 age group (2); 1990 (2), therefore, 1981 is the inverse of the period effect 1981–1990; Left-libertarian (1); Edu (low) is a dummy variable where 1 means the respondent left school before the age of 17; Working class is a dummy variable where 1 means the respondent is an unskilled, semi-skilled or skilled manual worker; Left and right are dummy variables derived from the left-right scale where left (1) means values 0/1 and right (1) means values 9/10.

Table 6.10 Logistic regression on boycotting, ESS, by country (APC and all controls)

	BEL	DNK	FRA	DEU	IRL	ITA	NLD	GBR	ESP	SWE
Pre-WWII	-0.64	-0.68**	-0.93***	-1.09***	-1.39*	-0.82	-0.54	-0.42**	-1.43*	-0.87***
Baby-boom	0.34*	0.19	0.23*	0.08	0.52**	0.35	0.27	0.04	0.66**	0.16
80s gen.	0.37	-0.03	0.30	0.07	0.50*	0.31	0.27	-0.24	0.83***	0.22
90s gen.	-0.35	0.16	-0.23	-0.29	0.58*	-0.07	0.53	-0.49*	0.73*	0.18
18–33	0.55	-0.28	0.13	0.02	-0.51*	-0.81*	-0.47*	-0.07	0.02	0.00
51+	0.22	-0.18	0.22	-0.14	-0.19	-0.39	0.17	0.17	0.28	-0.02
2002	0.31**	-0.30***	-0.21*	0.22**	0.26*	0.21	0.32***	0.29***	-0.57***	-0.11
2006	0.12	-0.21*	-0.25**	0.06	0.12		0.09	0.11	-0.38**	-0.24**
Edu (low)	-0.54***	-0.66***	-0.73***	-0.69***	-0.79***	-0.82***	-0.68***	-0.59***	-0.92***	-0.37***
Male	0.09	-0.17*	-0.03	-0.07	0.18	-0.13	-0.14	-0.06	0.05	-0.23***
Working cl.	-1.01***	-0.25**	-0.61***	-0.61***	-0.82***	-0.39	-0.58***	-0.49***	-0.19	-0.22***
Left	0.49**	1.11***	0.52***	0.20	0.78**	0.50	1.26***	-0.20	0.37*	0.33**
Right	0.24	-0.50*	-0.22	-0.17	-0.2	-1.42*	-0.38	0.21	0.08	-0.32*
Left-auth.	-0.61***	-0.46***	-0.37***	-0.48***	-0.73***	-0.84***	-0.63***	-0.54***	-0.46***	-0.55***
Right-lib.	-0.14	-0.37***	0.22	0.02	-0.31	-0.43	-0.38**	-0.06	-0.21	-0.46***
Right-auth.	-0.72***	-0.62***	-0.18	-0.62***	-0.76***	-0.94**	-0.58***	-0.41***	-0.50**	-0.62***
Intercept	-1.85***	-0.14	-0.48*	-0.44*	-1.52***	-1.51***	-1.99***	-0.43*	-1.74***	0.05
Pseudo-RSq	0.06	0.05	0.06	0.05	0.07	0.08	0.05	0.04	0.08	0.04
LogLike	-1,559.57	-2,202.4	-2,646.78	-3,999.01	-1,812.67	-594.94	-1,723.46	-3,140.2	-1,425.49	-3,166.94
N	4,622	4,015	4,759	7,514	5,125	2,414	5,693	5,721	4,360	5,164

Notes

Models with age, period, cohort, education, gender, class, ideology and values.

Significance levels:

* $p \leq 0.05$.

** $p \leq 0.01$.

*** $p \leq 0.001$.

Reference categories: Post-WWII cohort (2); 34–50 age group (2); 2004 (2), therefore, 2002 is the inverse of the period effect 2002–2004; Left-libertarian (1); Edu (low) is a dummy variable where 1 means the respondent left school before the age of 17; Working class is a dummy variable where 1 means the respondent is an unskilled, semi-skilled or skilled manual worker; Left and right are dummy variables derived from the left-right scale where left (1) means values 0/1 and right (1) means values 9/10.

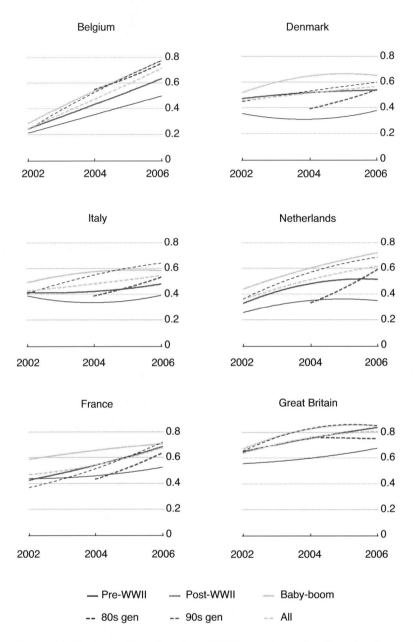

Belgium

Denmark

Italy

Netherlands

France

Great Britain

— Pre-WWII   — Post-WWII   Baby-boom

-- 80s gen   -- 90s gen   All

Figure 6.5 Signing petitions, by cohort, EVS (proportion saying 'have done'), over time.

Note
Best fit quadratic smoothed lines.

continued

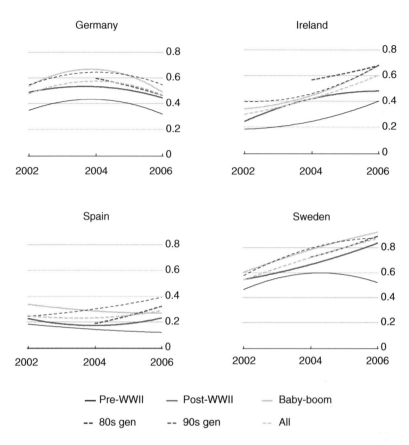

Figure 6.5 Continued

Across countries, and for both periods, the baby-boomers, '80s, and '90s generations tend to engage in this activity the most, and the older two cohorts the least. These differences are more marked in 2002–2006, suggesting the presence of age effects: as the older cohorts age, they tend to participate less. Again, while period effects tend to vary between countries they tend to be relatively similar between the different cohorts within a country. Turning to the identified models in Table 6.11 for the EVS, in eight out of ten countries the baby-boomers are significantly more likely than the post-WWII cohort to sign a petition; the '80s generation is only significantly more likely than the post-WWII cohort to sign a petition in five out of ten countries (though this effect is no longer significant when controlling for education in two of these countries); and the '90s generation is significantly more likely than the post-WWII generation to petition only in two countries, whereas it is significantly less likely to do so in two others.

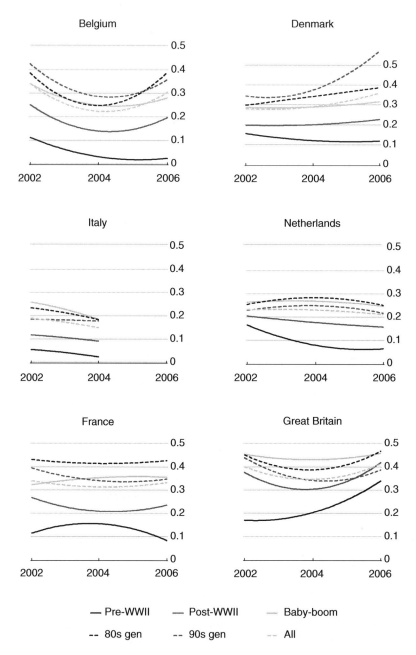

Figure 6.6 Signed a petition in the last twelve months, by cohort, ESS (proportion saying 'yes'), over time.

Note
Best fit quadratic smoothed lines.

continued

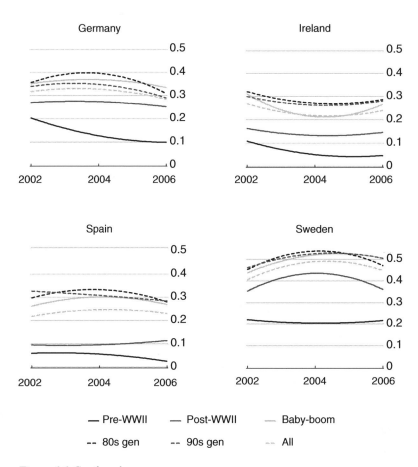

Figure 6.6 Continued

The results for petitioning for 2002–2006 from Table 6.12 provide some evidence for the modernisation thesis: all three younger cohorts are more likely than the post-WWII cohort to petition in four countries; but now the baby-boomers are significantly more likely than the post-WWII to engage in this elite-challenging activity in all ten countries. As such, while differences between younger and older cohorts in this repertoire appear to have exacerbated in the Noughties, the greatest differences are still between the post-WWII and the baby-boom cohorts, not the younger ones, as one would expect if cohort replacement is supposed to be bringing about 'a major change' in participation patterns. As usual, having a lower education has a strong negative effect on participation and including education in Model(s) 2 reduces the coefficient size and reduces differences between the post-WWII and younger cohorts; again, more so for the '80s and '90s generation than the baby-boomers, suggesting that education has less of a role for explaining their higher participatory patterns than for subsequent cohorts.

Table 6.11 Logistic regression on signing a petition, EVS, by country (APC and education)

	BEL		DNK		FRA		DEU		IRL	
	Model 1	Model 2	Model 1	Model 2	Model 1	Model 2	Model 1	Model 2	Model 1	Model 2
Pre-WWII	-0.23	-0.18	-0.56***	-0.53***	-0.32*	-0.27	-0.41***	-0.39***	-0.52***	-0.49**
Baby-boom	0.47***	0.43***	0.40**	0.30*	0.49***	0.39**	0.43***	0.39***	0.32*	0.26
80s gen.	0.79***	0.65***	0.21	0.03	0.16	0.02	0.66***	0.55**	0.45*	0.30
90s gen.	0.93***	0.72***	0.04	-0.19	0.03	-0.15	0.43	0.23	0.54*	0.33
18–33	-0.51***	-0.54***	-0.25	-0.23	-0.19	-0.28*	-0.36**	-0.38**	-0.04	-0.13
51+	-0.27*	-0.16	-0.12	-0.04	0.04	0.09	-0.11	-0.06	-0.1	-0.04
1981	-0.96***	-0.93***	-0.14	-0.17	-0.24*	-0.21*	-0.30***	-0.64***	-0.50***	-0.45***
1999	0.65***	0.63***	0.22*	0.41***	0.60***	0.58***	-0.51***	-0.50***	0.53***	0.58***
Edu (low)		-0.71***		-0.70***		-0.68***		-0.66***		-0.70***
Intercept	-0.07	0.20	0.07	0.31*	0.09	0.46***	0.25*	0.70***	-0.42**	0.01
Pseudo-RSq	0.09	0.10	0.02	0.04	0.04	0.05	0.02	0.04	0.06	0.08
LogLike	-3,242.85	-3,188.27	-1,982.53	-1,950.16	-2,293.6	-2,255.02	-2,798.37	-2,758.1	-1,900.87	-1,866.37
N	5,136	5,136	2,932	2,932	3,505	3,505	4,145	4,145	2,969	2,969

	ITA		NLD		GBR		ESP		SWE	
	Model 1	Model 2	Model 1	Model 2	Model 1	Model 2	Model 1	Model 2	Model 1	Model 2
Pre-WWII	-0.12	-0.09	-0.36*	-0.30	-0.44**	-0.43**	-0.14	-0.08	-0.29	-0.25
Baby-boom	0.21	0.04	0.56***	0.49***	0.45*	0.43*	0.23	0.15	0.49**	0.47**
80s gen.	0.22	-0.07	0.47*	0.29	0.75**	0.72**	0.04	-0.17	0.58*	0.56*
90s gen.	-0.23	-0.60**	0.04	-0.16	0.32	0.29	-0.33	-0.62**	0.57	0.53
18–33	-0.04	-0.11	-0.28	-0.35*	-0.53**	-0.57**	0.36**	0.26	-0.17	-0.22
51+	-0.42***	-0.33**	-0.26	-0.21	-0.14	-0.11	-0.28*	-0.17	-0.09	-0.03
1981	-0.16	0.04	-0.52***	-0.52***	-0.52***	-0.51***	0.08	0.01	-0.65***	-0.55***
1999	0.38***	0.43***	0.38***	0.33***	0.11	0.10	0.40***	0.44***	0.82***	0.83***
Edu (low)		-1.02***		-0.73***		-0.40***		-0.94***		-0.39***
Intercept	-0.04	0.53***	-0.03	0.32*	1.20***	1.50***	-1.31***	-0.69***	0.79***	0.89***
Pseudo-RSq	0.02	0.06	0.05	0.07	0.04	0.04	0.02	0.05	0.09	0.09
LogLike	-3,276.59	-3,157.91	-1,956.9	-1,922.29	-1,849.27	-1,840.54	-2,656.79	-2,577.14	-1,407.11	-1,400.41
N	4,837	4,837	2,978	2,978	3,287	3,287	4,870	4,870	2,539	2,539

Notes

Model 1: age, period and cohort; Model 2: age, period, cohort and education.

Significance levels:

* $p \leq 0.05$.

** $p \leq 0.01$.

*** $p \leq 0.001$.

Reference categories: Post-WWII cohort (2); 34–50 age group (2); 1990 (2), therefore, 1981 is the inverse of the period effect 1981–1990; Edu (low) is a dummy variable where 1 means the respondent left school before the age of 17.

Table 6.12 Logistic regression on signing a petition, ESS, by country (APC and education)

	BEL		DNK		FRA		DEU		IRL	
	Model 1	Model 2	Model 1	Model 2	Model 1	Model 2	Model 1	Model 2	Model 1	Model 2
Pre-WWII	-1.26***	-1.20***	-0.46*	-0.42	-0.73***	-0.66**	-0.74***	-0.55**	-0.69*	-0.56
Baby-Boom	0.45***	0.30*	0.43***	0.37**	0.58***	0.48***	0.39***	0.27***	0.72***	0.64***
80s Gen.	0.56**	0.34	0.50**	0.43*	0.86***	0.67***	0.37**	0.25	0.67***	0.57**
90s Gen.	0.43	0.13	1.08***	0.99***	0.46*	0.23	0.25	0.12	0.68***	0.57*
18–33	0.24	0.24	-0.25	-0.24	0.19	0.12	-0.02	-0.01	-0.02	-0.05
51+	-0.21	-0.19	-0.19	-0.17	0.03	0.13	-0.07	-0.04	-0.28	-0.20
2002	0.60***	0.60***	-0.08	-0.08	0.11	0.09	-0.10	-0.09	0.27***	0.25**
2006	0.42***	0.42***	0.30***	0.32***	0.06	-0.03	-0.25***	-0.26***	0.12	0.10
Edu (low)		-0.87***		-0.42***		-0.84***		-0.84***		-0.70***
Intercept	-1.56***	-1.18***	-1.24***	-1.12***	-1.25***	-0.83***	-0.88***	-0.67***	-1.67***	-1.47***
Pseudo-RSq	0.04	0.06	0.03	0.04	0.02	0.04	0.01	0.03	0.03	0.04
LogLike	-2,659.00	-2,603.86	-2,378.64	-2,368.56	-2,948.66	-2,883.2	-4,581.25	-4,513.32	-2,782.56	-2,751.71
N	4,624	4,624	4,012	4,012	4,758	4,758	7,516	7,516	5,150	5,150

	ITA		NLD		GBR		ESP		SWE	
	Model 1	Model 2	Model 1	Model 2	Model 1	Model 2	Model 1	Model 2	Model 1	Model 2
Pre-WWII	-0.98	-0.87	-0.61**	-0.48*	-0.66***	-0.60***	-0.69*	-0.63*	-0.78***	-0.73***
Baby-Boom	0.70***	0.53*	0.34**	0.25*	0.36***	0.26**	1.18***	1.05***	0.38***	0.31***
80s Gen.	0.23	-0.05	0.25	0.07	0.47**	0.30	1.15***	0.93***	0.26	0.18
90s Gen.	0.21	-0.20	0.08	-0.13	0.24	0.08	1.23***	0.94***	0.33	0.23
18–33	-0.33	-0.44	0.04	0.01	-0.01	-0.02	-0.05	-0.07	-0.03	-0.04
51+	-0.45*	-0.41	-0.15	-0.08	0.22	0.28	-0.21	-0.11	-0.16	-0.13
2002	0.29*	0.35**	-0.04	-0.07	0.22**	0.19*	0.04	0.07	-0.30***	-0.31***
2006			-0.17	-0.22*	0.26***	0.21**	-0.14	-0.16	-0.16*	-0.18*
Edu (low)		-1.08***		-0.73***		-0.58***		-0.74***		-0.28***
Intercept	-1.87***	-1.26***	-1.26***	-0.94***	-0.87***	-0.63***	-1.91***	-1.43***	-0.16	-0.03
Pseudo-RSq	0.03	0.06	0.01	0.02	0.01	0.02	0.06	0.07	0.02	0.02
LogLike	-1,045.95	-1,007.95	-3,026.53	-2,983.31	-3,817.47	-3,783.22	-2,294.82	-2,252.88	-3,464.36	-3,457.09
N	2,407	2,407	5,693	5,693	5,721	5,721	4,370	4,370	5,140	5,140

Notes

Model 1: age, period and cohort; Model 2: age, period, cohort and education.

Significance levels:

* $p \leq 0.05$.

** $p \leq 0.01$.

*** $p \leq 0.001$.

Reference categories: Post-WWII cohort (2); 34–50 age group (2); 2004 (2), therefore, 2002 is the inverse of the period effect 2002–2004; Edu (low) is a dummy variable where 1 means the respondent left school before the age of 17.

The results for the full models presented in Table 6.13 and 6.14 show that, as with boycotting, gender inequalities weaken for this mode of engagement between 1981–1999 and 2002–2006. In Ireland, Great Britain, Spain and Sweden and Italy, and the Netherlands for 2002–2006 there is no class bias for this activity. As with other forms of protest activism, strong left-wing identifiers tend to be more active, but in France, this is also true of individuals identifying with the right. Moreover, as with boycotting, libertarians both of the left and right tend to engage in this activity more than authoritarians of either colour. This is almost universally true for the 2002–2006 period whereas, for 1981–1999, left-libertarians were still somewhat more likely than right-libertarians to engage in this repertoire; this was also true for joining a boycott.

Participation in SMOs

The final indicator of elite-challenging participation analysed in this chapter is participation in new social movements. Figure 6.7 plots levels of participation in SMOs for the period 1981–1999. More than for any other indicator analysed in this study, cohorts tend to be very similar in their levels of participation. Again, period effects vary by country, but are similar within countries. In most countries, the '90s generation exhibits the lowest levels of participation in this activity, which again, is not what would be expected if an intergenerational shift was causing the rise in participation in this repertoire. And indeed, in most countries, participation in NSMs rises steeply for 1981–1990 but either declines or rises more smoothly in the 1990–1999 period (as already discussed in Chapter 4). This type of participation rises steeply across cohorts in Belgium, the Netherlands and Sweden (except for the pre-WWII generation in 2006 in Sweden probably due to ageing) but in all these countries the '90s generation participates less than the baby-boomers, post-WWII cohort and '80s generation. Therefore, Figure 6.7 gives some preliminary evidence that younger cohorts are not significantly more likely than older cohorts to engage in this elite-challenging activity. Instead, the rising levels of participation in this activity (where they occur) seem to be due to period effects affecting the population as a whole, and not intergenerational differences in participation. Therefore, theories which explain the rise in new social movements based on varying political contexts, and opportunity structures in different national contexts, appear more promising than theories which focus on more generalised structural changes, whether in the form of the rise of a 'new class' and 'decommodified groups' (Offe 1987) or the changing value structures of 'younger cohorts'. Inglehart (1977, 1990) proposes that as a result of the unprecedented degree of economic security the "post-WWII generation" developed post-materialist values emphasising self-esteem, intellectual and aesthetic satisfaction, as opposed to economic development.

Coming from the perspective of the classic Marxist understanding of society as characterised by conflict, Touraine (1971, 1981) understands class conflict in particular as displaced by conflict over the control of knowledge, where NSMs

Table 6.13 Logistic regression on signing a petition, EVS, by country (APC and all controls)

	BEL	DNK	FRA	DEU	IRL	ITA	NLD	GBR	ESP	SWE
Pre-WWII	-0.18	-0.51***	-0.25	-0.35**	-0.47**	-0.09	-0.25	-0.39*	-0.04	-0.22
Baby-boom	0.43***	0.23	0.32*	0.34**	0.23	0.00	0.43**	0.41*	0.10	0.47**
80s gen.	0.64***	0.00	-0.04	0.55***	0.25	-0.06	0.32	0.70**	-0.23	0.58*
90s gen.	0.73**	-0.19	-0.16	0.23	0.25	-0.54*	-0.06	0.28	-0.64**	0.55
18–33	-0.51***	-0.22	-0.27*	-0.42**	-0.13	-0.13	-0.39**	-0.60**	0.20	-0.21
51+	-0.15	-0.03	0.08	-0.03	-0.01	-0.32**	-0.22	-0.04	-0.11	-0.02
1981	-0.99***	-0.29**	-0.37***	-0.74***	-0.41***	0.04	-0.59***	-0.52***	0.04	-0.68***
1999	0.56***	0.33***	0.50***	-0.55***	0.53***	0.43***	0.22*	0.07	0.44***	0.77***
Edu (low)	-0.56***	-0.60***	-0.64***	-0.57***	-0.70***	-0.89***	-0.55***	-0.36***	-0.87***	-0.42***
Male	0.37***	0.01	0.20**	0.19**	0.22**	0.21**	0.24**	0.04	0.42***	-0.23*
Working cl.	-0.40***	-0.20*	-0.20*	-0.23**	-0.09	-0.27***	-0.44***	-0.14	-0.14	-0.15
Left	0.54***	0.92***	0.85***	0.75***	0.77***	0.73***	0.82***	0.11	0.75***	0.45*
Right	-0.05	-0.21	0.47*	0.02	-0.13	-0.14	-0.11	-0.87***	0.16	-0.35*
Left-auth.	-0.24*	-0.67***	-0.45***	-0.54***	-0.48***	-0.41***	-0.52***	-0.32**	-0.51***	-0.32*
Right-lib.	-0.11	-0.36***	-0.36***	-0.52***	0.03	0.13	-0.35**	-0.12	-0.25*	-0.18
Right-auth.	-0.32*	-0.44***	-0.59***	-0.62***	-0.17	-0.15	-0.67***	-0.33*	-0.45***	-0.29
Intercept	0.28*	0.66***	0.72***	1.12***	0.13	0.52***	0.59***	1.71***	-0.72***	1.25***
Pseudo-RSq	0.12	0.06	0.07	0.05	0.09	0.08	0.09	0.05	0.08	0.10
LogLike	-3,139.79	-1,916.85	-2,202.44	-2,716.98	-1,844.05	-3,093.82	-1,867.46	-1,819.9	-2,502.94	-1,379.08
N	5,133	2,932	3,505	4,145	2,965	4,837	2,977	3,286	4,870	2,525

Notes
Models with age, period, cohort, education, gender, class, ideology and values.
Significance levels:
* p≤0.05.
** p≤0.01.
*** p≤0.001.
Reference categories: Post-WWII cohort (2); 34–50 age group (2); 1990 (2), therefore, 1981 is the inverse of the period effect 1981–1990; Left-libertarian (1); Edu (low) is a dummy variable where 1 means the respondent left school before the age of 17; Working class is a dummy variable where 1 means the respondent is an unskilled, semi-skilled or skilled manual worker; Left and right are dummy variables derived from the left-right scale where left (1) means values 0/1 and right (1) means values 9/10.

Table 6.14 Logistic regression on signing a petition, ESS, by country (APC and all controls)

	BEL	DNK	FRA	DEU	IRL	ITA	NLD	GBR	ESP	SWE
Pre-WWII	-1.22***	-0.46*	-0.63**	-0.56**	-0.56	-0.87	-0.45*	-0.65***	-0.60	-0.73***
Baby-boom	0.25*	0.28	0.41***	0.25**	0.62***	0.47*	0.20	0.21*	0.99***	0.31***
80s gen.	0.30	0.37*	0.62***	0.22	0.53**	-0.16	0.03	0.26	0.85***	0.18
90s gen.	0.07	0.96***	0.19	0.07	0.57*	-0.28	-0.14	0.01	0.86***	0.24
18–33	0.24	-0.27	0.09	-0.02	-0.11	-0.47	0.00	0.00	-0.08	-0.08
51+	-0.19	-0.17	0.11	0.01	-0.21	-0.43	-0.08	0.29	-0.11	-0.12
2002	0.67***	-0.08	0.08	-0.08	0.26**	0.34**	-0.04	0.21**	0.09	-0.30***
2006	0.44***	0.28**	0.01	-0.26***	0.09		-0.20*	0.22**	-0.14	-0.21**
Edu (low)	-0.74***	-0.35***	-0.73***	-0.68***	-0.57***	-1.04***	-0.69***	-0.46***	-0.63***	-0.26***
Male	-0.09	-0.20**	0.04	-0.08	-0.05	0.19	-0.10	-0.17**	0.15	-0.21***
Working cl.	-0.60***	-0.29***	-0.40***	-0.56***	-0.45***	-0.17	-0.20	-0.41***	-0.33***	-0.11
Left	0.15	0.92***	0.64***	0.59***	0.40	0.58**	0.78***	-0.03	0.33*	0.29*
Right	0.11	-0.40*	-0.14	-0.01	0.06	0.30	-0.86***	0.28	-0.02	-0.14
Left-auth.	-0.43***	-0.38***	-0.44***	-0.49***	-0.49***	-0.63***	-0.48***	-0.36***	-0.55***	-0.37***
Right-lib.	-0.05	-0.33**	-0.20	-0.20	-0.37*	-0.29	-0.24*	-0.26	0.03	-0.36***
Right-auth.	-0.66***	-0.50***	-0.43***	-0.58***	-0.57***	-1.09***	-0.41***	-0.44***	-0.61***	-0.56***
Intercept	-0.73***	-0.57***	-0.57***	-0.15	-0.94***	-0.79*	-0.59**	-0.12	-1.08***	0.43***
Pseudo-RSq	0.08	0.06	0.06	0.05	0.05	0.09	0.04	0.03	0.09	0.03
LogLike	-2,542.81	-2,326.39	-2,828.54	-4,420.75	-2,703.19	-981.05	-2,935.69	-3,739.8	-2,213.41	-3,417.26
N	4,613	4,012	4,758	7,516	5,128	2,407	5,693	5,721	4,370	5,140

Notes
Models with age, period, cohort, education, gender, class, ideology and values.
Significance levels:
* $p \leq 0.05$.
** $p \leq 0.01$.
*** $p \leq 0.001$.
Reference categories: Post-WWII cohort (2); 34–50 age group (2); 2004 (2), therefore, 2002 is the inverse of the period effect 2002–2004; Left-libertarian (1); Edu (low) is a dummy variable where 1 means the respondent left school before the age of 17; Working class is a dummy variable where 1 means the respondent is an unskilled, semi-skilled or skilled manual worker; Left and right are dummy variables derived from the left-right scale where left (1) means values 0/1 and right (1) means values 9/10.

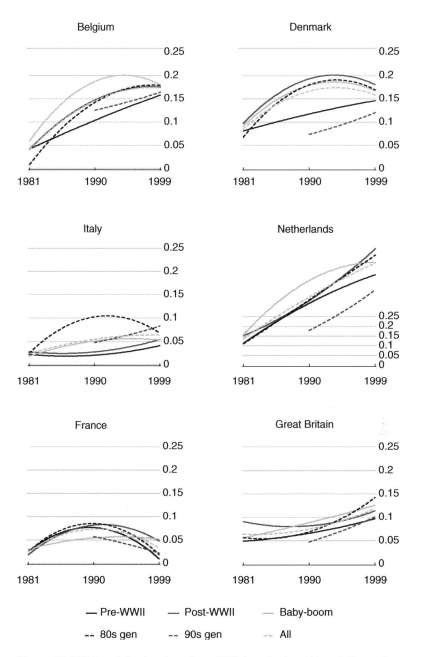

Figure 6.7 NSM participation, by cohort, EVS (member/unpaid work for environment or development/human rights organisations), over time.

Note
Best fit quadratic smoothed lines.

continued

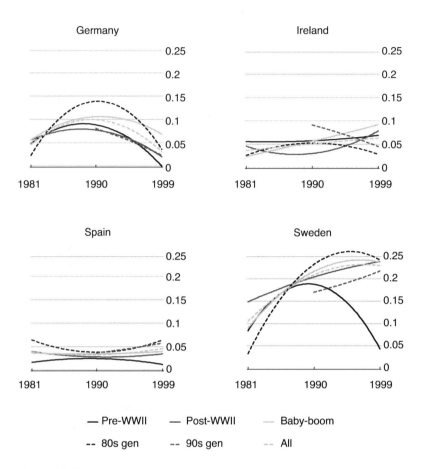

Figure 6.7 Continued

are seen as representing the interests of those well-educated sectors of society who are nevertheless marginalised. Similarly, for Melucci (1989, 1996), NSMs develop as forms of contestation in the cultural realm in order to push others to recognise something which they themselves recognise. Because these theories focus on explanatory mechanisms which are broadly affecting all advanced industrialised nations, they cannot explain why participation in new social movements is higher in some countries compared to others, or why certain countries might exhibit very low levels of participation in new social movements.

Against this trend in the literature, McAdam *et al.* (1996) argue that it is not only the case that a new socio-cultural context breeds the ascendancy of social movements. Rather, the authors outline a synthesis where they argue that while movements are "set in motion by social changes that render the established political order more receptive to challenge" and that "political opportunities" are a necessary prerequisite for action, they can only be taken advantage of given sufficient organisation, where these two processes are mediated through the shared meanings of movement adherents (McAdam *et al*. 1996: 8). Heartfield (2003) points out that it is unlikely that the environmental, or even anti-globalisation movement, could have risen to prominence without the vacuum created by the defeat of organised labour. In the 1990s, social-democratic parties regained office across Europe by moving to the centre and casting away their socialist appeal. In West Germany, the Green Party's electoral breakthrough came in 1983 when they won 7 per cent of the vote (over the 5 per cent threshold of Parliament) just as the Social Democratic Party dropped 5 per cent after facing down a wave of industrial militancy (Heartfield 2003: 278). Applying the McAdam *et al.* (1996) framework, the reason for the rise in NSMs since the late 1960s is to be understood in terms of those political opportunities given by the socio-cultural climate, as well as in terms of the organisation and cohesion of social actors around what they understand to be the movements' shared concerns. Most importantly, McAdam *et al.* (1996) emphasise that while "type of opportunity may dictate the broad category of movement", "the formal and ideological properties of the movement are apt to be more directly influenced by the organizational forms and ideological templates available to insurgents" (1996: 11). Because of its breadth, McAdam *et al.*'s (1996) framework seems the most useful for understanding why movements emerge in certain countries at specific times. While this is not a question that is pursued in this study, it is worth noting that nation-specific political context variables such as opportunity structure, and factors such as ideological frames, and elite openness, are key for explaining the rise or the absence of new social movements in certain countries.

The results for the identified models presented in Table 6.15 show that in no country is any one of the younger cohorts more likely than the post-WWII cohort to participate in new social movements. Younger cohorts are significantly less likely than the post-WWII cohort to participate in SMOs. A more detailed discussion of some potential reasons for why we observe this result is provided in the next chapter. At this stage, however, we turn to the full model in Table 6.16. The effects of the predictor variables are relatively similar to those for petitioning and boycotting. Gender inequalities are negligible in this mode of engagement. However, participation in new social movements appears to be strongly biased against people in manual occupations. This might not be particularly surprising, given their flagship concerns are meant to be those of the 'new middle class'. More surprisingly, only in four out of ten countries do left-libertarians engage more than individuals with other value priorities in this repertoire. Similarly, strong left-wing politicisation is not a particularly strong predictor of participation. As such, these results might further suggest that participation in NSMs is more closely related to country-level than individual-level factors: in those countries where they are popular they attract individuals from diverse constituencies, regardless of their specific value priorities.

Table 6.15 Logistic regression on NSM participation, EVS, by country (APC and education)

	BEL		DNK		FRA		DEU		IRL	
	Model 1	Model 2	Model 1	Model 2	Model 1	Model 2	Model 1	Model 2	Model 1	Model 2
Pre-WWII	-0.20	-0.14	-0.47*	-0.42*	-0.49	-0.41	0.12	0.18	0.32	0.42
Baby-boom	0.07	0.03	0.13	-0.03	0.47	0.33	0.22	0.16	-0.03	-0.20
80s gen.	-0.10	-0.22	0.26	-0.01	0.27	0.11	0.29	0.15	-0.37	-0.70
90s gen.	-0.12	-0.29	-0.22	-0.58	-0.01	-0.18	-0.23	-0.45	-0.04	-0.45
18–33	-0.18	-0.21	-0.13	-0.06	-0.13	-0.25	-0.02	-0.04	-0.01	-0.12
51+	-0.19	-0.1	0.36	0.50*	0.61	0.71	-0.21	-0.16	-0.14	-0.03
1981	-1.42***	-1.38***	-0.61***	-0.66***	-0.91***	-0.85**	-0.76***	-1.11***	-0.32	-0.23
1999	0.09	0.07	-0.04	0.22	-0.73***	-0.79***	-1.17***	-1.15***	0.06	0.11
Edu (low)		-0.64***		-1.05***		-1.01***		-0.78***		-1.33***
Intercept	-1.49***	-1.27***	-1.75***	-1.47***	-2.96***	-2.54***	-2.25***	-1.78***	-2.85***	-2.18***
Pseudo-RSq	0.03	0.04	0.02	0.05	0.03	0.05	0.03	0.05	0.01	0.05
LogLike	-2,154.07	-2,131.36	-1,173.72	-1,142.9	-588.57	-575.39	-1,043.7	-1,027.58	-572.02	-548.52
N	5,411	5,411	3,035	3,035	3,595	3,595	4,313	4,313	3,058	3,058

	ITA		NLD		GBR		ESP		SWE	
	Model 1	Model 2	Model 1	Model 2	Model 1	Model 2	Model 1	Model 2	Model 1	Model 2
Pre-WWII	-0.14	-0.08	-0.29	-0.24	-0.06	0.01	-0.15	-0.04	-0.28	-0.21
Baby-boom	-0.15	-0.35	0.08	0.00	-0.24	-0.37	-0.57*	-0.70*	-0.41*	-0.46*
80s gen.	0.08	-0.20	-0.07	-0.24	-0.56	-0.80*	-0.37	-0.66	-0.39	-0.44
90s gen.	-0.28	-0.61	-0.73*	-0.92**	-0.96	-1.15*	-0.65	-1.03*	-0.35	-0.43
18–33	0.47	0.40	-0.08	-0.14	0.25	0.08	0.47	0.32	-0.09	-0.16
51+	-0.32	-0.22	0.04	0.11	-0.47	-0.34	-0.70*	-0.53	-0.36	-0.27
1981	-0.77***	-0.58*	-1.18***	-1.18***	-0.55**	-0.49*	0.05	-0.05	-0.87***	-0.71***
1999	0.28	0.30	0.81***	0.76***	0.33	0.31	0.38	0.39	0.07	0.07
Edu (low)		-1.04***		-0.72***		-1.63***		-1.34***		-0.75***
Intercept	-2.97***	-2.46***	-0.57***	-0.24	-2.02***	-1.03***	-3.10***	-2.30***	-0.95***	-0.79***
Pseudo-RSq	0.03	0.05	0.10	0.11	0.01	0.09	0.01	0.05	0.03	0.04
LogLike	-988.39	-965.7	-1,717.14	-1,690.08	-922.26	-850.84	-864.34	-830.45	-1,160.78	-1,146.19
N	5,215	5,215	3,048	3,048	3,327	3,327	5,767	5,767	2,584	2,584

Notes

Model 1: age, period and cohort; Model 2: age, period, cohort and education.

Significance levels:

* $p \leq 0.05$.

** $p \leq 0.01$.

*** $p \leq 0.001$.

Reference categories: Post-WWII cohort (2); 34–50 age group (2); 1990 (2), therefore, 1981 is the inverse of the period effect 1981–1990; Edu (low) is a dummy variable where 1 means the respondent left school before the age of 17.

Table 6.16 Logistic regression on NSM participation, EVS, by country (APC and all controls)

	BEL	DNK	FRA	DEU	IRL	ITA	NLD	GBR	ESP	SWE
Pre-WWII	-0.15	-0.38	-0.47	0.23	0.40	-0.08	-0.24	0.04	-0.02	-0.24
Baby-boom	0.04	-0.12	0.29	0.10	-0.18	-0.41	0.01	-0.47	-0.73*	-0.42*
80s gen.	-0.24	-0.03	0.12	0.13	-0.65	-0.20	-0.17	-0.87*	-0.67	-0.33
90s gen.	-0.29	-0.55	-0.09	-0.47	-0.36	-0.57	-0.77*	-1.16*	-1.00	-0.26
18–33	-0.15	-0.01	-0.26	-0.05	-0.18	0.44	-0.21	0.14	0.30	-0.21
51+	-0.1	0.51*	0.73	-0.11	-0.01	-0.20	0.13	-0.37	-0.52	-0.27
1981	-1.47***	-0.82***	-0.97***	-1.16***	-0.18	-0.66**	-1.14***	-0.46*	0.00	-0.91***
1999	-0.04	0.06	-0.80***	-1.22***	0.02	0.31	0.67***	0.31	0.40	0.05
Edu (low)	-0.43***	-0.84***	-0.81***	-0.59***	-1.21***	-0.85***	-0.61***	-1.26***	-1.29***	-0.72***
Male	0.17	-0.09	0.05	0.22	0.05	0.15	-0.31***	0.01	0.00	-0.25*
Working cl.	-0.62***	-0.63***	-0.91***	-0.48**	-0.47*	-0.55**	-0.51***	-1.17***	-0.12	-0.51**
Left	0.29	0.88***	0.22	0.71***	0.89*	0.42*	0.14	0.46	0.48*	-0.05
Right	-0.14	-0.11	-0.04	0.03	0.36	-0.73	-0.39	-1.32*	-1.19*	-0.19
Left-auth.	-0.29*	-0.57**	-0.24	-0.54**	-0.46	-0.35	-0.50***	0.07	-0.14	0.35
Right-lib.	-0.30*	-0.43**	-0.84**	-0.40*	-0.17	-0.05	-0.13	0.18	0.01	-0.15
Right-auth.	-0.37**	-0.69***	-0.54*	-0.64***	-0.27	-0.29	-0.24	-0.21	0.21	-0.19
Intercept	-0.97***	-0.95***	-2.13***	-1.45***	-1.93***	-2.33***	0.17	-0.87**	-2.32***	-0.48*
Pseudo-RSq	0.06	0.07	0.07	0.06	0.06	0.06	0.13	0.12	0.06	0.05
LogLike	-2,099.77	-1,110.17	-562.55	-1,010.35	-541.92	-952.55	-1,660.75	-818.03	-824.78	-1,125.25
N	5,408	3,035	3,595	4,313	3,053	5,215	3,047	3,326	5,767	2,570

Notes

Models with age, period, cohort, education, gender, class, ideology and values.

Significance levels:

* $p \leq 0.05$.

** $p \leq 0.01$.

*** $p \leq 0.001$.

Reference categories: Post-WWII cohort (2); 34–50 age group (2); 1990 (2), therefore, 1981 is the inverse of the period effect 1981–1990; Left-libertarian (1); Edu (low) is a dummy variable where 1 means the respondent left school before the age of 17; Working class is a dummy variable where 1 means the respondent is an unskilled, semi-skilled or skilled manual worker; Left and right are dummy variables derived from the left-right scale where left (1) means values 0/1 and right (1) means values 9/10.

Conclusions

The results presented in this chapter show that the baby-boomers are in most countries significantly more likely than the post-WWII cohort to demonstrate and sign a petition and, to a lesser extent, to join a boycott. Differences between each of the '80s and '90s generations and the post-WWII cohort are much less marked than those between the baby-boomers and the post-WWII cohort for these activities. Where differences between the '80s/'90s cohort and the post-WWII generation are significant, they are generally accounted for by their higher education levels. The same is not generally true of the baby-boomers. Therefore, the argument that all the younger cohorts should be engaging in elite-challenging activities more than older cohorts is not universally supported with respect to protest activism based on the evidence presented here, and more so for demonstrating. This suggests that rather than modernisation, which should affect all cohorts, and more so younger ones, it is in fact formative experiences which set the baby-boomers apart from later cohorts. This is likely to be what explains their higher protest participatory patterns as suggested by Della Porta and Diani (2006).

Moreover, it appears that the fact that less politicised political contexts in the aftermath of the radical 1960s–70s has had a depressing impact on the likelihood of cohorts coming of age in later periods to demonstrate and participate in other protest activities. Therefore, the results presented in this chapter show that the context of formative years matters, and that the baby-boomers are still 'the protest generation' across Western Europe, and particularly given the results for demonstrating.

Differences between the '80s generation and the post-WWII cohort are more marked in the 2002–2006 period for boycotting and for petitioning, but even here differences between the baby-boomers and the post-WWII cohort are greater. Again, education plays a mediating role for participation, but less so for the baby-boomers than the other cohorts. Including education in the models showed that taking their higher education level into account, the '90s generation was significantly less likely than the post-WWII generation to boycott. As for participation in social movement organisations (SMOs), in no country is any one of the younger cohorts significantly more likely than the post-WWII cohort to participate in new social movements. Younger cohorts are significantly less likely than the post-WWII cohort to participate in SMOs. Gender inequalities are more or less inexistent for this mode of engagement.

However, participation in new social movements appears to be strongly biased against people in manual occupations. Yet this is not particularly surprising, given that their flagship concerns are meant to be those of the 'new middle class'. Moreover, in terms of the effects of the predictor variables for protest activities, and relative to their effects for different types of conventional participation, in Denmark and Sweden, Italy and Spain, and as was the case for party membership (Chapter 5), having a manual occupation did not have a negative effect on demonstrating and boycotting. This suggests that, at least in countries with strong social-democratic and/or left-wing traditions, class inequalities in participation are weak for these repertoires. Therefore, 'unconventional' participation might provide such generally under-represented groups with more opportunities to have a say in the running of society, or at the very least an 'oppositional space' in the democratic arena. Class inequalities are also negligible for petitioning in six out of ten countries, though this is probably due to the fact that this activity is virtually universal due to its cheapness and ubiquity. Moreover, while men are more likely to demonstrate, this effect is reversed or no longer significant for boycotting and petitioning the 2002–2006 period.

While left-libertarians are significantly more likely than the other three economic-social value groups to engage in protest activism in the 1981–1999 period, right-libertarians are about as likely to join boycotts and petition for the period 2002–2006. This suggests that social values may have become more prominent levers than economic considerations for engagement in these activities in more recent years. However, strong left-wing identifiers are in all cases more likely to engage in protest activities than others; and unlike with conventional participation, strong right-wing identifiers are, in several countries, significantly less likely than others to engage in elite-challenging participation. Therefore, there is some evidence that, as suggested by Inglehart (1990: 374), the meaning of 'Left' may have changed in more recent years to include value considerations, and that:

> Except in the very general sense that the Left (then as now) constitutes the side of the political spectrum that is seeking social change, the traditional and contemporary meanings of 'Left' are very different: the Old Left viewed both economic growth and technological progress as fundamentally good and progressive.

Instead:

> the New Left is suspicious of both. The Old Left has a working-class social base; the New Left has a predominantly middle-class base. To a great extent, the spread of new values and the rise of new issues have already reshaped the meaning of 'Left' and 'Right'.

He continues:

> To mass publics, the core meaning of the 'Left' is no longer simply state ownership of the means of production and related issues focussing on class conflict. Increasingly, it refers to a cluster of issues concerning the quality of the physical and social environment, the role of women, nuclear power.

Therefore, taken together, the results presented in this chapter suggest that the baby-boomers are distinctive in being significantly more likely than the post-WWII generation to engage in the various types of protest activities, and more so since their higher levels of participation are not generally accounted for simply by their higher levels of education relative to this older cohort. As such, the evidence presented in this chapter would suggest that at least for protest activism, the baby-boomers' formative experiences in the radicalising period of the late 1960s and 1970s have left a lasting imprint on their political behaviour many years later. However, neither the baby-boomers, or the even younger, '80s and '90s cohort are more likely than the post-WWII cohort to participate in new social movements. This means that not one of the three younger cohorts is significantly more likely than the post-WWII cohort to engage in this type of elite-challenging participation. Similarly to the results presented in Chapter 5 for conventional participation (where it was shown that younger cohorts were significantly more likely than older cohorts to contact a politician), this suggests that modernisation arguments, suggesting that similar influences should be drawing younger cohorts to engage more in elite-challenging participation and less in elite-directed activities than older generations, do not hold across indicators included in these two groups in theory. Therefore, it seems that other, more specific, mechanisms might fare better for explaining cohort differences in participation. Some tentative propositions for these were sketched in the discussion of the results in this chapter and the previous one. In the next chapter, by analysing cohort differences across Western Europe for eight different indicators of political participation side by side, we attempt to provide a more unified and consistent account of the proposed answers, particularly in respect to the differences in cohort effect patterns between protest activism and participation and voluntary work in social movement organisations.

Note

1 These are best fit quadratic smoothed lines.

References

Barnes, S. and M. Kaase (1979). *Political Action: Mass Participation in Five Western Societies*. Thousand Oaks, CA, Sage.
Della Porta, D. and M. Diani (2006). *Social Movements: An Introduction, 2nd Edition*. Oxford, Blackwell.
Franklin, M. N. (2004). *Voter Turnout and the Dynamics of Electoral Competition in Established Democracies since 1945*. Cambridge, Cambridge University Press.
Heartfield, J. (2003). "Capitalism and Anti-Capitalism". *Interventions* 5(2): 271–89.
Inglehart, R. (1977). *The Silent Revolution: Changing Values and Political Styles among Western Publics*. Princeton, Princeton University Press.
Inglehart, R. (1990). *Culture Shift in Advanced Industrial Society*. Princeton, Princeton University Press.
Inglehart, R. and G. Catterberg (2002). "Trends in Political Action: The Developmental Trend and the Post-Honeymoon Decline". *International Journal of Comparative Sociology* 43: 300–16.
Inglehart, R. and C. Welzel (2005). *Modernization, Cultural Change and Democracy: The Human Development Sequence*. Cambridge, Cambridge University Press.

Mason, K. O., W. M. Mason, H. H. Winsborough and W. K. Poole (1973). "Some Methodological Issues in Cohort Analysis of Archival Data". *American Sociological Review* 38(2): 242–58.

McAdam, D., J. McCarthy and M. N. Zald (1996). *Comparative Perspectives on Social Movements: Political Opportunities, Mobilising Structures and Cultural Framing.* Cambridge, Cambridge University Press.

Melucci, A. (1989). *The Nomads of the Present: Social Movements and Individual Needs in Contemporary Society.* London, Hutchinson Radius.

Melucci, A. (1996). *Challenging Codes: Collective Action in the Information Age.* Cambridge, Cambridge University Press.

Offe, C. (1987). Challenging the Boundaries of Institutional Politics: Social Movements since the 1960s. *Changing the Boundaries of the Political.* C. Maier. Cambridge, Cambridge University Press: 63–104.

Rodgers, W. L. (1982). "Estimable Functions of Age, Period and Cohort Effects". *American Sociological Review* 47: 774–87.

Touraine, A. (1971). *The Post-Industrial Society.* New York, Random House.

Touraine, A. (1981). *The Voice and the Eye.* Cambridge, Cambridge University Press.

Van Aelst, P. and S. Walgrave (2001). "Who is that (Wo)man in the Street? From the Normalisation of Protest to the Normalisation of the Protester". *European Journal of Political Research* 39: 461–86.

7 Explaining generational differences in political participation in Western Europe

Chapters 4–6 showed that for the same indicators, period effects varied across countries. On the other hand, Chapters 5 and 6 showed that cohort and age effects are relatively similar across Western Europe for each individual indicator of political participation analysed in detail in this study. This chapter brings together this study's findings for Western Europe for all the various types of activities, including party membership and demonstrating. The research question guiding the analyses in this chapter is: Are younger cohorts less likely than older cohorts to participate in conventional forms of participation while at the same time more likely to participate in unconventional forms of participation? By analysing data from the entire sample, this chapter reflects on whether the patterns uncovered in the country-by-country analyses in Chapters 5–6 are replicated for the whole of Western Europe.

Since results from Chapters 4–6 showed that while there is substantial variation between countries in terms of period effects, that cohort, age and other variable effects are relatively stable across Western Europe for each individual indicator, this chapter generalises the results for the whole of Western Europe. It shows that the patterns suggested by the country-by-country analyses in the previous chapters hold across all ten. More specifically, this chapter shows that younger cohorts are significantly less likely than the post-WWII cohort to join a party and vote, but are significantly more likely than older cohorts to contact a politician. As such, younger cohorts are not less likely than older cohorts to participate in all types of 'elite-directed' participation as suggested by the modernisation account. Furthermore, for unconventional participation, younger cohorts are significantly more likely than older cohorts to engage in protest activism, but, amongst the younger cohorts, the baby-boomers are significantly more likely than the '80s and '90s cohorts to demonstrate and occupy and significantly more likely than the '90s generation to join a boycott. Younger cohorts are significantly less likely than older cohorts to participate in new social movements (or SMOs). Therefore, this indicates that, across Western Europe, younger cohorts are not more likely than older cohorts to participate in all types of 'elite-challenging' participation.

Moreover, in the second section of the analysis we plot the smoothed cohort effects for the various types of participation to test the sensitivity of our results to the cohort classification schema. The focus of this chapter is to summarise the results from Chapters 5 and 6. It aims to show that while cohort effects for each activity are similar across countries, they vary by type of activity with younger cohorts being more likely than older cohorts to participate in some activities whereas the reverse is true for other political actions. The central focus in this respect is in showing that the direction of cohort effects does not map onto the conventional-unconventional or elite-directed-elite-challenging distinctions and that actually, younger cohorts are significantly more likely than older cohorts to engage in certain conventional actions and less likely than older cohorts to participate in specific types of elite-challenging participation. The chapter also shows that the baby-boomers are significantly more likely than the '80s and '90s generations to engage in social, confrontational-demonstrative unconventional activities (and, than just the '90s cohorts, to join boycotts). This is not what would be expect based on the argument that due to societal modernisation, rising levels of post-materialism and increasing 'cognitive mobilisation' lead younger cohorts to reject elite-directed forms of participation in favour of more elite-challenging types of participation associated with the rise of NSMs and protest politics. As such, evidence does not show a monotonic strictly increasing cohort effect with each younger cohort being more likely to participate in protest activism than the next. Instead, results suggest that formative experiences matter for political participation patterns many years later (Grasso 2011, Grasso 2014). The baby-boomers, coming of age in the radical-ising period of the late 1960s and 1970s, stand out as 'the protest generation'.

Key themes and previous research

It is commonplace for scholars and commentators to argue that we have entered a 'post-political' age, where public disengagement from politics is widespread across advanced Western European democracies. However, other scholars counter that 'elite-challenging' or 'unconventional' political participation is becoming increasingly prevalent, particularly amongst young people, so that ignoring these repertoires in investigations of political participation results in underestimating actual engagement. Inglehart (1990) proposes what is perhaps the most comprehensive categorisation of different types of political activities in distinguishing between: (1) *elite-directed activities:* voting, party membership, other party-mediated activities, union membership; and (2) *elite-directing activities:* political discussion, participation in new social movements and protest activities such as demonstrations, boycotts, signing petitions, occupations, unofficial strikes, etc. (Inglehart 1990: 335–6). In later work, Inglehart uses the term *elite-challenging* (Inglehart and Catterberg 2002) to designate elite-directing activities, but political discussion is no longer designated as belonging to this repertoire. Therefore, I take *elite-challenging activities* to designate all those activities mentioned above with the exclusion of political discussion.

In previous chapters, I argued that it should not be assumed that cohort effects – and also period and age effects – operate in the same way in what are taken as 'similar' types of activities. Rather, this is something that should be tested empirically, by analysing each indicator of political participation in turn. This chapter, following the previous chapters, does not create scales but instead treats each indicator as a distinct dependent variable. The only exception to this practice is NSM/SMO participation, which is composed of several survey items. This variable takes a value of 1 if individuals did any of the following four activities: joined an environmental, conservation, ecology/animal rights organisation, joined a third world development/human rights organisation, did unpaid voluntary work for an environment, conservation, ecology/animal rights organisation, did unpaid work for a third world development or human rights organisation. This is because each of these activities is particularly infrequent in the sample. Regarding cohort effects on different types of political participation, I argued that if Mannheim's (1928) account that generations are firmly located within socio-historical contexts is correct, then it would be expected that different generations exhibit different patterns of participation based on the period of their 'formative years'. The generations coming of age in the classic period of party cleavage congealment (Lipset and Rokkan 1967), broadly, before the transformations of the mid-to-late 1960s, should be more likely to be members of political parties and to vote than those generations that came of age in subsequent historical periods. On the other hand, the generation that came of age in the radicalising period of the late 1960s and 1970s, the baby-boomers, should be more likely than older cohorts to engage in demonstrations, and possibly to be involved in new social movements.

While there are good reasons to think that the 1960s generation might be more radical than previous generations due to the period of their formative years, it is not clear that this would extend to generations coming of age in later periods. Since Della Porta and Diani (2006: 69) write that "political contexts subsequently differed greatly", then so might have the socialisation experiences of cohorts coming of age after the radicalising period of the late 1960 and 1970s. It follows that there is no clear reason to believe that "the 1960s generation would have passed on ... these new conceptualisations to younger groups". On the other hand, the mechanism which Inglehart and Catterberg (2002: 303) propose is one which centres on rising education levels (and as a result, rising post-materialist values). On this reading, while the socialisation experiences of the '80s and '90s cohorts might not in and of themselves encourage elite-directing activities, their relatively higher education levels would explain their higher levels of participation in these activities relative to older cohorts. It is of interest to examine cohort differences in unconventional participation, particularly to see whether the generations coming of age in the 1980s and 1990s engage in unconventional activities more than the 1960s generation and how far this is related to their higher education levels and perhaps their 'new values'.

A different type of argument characterises the socio-historic period of socialisation of the 1980s and 1990s as potentially having a depressing effect on the political participation of these generations, if the generational thesis is correct. In his classic essay *The End of History?* Fukuyama (1989: 1) wrote that "In watching the flow of events over the past decade or so, it is hard to avoid the feeling that something very fundamental has happened in world history" and that this "end of history will be a very sad time" since:

The struggle for recognition, the willingness to risk one's life for a purely abstract goal, the worldwide ideological struggle that called forth daring, courage, imagination, and idealism, will be replaced by economic calculation, the endless solving of technical problems, environmental concerns, and the satisfaction of sophisticated consumer demands.

(1989: 1)

For Fukuyama then, the end of the Cold War and the ideological struggle between Left and Right marked the replacement of "the willingness to risk one's life for a purely abstract goal" with more mundane, managerial-practical preoccupations. It might be concluded from this that the end of the Cold War also marked the demise of some of the more significant motivations for individuals to participate in politics. Without ideological struggle, it seems, a key element of what has traditionally motivated individuals to participate in politics dissipates. Therefore, it might be expected that this new political context should have some influence on the political socialisation process of young adults coming of age in the wake of these historical events.

For example, Clarke *et al.* (2004) show that in Britain, the Thatcher and Blair generation are less likely to participate than older generations. The authors argue that their age, period and cohort analysis shows that:

The available evidence is quite consistent that the Thatcher era – a period characterised by insistent advocacy of market rather than government solution to societal problems, and a more general emphasis on the individual rather than collective good – had important negative effects on public attitudes towards electoral participation.

(Clarke *et al.* 2004: 270–1)

The 1980s were marked by the ascendancy of more 'capitalist values' and the demise of the traditional Left across Western Europe. They were also characterised by economic crisis and higher levels of unemployment affecting young people entering the job market (cf. Becker's classification of the '80s generation as the 'Lost generation'). Consequently, it could be argued that this generation might exhibit lower levels of participation than the baby-boomers. Since the '90s generation came of age in a period marked by the 'end of ideology', then perhaps the lower levels of left-right ideological polarisation in society at the time of their formative years might have led them to be less politically active than the baby-boomers. This could be the case despite rising education levels and thus greater 'cognitive mobilisation' levels amongst this cohort (Grasso 2013).

Findings

Tables 7.1 and 7.2 present the multi-level model parameter estimates for conventional political participation across Western Europe. For every indicator of participation, including education in Model(s) 2 and the other predictors in Model(s) 3, significantly improves model fit. The optimal measure of fit for multi-level models is Akaike's Information Criterion, since it incorporates penalties for a greater number of parameters[1]. Tables 7.1 and 7.2 show that patterns are broadly similar to those uncovered in the country-by-country analyses from Chapter 5. Younger cohorts are significantly less likely than older cohorts to vote and to join parties. They are also significantly more likely to contact a politician. The central difference between these models and those from Chapter 5 is that the differences between the baby-boomers and the post-WWII cohort for both party membership and voting are emphasised. Here, the baby-boomers are significantly less likely than the post-WWII cohort to join parties and to vote. Further, testing for coefficient differences[2] not captured in these models shows that in all of the six models for party membership (Models 1–3 for the EVS and 1–3 for the ESS), both the '80s and '90s generations are significantly less likely than the baby-boomers to join parties. However, differences between the '80s and '90s generation are not significant. This would suggest that events taking place since the end of the 1970s could have had a negative impact on the propensity of cohorts experiencing their formative years in this period to get involved with parties. The demise of the Left and the rise of neoliberalism could have meant that younger people (who tend to be more left wing) had fewer incentives to join parties in their formative years and so never learned this political 'habit'. In their study of political participation in Britain, Clarke *et al.* (2004: 270–1) cite the "insistent advocacy of market rather than government solutions to societal problems, and a more general emphasis on the individual rather than collective good" in this period as having negative effects on the participation patterns of the Thatcher and Blair generation; the authors show that these effects are long-lasting since they "have not abated since New Labour came to power in 1997". Moreover, the results presented in Table 7.1 show that the effects of the other predictor variables are also very similar across the EVS and ESS models for party membership. Being less educated has a negative effect as does having a manual occupation; being male and highly politicised have strong positive effects on party membership; left-authoritarians and right-libertarians are significantly less likely than left-libertarians to join parties. Interestingly, for 1981–1999 EVS, strongly left-wing individuals were more likely than strongly right-wing individuals to join parties; on the other hand, there were no significant differences between these two groups for the 2002–2006 period.[3] The results from Table 7.2 for the multi-level models on voting and for contacting a politician show that the effects of the other predictor variables are similar to those for party membership.

However, being strongly left wing does not have a positive effect on turnout and right-libertarians are significantly more likely than left-libertarians to vote whereas both types of authoritarians are less likely to do so; they are also less likely than left-libertarians to contact a politician and being highly politicised on either extremity of the left-right spectrum has a positive effect on this activity. Two more things are worth mentioning from Table 7.2. For voting, there are age effects that confound the cohort effects for younger cohorts. However, these are in the opposite direction to those for the pre-WWII cohort effect – I will reflect

Table 7.1 Multi-level parameter estimates for party membership (EVS and ESS)

Fixed effects	Party membership EVS			Party membership ESS		
	N = 39,353, 10			N = 49,532, 10		
	Model 1 Estimate (s.e.)	Model 2 Estimate (s.e.)	Model 3 Estimate (s.e.)	Model 1 Estimate (s.e.)	Model 2 Estimate (s.e.)	Model 3 Estimate (s.e.)
Constant γ'_{00}	−2.59(.18)***	−2.25(.17)***	−2.57(.19)***	−2.76(.17)***	−2.58(.17)***	−2.84(.18)***
Cohort						
Pre-WWII	0.02(.08)	0.07(.07)	0.05(.08)	0.09(.08)	0.16(.08)	0.19(.08)*
Post-WWII r.c.						
Baby-boomers	−0.20(.08)*	−0.27(.08)***	−0.29(.08)***	−0.23(.06)***	−0.30(.06)***	−0.27(.06)***
80s generation	−0.61(.12)***	−0.76(.12)***	−0.70(.12)***	−0.63(.11)***	−0.73(.11)***	−0.68(.11)***
90s generation	−0.96(.17)***	−1.14(.17)***	−1.02(.17)***	−0.99(.18)***	−1.11(.18)***	−1.08(.18)***
Age group						
18–33	−0.15(.09)	−0.20(.09)*	−0.24(.09)**	0.08(.16)	0.07(.16)	0.08(.16)
34–50 r.c.						
51+	−0.13(.08)	−0.59(.08)	−0.09(.08)	0.13(.09)	0.17(.09)	0.17(.09)
Survey year						
1981/2002*	−0.03(.10)	−0.02(.11)	−0.04(.11)	−0.01(.06)	−0.02(.06)	−0.01(.06)
1990/2004* r.c						
1999/2006*	−0.10(.12)	−0.09(.12)	−0.14(.12)	0.01(.06)	−0.00(.06)	0.00(.06)
Education (low)		−0.77(.05)***	−0.60(.06)***		−0.41(.05)***	−0.28(.05)***
Male			0.70(.05)***			0.58(.04)***
Working class			−0.47(.05)***			−0.37(.05)***
Left			1.11(.07)***			0.95(.08)***
Right			0.74(.09)***			0.90(.08)***

Political values

	Variance (std. d.)	Variance (std. d.)	Variance (std. d.)	Variance (std. d.)	Variance (std. d.)	Variance (std. d.)
Left-libertarian r.c.						
Left-authoritarian			−0.24(.07)***			−0.26(.06)***
Right-libertarian			−0.24(.07)***			−0.16(.08)*
Right-authoritarian			−0.12(.07)			−0.10(.06)

Random effects	Variance (std. d.)	Variance (std. d.)	Variance (std. d.)	Variance (std. d.)	Variance (std. d.)	Variance (std. d.)
Between-country var σ^2_u	0.29(.54)	0.24(.49)	0.29(.54)	0.18(.42)	0.17(.42)	0.20(.44)
Survey year						
1981/2002* r.c.						
1990/2004*	0.06(.25)	0.09(.29)	0.07(.26)	0.01(.09)	0.01(.10)	0.01(.11)
1999/2006*	0.10(.32)	0.12(.34)	0.11(.33)	0.01(.07)	0.01(.08)	0.01(.09)
AIC	15,556	15,345	14,780	18,749	18,682	18,207
BIC	15,685	15,482	14,978	18,881	18823	18,410
LogLikelihood	−7,763	−7,656	−7,367	−9,359	−9325	−9,080
Deviance	15,526	15,313	14,734	18,719	18,650	18,161

Notes

Significance levels:

* $p \leq 0.05$.

** $p \leq 0.01$.

*** $p \leq 0.001$.

Reference categories: Post-WWII cohort (2); 34–50 age group (2); 1990/2004 (2), therefore, 1981/2002 is the inverse of the period effect 1981–1990/2002–2004; Left-libertarian (1); Edu (low) is a dummy variable where 1 means the respondent left school before the age of 17 or completed less than eleven years in FTE; Working class is a dummy variable where 1 means the respondent is an unskilled, semi-skilled or skilled manual worker; Left and right are dummy variables derived from the left-right scale, respectively, values 0/1 and values 9/10.

Table 7.2 Multi-level parameter estimates for voting and contacting a politician (ESS)

Fixed effects	Voting ESS			Contacting a politician ESS		
	N = 49,284, 10			N = 49,554, 10		
	Model 1	Model 2	Model 3	Model 1	Model 2	Model 3
	Estimate (s.e.)	Estimate (s.e.)	Estimate (s.e.)	Estimate (s.e.)	Estimate (s.e.)	Estimate (s.e.)
Constant γ_{00}	-2.00(.18)***	-2.36(.18)***	-2.44(.19)***	-1.78(.09)***	-1.50(.09)***	-1.54(.10)***
Cohort						
Pre-WWII	-0.51(.06)***	-0.41(.06)***	-0.42(.06)***	-0.55(.07)***	-0.43(.07)***	-0.43(.07)***
Post-WWII r.c.						
Baby-boomers	-0.17(.05)***	-0.30(.05)***	-0.30(.05)***	0.35(.04)***	0.24(.04)***	0.24(.04)***
80s generation	-0.41(.07)***	-0.61(.07)***	-0.61(.07)***	0.26(.06)***	0.10(.06)	0.12(.06)
90s generation	-0.64(.09)***	-0.88(.09)***	-0.89(.09)***	0.18(.08)*	0.00(.08)	0.00(.08)
Age group						
18–33	-0.31(.06)***	-0.34(.06)***	-0.33(.06)***	-0.30(.07)***	-0.32(.07)***	-0.31(.07)***
34–50 r.c.						
51+	0.22(.06)***	0.29(.06)***	0.28(.06)***	-0.04(.05)	0.01(.05)	0.01(.05)
Survey year						
2002	0.05(.06)	0.04(.07)	0.05(.07)	0.09(.05)	0.08(.05)	0.09(.05)
2004 r.c.						
2006	0.02(.06)	-0.00(.07)	-0.00(.06)	0.05(.05)	0.03(.04)	0.03(.05)
Education (low)		-0.70(.03)***	-0.56(.03)***		-0.67(.03)***	-0.54(.03)***
Male			0.10(.03)***			0.36(.02)***
Working class			-0.44(.03)***			-0.40(.03)***
Left			0.11(.06)			0.37(.05)***
Right			0.49(.08)***			0.26(.06)***

Political values

	Variance (std. d.)	Variance (std. d.)	Variance (std. d.)	Variance (std. d.)	Variance (std. d.)	Variance (std. d.)
Left-libertarian r.c.						
Left-authoritarian			-0.10(.03)**			-0.22(.03)***
Right-libertarian			0.14(.05)***			-0.01(.04)
Right-authoritarian			-0.11(.04)**			-0.13(.04)***

Random effects	Variance (std. d.)	Variance (std. d.)	Variance (std. d.)	Variance (std. d.)	Variance (std. d.)	Variance (std. d.)
Between-country var σ_u^2	0.29(.54)	0.29(.54)	0.29(.54)	0.05(.23)	0.05(.23)	0.06(.25)
Survey year						
2002	0.04(.19)	0.03(.19)	0.03(.18)	0.02(.12)	0.12(.11)	0.01(.12)
2004 r.c.						
2006	0.03(.16)	0.03(.17)	0.03(.17)	0.01(.10)	0.01(.10)	0.01(.11)
AIC	43,073	42,525	42,175	43,879	43,412	42,930
BIC	43,205	42,666	42,377	44,011	43,553	43,113
LogLikelihood	−21,522	−21,247	−21,064	−21,924	−21,690	−21,442
Deviance	43,043	42,493	42,129	43,849	43,380	42,884

Notes

Significance levels:

* $p \leq 0.05$.

** $p \leq 0.01$.

*** $p \leq 0.001$.

Reference categories: Post-WWII cohort (2); 34–50 age group (2); 2004 (2), therefore, 2002 is the inverse of the period effect 2002–2004; Left-libertarian (1); Edu (low) is a dummy variable where 1 means the respondent left school before the age of 17 or completed less than eleven years in FTE; Working class is a dummy variable where 1 means the respondent is an unskilled, semi-skilled or skilled manual worker; Left and right are dummy variables derived from the left-right scale, respectively, values 0/1 and values 9/10.

on the implications of this in more detail when I plot the smoothed cohort effects with GAMs in the next section of the analysis.

For contacting a politician, testing for coefficient differences (via the Wald test post-regression) shows that differences between the baby-boomers and both the '80s and '90s generation become significant when controlling for education levels. As discussed in more detail in Chapter 5, and reflected in the results from Models 2 and 3, higher education levels account for why the '80s and '90s cohorts engage in this activity more than the post-WWII cohort. However, the baby-boomers appear to be more active than older cohorts in this activity for other reasons: most likely something about their formative years that is not accounted for in these models.

Moving onto the results for the indicators of unconventional political participation, starting with demonstrating, the results presented in Table 7.3 show that younger cohorts are significantly more likely than older cohorts to engage in this activity (though education mediates this effect for the '80s and '90s generation); young people tend to be more likely to engage in this activity than middle age people (though this difference appears less marked for 1981–1999); old people tend to engage in this activity less than middle age people (though this effect is somewhat less marked for 2002–2006); having a lower education and being working class have a negative effect on demonstrating (confirming findings that this activity has not been 'democratised') (Van Aelst and Walgrave 2001). Being strongly left wing has a positive effect on demonstrating, whereas being strongly right wing has a negative effect on engaging in this activity. Left-libertarians are significantly more likely than individuals with the other three sets of values to engage in this activity. This would seem to confirm the arguments of authors suggesting that post-materialist values are really just a poor proxy for progressive liberal values (Brooks and Manza 1994; Evans and De Graaf 1996).

Testing for coefficient differences (post-regression via the Wald test) for all six models for demonstrating (Models 1–3 for the EVS and 1–3 for the ESS) shows that the '80s and '90s generation are significantly less likely than the baby-boomers to demonstrate. There are no significant differences between the '80s and '90s generation. However, based on the modernisation account that post-materialist value-change drives rising levels of elite-challenging participation, it would be expected that each younger cohort would participate in these sorts of activities more than the previous one, or at least at about the same level. As such, Della Porta and Diani's (2006) argument that the 1960s generation was deeply impressed by the "dramatic transformations, even a revolution" of their formative years is supported by the findings. But the authors also claim that "the 1960s generation would have passed on – at least in part – these new conceptualisations to younger groups, even though political contexts subsequently differed greatly" (Della Porta and Diani 2006: 69). Here the results would suggest that the changing political context meant that subsequent generations were not as likely to demonstrate as the baby-boomers across Western Europe. Therefore, 'the protest generation' is distinctive in this respect. They were not the first wave of a rising tide of protest, but rather quite a unique activist generation.

The results for the models on boycotting (Table 7.4) and those for petitioning (Table 7.5) show that the effect of the other predictor variables (not age, period and cohort) in Model 3, on these other 'elite-directing' activities, are more or less identical to those for demonstrating. The interesting exception is that for 2002–2006, women are significantly more likely than men to engage in these activities. However, the effect is only slight, which suggests that both genders engage in these activities at about the same level in subsequent years. Cohort and age effects on demonstrating also present some interesting differences. For example, the baby-boomers are in all models significantly more likely to boycott than the post-WWII cohort. However, controlling for education in Model 2 shows the '90s generation is significantly less likely than the post-WWII cohort to boycott for 1981–1999, or about as likely to boycott for 2002–2006. Testing for coefficient differences (Wald test) shows that in all six models for boycotting, the baby-boomers are significantly more likely than the '90s generation to join a boycott. For 1981–1999 the baby-boomers are significantly more likely than both the '80s and '90s cohorts, to engage in this activity (Models 1–3). Again, the baby-boomers and not the '80s and '90s cohorts are the most likely to engage in another type of elite-challenging activity. However, testing for coefficient differences for petitioning reveals that there are no significant differences between the baby-boomers, '80s and '90s cohorts. Therefore, taken together these results show that across the six models for each of the three indicators, the baby-boomers are significantly more likely than the '80s and '90s cohorts to demonstrate; that they are significantly more likely than the '90s cohort to boycott, but about as prone to this activity as the '80s cohort; and about as likely as the '80s and '90s cohort to petition. Once again, education plays a mediating role in explaining differences in elite-challenging participation between the '80s and '90s cohorts and the post-WWII generation, but not for differences between the latter cohort and the baby-boomers. This suggests that these persistent cohort effects may reflect something special about their formative experiences in the radicalising period of the late 1960s and 1970s. 'Cognitive mobilisation' appears to play a role in explaining why the '80s and '90s cohorts engage in unconventional activism more than older cohorts. However, the baby-boomers are significantly more likely to engage in these activities than older cohorts for reasons not accounted for by their higher education levels. It is likely, as suggested by Della Porta and Diani (2006), that the formative experiences of the baby-boomers in the radicalising late 1960s and 1970s would have left a lasting imprint on their patterns of participation many years later.

The final indicator of elite-challenging participation analysed in this section is participation in new social movements (NSMs), or more appropriately, since we are looking at participation in environmental, animal rights, development and human rights organisations, participation in SMOs (Kriesi and Wisler 1996). The results from Chapter 6 showed that, in four countries, the youngest cohorts were significantly less likely than older cohorts to participate in SMOs. The results from the multi-level models presented in Table 7.6 for participation in new social movements show that, across Models 1–3, the '90s generation is

Table 7.3 Multi-level parameter estimates for demonstrating (EVS and ESS)

Fixed effects	Demonstrating EVS			Demonstrating ESS		
	N = 37,214, 10			N = 49,506, 10		
	Model 1	Model 2	Model 3	Model 1	Model 2	Model 3
	Estimate (s.e.)	Estimate (s.e.)	Estimate (s.e.)	Estimate (s.e.)	Estimate (s.e.)	Estimate (s.e.)
Constant γ_{00}	−1.33(.11)***	−0.93(.10)***	−0.70(.11)***	−2.85(.25)***	−2.56(.26)***	−2.26(.25)***
Cohort						
Pre-WWII	−0.34(.05)***	−0.29(.05)***	−0.25(.06)***	−0.76(.13)***	−0.66(.14)***	−0.59(.14)***
Post-WWII r.c.						
Baby-boomers	0.43(.05)***	0.35(.05)***	0.27(.05)***	0.68(.06)***	0.56(.06)***	0.52(.06)***
80s generation	0.28(.06)***	0.12(.06)	0.07(.07)	0.53(.09)***	0.36(.09)***	0.32(.09)***
90s generation	0.22(.08)**	0.02(.08)	0.03(.09)	0.34(.12)**	0.13(.12)	0.12(.12)
Age group						
18–33	0.11(.05)*	0.05(.05)	0.01(.05)	0.30(.09)**	0.29(.09)**	0.26(.10)**
34–50 r.c.						
51+	−0.20(.05)***	−0.13(.05)*	−0.11(.05)*	−0.17(.07)*	−0.11(.07)	0.10(.07)
Survey year						
1981/2002*	−0.37(.08)***	−0.37(.09)***	−0.57(.10)***	0.01(.14)	0.00(.14)	0.01(.14)
1990/2004* r.c						
1999/2006*	0.23(.09)**	0.24(.08)**	0.17(.07)*	−0.13(.13)	−0.15(.13)	−0.17(.13)
Education (low)		−0.80(.03)***	−0.75(.03)***		−0.70(.05)***	−0.62(.05)***
Male			0.56(.03)***			0.29(.03)***
Working class			−0.23(.03)***			−0.29(.04)***
Left			1.11(.05)***			1.10(.06)***
Right			−0.26(.07)***			−0.02(.10)

Political values

	Variance (std. d.)	Variance (std. d.)	Variance (std. d.)	Variance (std. d.)	Variance (std. d.)	Variance (std. d.)
Left-libertarian r.c.						
Left-authoritarian			$-0.67(.07)$***			$-0.50(.04)$***
Right-libertarian			$-0.60(.04)$***			$-0.51(.06)$***
Right-authoritarian			$-0.81(.04)$***			$-0.93(.06)$***
Random effects						
Between-country var σ_u^2	0.11(.33)	0.09(.29)	0.08(.29)	0.53(.73)	0.62(.79)	0.56(.75)
Survey year						
1981/2002*	0.05(.23)	0.06(.25)	0.08(.28)	0.18(.43)	0.18(.43)	0.19(.43)
1990/2004* r.c						
1999/2006*	0.06(.25)	0.05(.23)	0.03(.18)	0.14(.37)	0.14(.38)	0.15(.39)
AIC	39,533	38,744	36,824	26,206	25,950	25,151
BIC	39,661	38,880	37,020	26,338	26,091	25,354
LogLikelihood	−19,752	−19,356	−18,389	−13,088	−12,959	−12,553
Deviance	39,503	38,712	36,778	26,176	25,918	25,105

Notes
Significance levels:
* $p \leq 0.05$.
** $p \leq 0.01$.
*** $p \leq 0.001$.
Reference categories: Post-WWII cohort (2); 34–50 age group (2); 1990/2004 (2); therefore, 1981/2002 is the inverse of the period effect 1981–1990/2002–2004; Left-libertarian (1); Edu (low) is a dummy variable where 1 means the respondent left school before the age of 17 or completed less than eleven years in FTE; Working class is a dummy variable where 1 means the respondent is an unskilled, semi-skilled or skilled manual worker; Left and right are dummy variables derived from the left-right scale, respectively, values 0/1 and values 9/10.

Table 7.4 Multi-level parameter estimates for boycotting (EVS and ESS)

Fixed effects	Boycotting EVS			Boycotting ESS		
	N = 36,081, 10			N = 49,420, 10		
	Model 1	Model 2	Model 3	Model 1	Model 2	Model 3
	Estimate (s.e.)	Estimate (s.e.)	Estimate (s.e.)	Estimate (s.e.)	Estimate (s.e.)	Estimate (s.e.)
Constant γ_{00}	−2.27(.13)***	−1.91(.13)***	−1.61(.14)***	−1.75(.22)***	−1.43(.21)***	−0.95(.22)***
Cohort						
Pre-WWII	−0.46(.08)***	−0.41(.08)***	−0.35(.09)***	−0.79(.08)***	−0.67(.08)***	−0.67(.08)***
Post-WWII r.c.						
Baby-boomers	0.41(.07)***	0.33(.07)***	0.24(.07)***	0.38(.04)***	0.24(.04)***	0.20(.04)***
80s generation	0.28(.09)**	0.13(.09)	0.08(.09)	0.38(.06)***	0.20(.06)**	0.15(.06)*
90s generation	−0.08(.12)	−0.26(.13)*	−0.24(.12)*	0.24(.09)**	0.03(.08)	−0.03(.08)
Age group						
18–33	0.08(.06)	0.02(.06)	−0.02(.06)	−0.03(.06)	−0.05(.06)	−0.06(.06)
34–50 r.c.						
51+	−0.30(.07)***	−0.22(.07)**	−0.22(.07)**	0.07(.05)	−0.00(.05)	0.00(.05)
Survey year						
1981/2002*	−0.33(.15)*	−0.33(.15)*	−0.50(.16)**	0.03(.09)	0.02(.09)	0.03(.09)
1990/2004* r.c.						
1999/2006*	0.38(.14)**	−0.39(.14)**	0.30(.14)*	−0.00(.06)	−0.02(.06)	−0.02(.06)
Education (low)		−0.77(.04)***	−0.67(.04)***		−0.78(.03)***	−0.65(.03)***
Male			0.45(.04)***			−0.07(.02)**
Working class			−0.33(.05)***			−0.48(.03)***
Left			1.09(.06)***			0.48(.05)***
Right			−0.30(.11)**			−0.20(.07)**

Political values

	Variance (std. d.)	Variance (std. d.)	Variance (std. d.)	Variance (std. d.)	Variance (std. d.)	Variance (std. d.)
Left-libertarian r.c.						
Left-authoritarian			−0.82(.06)***			−0.53(.03)***
Right-libertarian			−0.57(.05)***			−0.18(.04)***
Right-authoritarian			−0.88(.06)***			−0.53(.04)***
Random effects						
Between-country var σ_u^2	0.12(.35)	0.12(.34)	0.15(.39)	0.44(.66)	0.42(.65)	0.45(.67)
Survey year						
1981/2002*	0.20(.45)	0.19(.43)	0.24(.49)	0.07(.27)	0.07(.26)	0.07(.27)
1990/2004* r.c						
1999/2006*	0.16(.41)	0.18(.43)	0.18(.42)	0.03(.17)	0.03(.17)	0.03(.18)
AIC	23,418	23,063	21,941	46,397	45,735	44,914
BIC	23,545	23,199	22,137	46,529	45,875	45,116
LogLikelihood	−1,694	−11,515	−10,948	−23,183	−22,851	−22,434
Deviance	23,388	23,031	21,895	46,367	45,703	44,868

Notes
Significance levels:
* $p \leq 0.05$.
** $p \leq 0.01$.
*** $p \leq 0.001$.

Reference categories: Post-WWII cohort (2); 34–50 age group (2); 1990/2004 (2), therefore, 1981/2002 is the inverse of the period effect 1981–1990/2002–2004; Left-libertarian (1); Edu (low) is a dummy variable where 1 means the respondent left school before the age of 17 or completed less than eleven years in FTE; Working class is a dummy variable where 1 means the respondent is an unskilled, semi-skilled or skilled manual worker; Left and right are dummy variables derived from the left-right scale, respectively, values 0/1 and values 9/10.

Table 7.5 Multi-level parameter estimates for petitioning (EVS and ESS)

Fixed effects	Petitioning EVS			Petitioning ESS		
	N = 37,198, 10			N = 49,391, 10		
	Model 1	Model 2	Model 3	Model 1	Model 2	Model 3
	Estimate (s.e.)	Estimate (s.e.)	Estimate (s.e.)	Estimate (s.e.)	Estimate (s.e.)	Estimate (s.e.)
Constant γ_{00}	-0.07(.21)	-0.45(.21)*	-0.67(.22)**	-1.22(.15)***	-0.93(.15)***	-0.48(.15)**
Cohort						
Pre-WWII	-0.32(.04)***	-0.29(.04)***	-0.27(.04)***	-0.70(.06)***	-0.59(.06)***	-0.59(.06)***
Post-WWII r.c.						
Baby-boomers	0.38(.04)***	0.31(.04)***	0.27(.04)***	0.48(.03)***	0.37(.03)***	0.33(.03)***
80s generation	0.34(.06)***	0.19(.06)***	0.17(.06)**	0.50(.05)***	0.33(.05)***	0.30(.05)***
90s generation	0.15(.08)*	-0.04(.08)	-0.03(.07)	0.44(.07)***	0.25(.07)***	0.21(.07)**
Age group						
18–33	-0.14(.04)***	-0.20(.04)***	-0.21(.04)***	0.01(.05)	-0.01(.05)	-0.02(.05)
34–50 r.c.						
51+	-0.21(.04)***	-0.13(.04)**	-0.12(.04)**	-0.12(.04)**	-0.06(.04)	-0.06(.04)
Survey year						
1981/2002*	-0.43(.10)***	-0.43(.10)***	-0.49(.10)***	0.11(.08)	0.10(.08)	0.11(.08)
1990/2004* r.c						
1999/2006*	0.41(.13)**	0.43(.12)***	0.38(.12)**	0.07(.07)	0.06(.08)	0.05(.07)
Education (low)		-0.72(.03)***	-0.63(.03)***		-0.67(.03)***	-0.58(.03)***
Male			0.19(.02)***			-0.08(.02)***
Working class			-0.26(.03)***			-0.38(.03)***
Left			0.70(.05)***			0.48(.05)***
Right			-0.10(.05)			-0.12(.06)*

Political values

	Variance (std. d.)	Variance (std. d.)	Variance (std. d.)	Variance (std. d.)	Variance (std. d.)	Variance (std. d.)
Left-libertarian r.c.						
Left-authoritarian			−0.49(.03)***			−0.45(.03)***
Right-libertarian			−0.25(.03)***			−0.26(.04)***
Right-authoritarian			−0.42(.03)***			−0.55(.03)***
Random effects						
Between-country var σ_u^2	0.42(.65)	0.43(.67)	0.45(.67)	0.20(.45)	0.19(.43)	0.20(.45)
Survey year						
1981/2002*	0.09(.30)	0.10(.31)	0.10(.31)	0.06(.24)	0.06(.24)	0.06(.24)
1990/2004* r.c						
1999/2006*	0.15(.39)	0.14(.38)	0.13(.36)	0.04(.21)	0.05(.22)	0.05(.22)
AIC	46,951	46,138	45,412	58,256	57,548	56,695
BIC	47,079	46,274	45,608	58,388	57,689	56,898
LogLikelihood	−23,461	−23,053	−22,683	−29,113	−28,758	−28,325
Deviance	46,921	46,106	45,366	58,226	57,516	56,649

Notes
Significance levels:
* $p \leq 0.05$.
** $p \leq 0.01$.
*** $p \leq 0.001$.

Reference categories: Post-WWII cohort (2); 34–50 age group (2); 1990/2004 (2), therefore, 1981/2002 is the inverse of the period effect 1981–1990/2002–2004 (2); Left-libertarian (1). Edu (low) is a dummy variable where 1 means the respondent left school before the age of 17 or completed less than eleven years in FTE; Working class is a dummy variable where 1 means the respondent is an unskilled, semi-skilled or skilled manual worker; Left and right are dummy variables derived from the left-right scale, respectively, values 0/1 and values 9/10.

Table 7.6 Multi-level parameter estimates for NSM participation and occupying (EVS)

Fixed effects	NSM participation N = 39,353, 10			Occupying EVS N = 36,543, 10		
	Model 1 Estimate (s.e.)	Model 2 Estimate (s.e.)	Model 3 Estimate (s.e.)	Model 1 Estimate (s.e.)	Model 2 Estimate (s.e.)	Model 3 Estimate (s.e.)
Constant γ_{00}	-2.07(.26)***	-1.64(.24)***	-1.35(.24)***	-3.86(.26)***	-3.62(.27)***	-3.56(.27)***
Cohort						
Pre-WWII	-0.19(.07)**	-0.12(.07)	-0.12(.07)	-0.54(.14)***	-0.51(.14)***	-0.46(.14)**
Post-WWII *r.c.*						
Baby-boomers	-0.03(.07)	-0.12(.07)	-0.14(.07)*	0.65(.11)***	0.59(.11)***	0.56(.11)***
80s generation	-0.08(.09)	-0.27(.09)**	-0.24(.09)**	0.38(.14)**	0.27(.14)	0.17(.14)
90s generation	-0.36(.12)**	-0.57(.13)***	-0.50(.12)***	0.03(.19)	-0.10(.19)	-0.13(.20)
Age group						
18–33	-0.00(.07)	-0.06(.07)	-0.06(.07)	0.09(.10)	0.05(.10)	-0.02(.10)
34–50 *r.c.*						
51+	-0.14(.07)*	-0.05(.07)	-0.04(.07)	-0.11(.11)	-0.06(.11)	-0.02(.12)
Survey year						
1981	-0.73(.14)***	-0.73(.15)***	-0.78(.14)***	-0.03(.10)	-0.00(.09)	-0.19(.11)
1990 *r.c.*						
1999	-0.03(.17)	0.05(.17)	-0.02(.17)	0.27(.12)*	-0.29(.13)*	-0.20(.11)
Education (low)		-0.95(.04)***	-0.79(.05)***		-0.50(.06)***	-0.43(.07)***
Male			-0.02(.04)			0.62(.06)***
Working class			-0.58(.05)***			0.20(.06)**
Left			0.43(.07)***			1.27(.07)***
Right			-0.21(.09)*			-0.22(.19)

Political values

	Variance (std. d.)	Variance (std. d.)	Variance (std. d.)	Variance (std. d.)	Variance (std. d.)	Variance (std. d.)
Left-libertarian r.c.						
Left-authoritarian			-0.33(.06)***			-0.72(.08)***
Right-libertarian			-0.20(.05)***			-0.59(.08)***
Right-authoritarian			-0.30(.05)***			-1.08(.10)***
Random effects	*Variance (std. d.)*	*Variance (std. d.)*	*Variance (std. d.)*	*Variance (std. d.)*	*Variance (std. d.)*	*Variance (std. d.)*
Between-country var σ^2_u	0.62(.79)	0.53(.73)	0.54(.04)	0.59(.77)	0.62(.79)	0.58(.76)
Survey year						
1981	0.17(.41)	0.19(.43)	0.18(.42)	0.04(.20)	0.01(.10)	0.04(.20)
1990 r.c.						
1999	0.27(.51)	0.26(.51)	0.26(.51)	0.08(.29)	0.10(.32)	0.05(.21)
AIC	22,445	21,945	21,669	11,051	10,993	10281
BIC	22,574	22,082	21,867	11,179	11,130	10,477
LogLikelihood	-11,207	-10,956	-10,812	-5,511	-5,481	-5,118
Deviance	22,415	21,913	21,623	11,021	10,961	10,235

Notes
Significance levels:
* $p \leq 0.05$.
** $p \leq 0.01$.
*** $p \leq 0.001$.

Reference categories: Post-WWII cohort (2); 34–50 age group (2); 1990 (2); therefore, 1981 is the inverse of the period effect 1981–1990; Left-libertarian (1); Edu (low) is a dummy variable where 1 means the respondent left school before the age of 17 or completed less than eleven years in FTE; Working class is a dummy variable where 1 means the respondent is an unskilled, semi-skilled or skilled manual worker; Left and right are dummy variables derived from the left-right scale, respectively, values 0/1 and values 9/10.

significantly less likely than the post-WWII generation to participate in new social movement organisations. Controlling for education levels shows that the '80s generation is also significantly less likely than the post-WWII generation to participate in new social movements. Including political values in Model 3 shows that the baby-boomers are significantly less likely than the post-WWII cohort to participate in NSMs. Taken together, these results would suggest that the higher levels of education amongst the '80s generation mean that they are about as likely as the post-WWII cohort to participate in SMOs. Instead, being more educated and being more left-libertarian explains why the baby-boomers are about as likely as the post-WWII cohort to participate in NSMs. Given that the post-WWII cohort was significantly more likely than younger cohorts also to join parties, these results could suggest that this generation is generally more likely than younger cohorts to participate in organisations, regardless of whether they are 'old' or 'new'.

Most importantly, these results show that younger cohorts are not significantly more likely than older cohorts to engage in all types of elite-challenging activities as suggested by the modernisation account. Insofar as the indicators employed here provide a reliable measure of new social movement participation, it appears that this mode of engagement exhibits quite different cohort effects to those for the other protest activities. Moreover, testing for coefficient differences across the three models shows that the '90s generation is significantly less likely than both the baby-boomers and '80s generation to participate in NSMs. In turn, this suggests that this generation is not continuing to participate in this type of activity as previous cohorts. Chapter 4 showed that while NSM participation rose in most countries in the period 1981–1990, it did not continue to rise for 1990–1999 in most countries and, indeed, fell significantly in several countries. Taken together, the findings from that chapter and those from this section would suggest that perhaps NSM participation rose for 1981–1990 as the post-WWII, baby-boomers and '80s generation took up these activities, but that this pattern did not continue or was reversed, in the 1990–1999 period as the post-WWII generation begun to be replaced by the '90s generation, which did not participate at the same rate, in later years. Or perhaps, this activity became less popular and all the cohorts participated in it less. Finally, the effects of the other predictor variables (not age, period and cohort) are more or less identical to those for boycotting and petitioning except that here men and women are about as likely to participate.

The results presented in the previous section provide an interesting summary of the results from the country-by-country analyses from Chapters 5 and 6 extended for the whole of Western Europe. However, it might be asked whether these results are sensitive to the particular theoretical categorisation of cohorts, based on the historic period in which respondents have spent the majority of their formative years, which I have been applying in this study. Rosow (1978: 69) points out that "the general bounding criteria for cohorts cannot be clearly established independent of specific analytic questions to delineate them". This study's distinctions between cohort categories are driven by theoretical considerations (as discussed in detail in Chapters 2 and 3). However, Spitzer (1973: 1358) points out that there is always going to be a boundary problem of where to delineate social generations in the "seamless continuum of daily births" and that there is always unavoidable ambiguity in terms of where to apply the 'cuts'. Rosow (1978: 69) also adds that even where there are specific analytic questions to inform these 'cuts', categorising cohorts based on the historic period of their formative years can still be difficult since "major historical events are soft and indistinct, cohorts may be clearest at their centres, but blurred and fuzzy at the edges". Given these theoretical considerations and the eternal 'blurriness' of cohort boundaries, this section applies generalised additive models (GAMs) to test the sensitivity of results to the specific categorisation of cohorts applied in this study (full details on this statistical technique are available in the Appendix). Evidence is provided that results are robust and not simply the artefact of what might be seen as potentially arbitrary cut-off points for the distinct historic periods of the formative experiences of the five cohorts identified here.

Figure 7.1 plots the smoothed cohort effect on party membership from the EVS 1981–1999. The figure shows that starting from a relatively high level, the

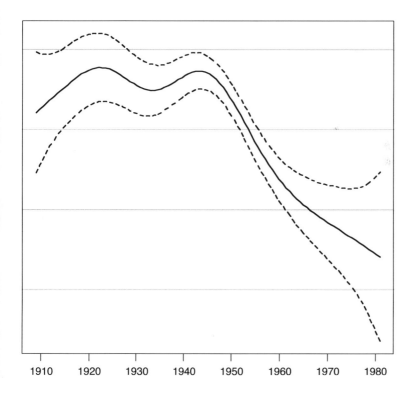

Figure 7.1 Party membership EVS, smoothed cohort effect (GAM).

Note
Generalised additive model; *y*-axis participation; *x*-axis years of birth.

curve slopes down steeply around the mid-1940s, which is just about around the time when the first baby-boomers would have been born, based on my cohort classification schema (i.e. 1947). This confirms the results from the random effects multi-level models for party membership presented in Table 7.1, that the baby-boomers, the '80s and '90s generation are all significantly less likely than the post-WWII cohort to be members of a party. Moreover, it shows that the pre-war generation also exhibit relatively high levels of party membership. This also supports the results from Table 7.1 that there were no significant differences between the pre-WWII and post-WWII cohorts in party membership. Additionally, confirming the results for significant coefficient differences discussed above, Figure 7.1 shows that the curve keeps sloping down over the years of birth of the '80s generation (1958–1968) and those of the '90s generation (1969–1981). This confirms that more recent cohorts are the least likely to join parties.

Figure 7.2 shows the smoothed cohort effects on voting from the ESS 2002–2006. Confirming the results from the multi-level model for voting presented in Table 7.2 that all cohorts were less likely than the post-WWII cohort

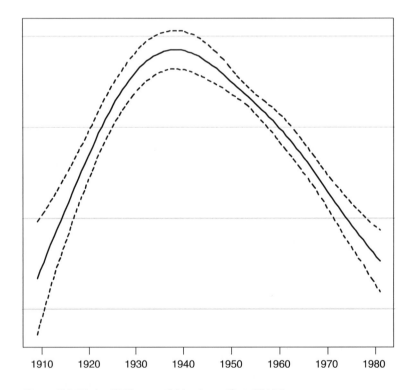

Figure 7.2 Voting EVS, smoothed cohort effect (GAM).

Note

Generalised additive model; *y*-axis participation; *x*-axis years of birth.

to vote, it shows that the peak is situated over the years of birth of the post-WWII cohort: 1926–1945. However, it is worth noting that the results presented in Table 7.2 from the multi-level model show that young people are less likely than middle age people to vote. As such, the downward sloping curve on the right-hand side could be in part attributed to this age effect, since individuals in the '90s generation were almost all in the young age group (the youngest members of this cohort were twenty-one in 2002 and the oldest thirty-seven in 2006). However, for the pre-WWII generation, the age effect would point in the opposite direction and therefore age effects should not confound the cohort effect in this case. The final indicator of conventional political participation examined in this study is contacting a politician, and again Figure 7.3 shows that the results presented in Table 7.2 are confirmed: that individuals born after the mid-1940s are more likely than older cohorts to engage in this type of conventional activity (though the multi-level models showed that for the '80s and '90s generations their higher participation levels in this respect are accounted for by their higher education levels). Here age effects from the multi-level model do not confound the cohort effects since old people are about as likely as

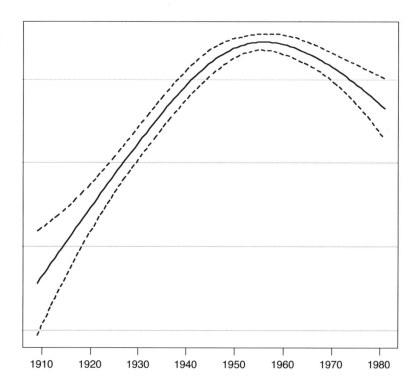

Figure 7.3 Contacting a politician ESS, smoothed cohort effect (GAM).

Note

Generalised additive model; *y*-axis participation; *x*-axis years of birth.

middle age people to contact a politician: in other words, cohort differences could not reflect age differences between the baby-boomers and the pre- and post-WWII cohorts. This confirms the evidence that individuals born since the mid-1940s are more likely than their predecessors to approach their representatives.

Moving on to the indicators of unconventional participation, Figure 7.4 plots the smoothed cohort effect for NSM participation; it shows that the peak is situated between the late 1930s and the early 1950s, sloping down steeply after the 1960s. The years of birth that map onto the peak straddle both the post-WWII and the baby-boomer cohort. Confirming the results from the multi-level models presented in Table 7.6, that the '90s generation was significantly less likely than the post-WWII cohort to participate in NSMs, is the fact that the curve slopes down steeply on the right-hand side right about when the first members of this cohort would have been born. The wide confidence intervals are likely to be due to the small number of cases. Moving onto protest activism, Figure 7.5 plots the smoothed cohort effect for demonstrating; Figure 7.6 that for boycotting; Figure 7.7 that for petitioning; and finally, Figure 7.8 that for occupying.

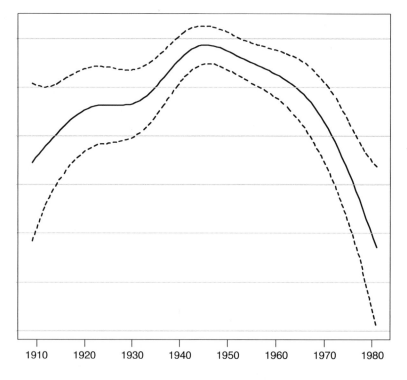

1910   1920   1930   1940   1950   1960   1970   1980

Figure 7.4 NSM participation EVS, smoothed cohort effect (GAM).

Note

Generalised additive model; *y*-axis participation; *x*-axis years of birth.

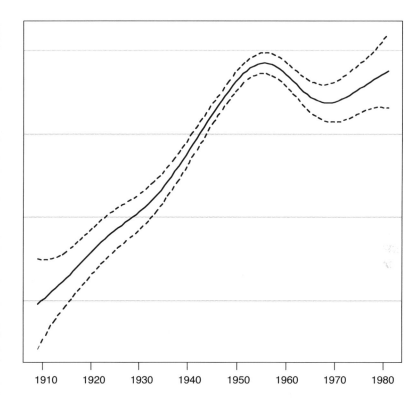

| 1910 | 1920 | 1930 | 1940 | 1950 | 1960 | 1970 | 1980 |

Figure 7.5 Demonstrating EVS, smoothed cohort effect (GAM).

Note
Generalised additive model; y-axis participation; x-axis years of birth.

They all show that in each case the peaks map on quite neatly to the years of birth of the baby-boomers; and that younger cohorts, with the exception of the '90s generation for boycotting, are significantly more likely than the post-WWII cohort to engage in protest activism. Therefore, the application of generalised additive models to map the smoothed cohort effects in this section shows that the results are not biased by the theoretically driven cohort classification applied in this study.

Conclusions

The results presented in this chapter show that the patterns suggested by the country-by-country analyses in Chapters 5 and 6 hold across Western Europe. More specifically, this chapter shows that younger cohorts are significantly less likely than the post-WWII cohort to join a party and vote, but they are significantly more likely than older cohorts to contact a politician. Younger cohorts

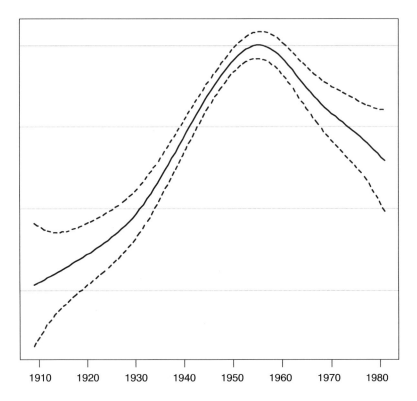

Figure 7.6 Boycotting EVS, smoothed cohort effect (GAM).

Note
Generalised additive model; *y*-axis participation; *x*-axis years of birth.

are thus not less likely than older cohorts to participate in all types of 'elite-directed' participation. Moreover, for unconventional participation, younger cohorts are significantly more likely than older cohorts to engage in protest activism. Yet, amongst the younger cohorts, the baby-boomers are significantly more likely than the '80s and '90s cohorts to demonstrate and significantly more likely than the '90s generation to participate in new social movements and to join a boycott. However, based on the modernisation argument that post-materialist value-change drives rising levels of elite-challenging participation, it would be expected that each younger cohort participate in these sorts of activities more than the previous one, or at least at about the same level. The evidence presented here shows that younger cohorts are significantly less likely than older cohorts to participate in new social movements (or SMOs). Therefore, this indicates that, across Western Europe, younger cohorts are not more likely than older cohorts to participate in all types of 'elite-challenging' participation. Moreover, by applying generalised additive models (GAMs) this chapter tests the sensitivity of results to the cohort categorisation applied in this study and

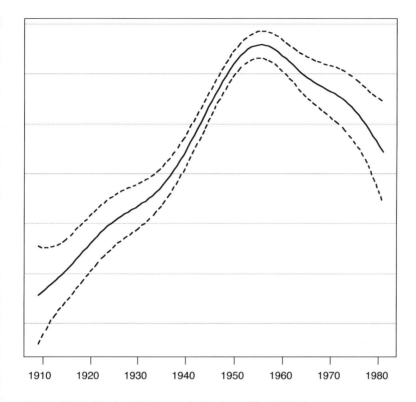

Figure 7.7 Petitioning EVS, smoothed cohort effect (GAM).

Note
Generalised additive model; *y*-axis participation; *x*-axis years of birth.

shows they are robust. Indeed, the results presented here show that the theoretical considerations that contributed to this cohort schema are upheld by the
observed patterns for the non-linear smoothed cohort effects. Members of the
post-WWII generation are those most likely to join a party, vote and participate
in new social movements; but the baby-boomers are significantly more likely
than both the '80s and '90s generation to engage in these activities. The baby-
boomers are significantly more likely than all the other cohorts to contact a politician; but also to engage in three out of four protest activities: demonstrating,
boycotting and occupying. As such, the results presented show that formative
experiences matter: based on this evidence, the baby-boomers, coming of age in
the radicalising period of the late 1960s and 1970s, once more stand out as 'the
protest generation'.

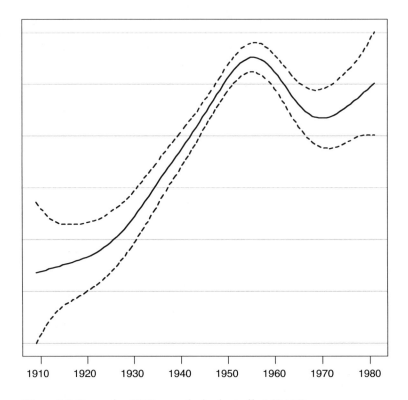

Figure 7.8 Occupying EVS, smoothed cohort effect (GAM).

Note
Generalised additive model; *y*-axis participation; *x*-axis years of birth.

Notes

1 But unlike the Schwarz's Bayesian Information Criterion there are no uncertainties in terms of which sample sizes should be used (Luke 2004).
2 This is accomplished post-regression via the Wald test.
3 Wald test post-regression Model 3 for both EVS 1981–1999 and ESS 2002–2006.

References

Brooks, C. and J. Manza (1994). "Do Changing Values Explain the New Politics? A Critical Assessment of the Postmaterialist Thesis". *The Sociological Quarterly* 35(4): 541–70.

Clarke, H., D. Sanders, M. Stewart and P. Whiteley (2004). *Political Choice in Britain*. Oxford, Oxford University Press.

Della Porta, D. and M. Diani (2006). *Social Movements: An Introduction, 2nd Edition*. Oxford, Blackwell.

Evans, G. and N. D. De Graaf (1996). "Why are the Young More Postmaterialist? A Cross-National Analysis of Individual and Contextual Influences on Postmaterial Values". *Comparative Political Studies* 28(4): 608–35.

Fukuyama, F. (1989). "The End of History?" *The National Interest.*

Grasso, M. T. (2011). *Political Participation in Western Europe.* Nuffield College, University of Oxford. D. Phil. Thesis.

Grasso, M. T. (2013). "The Differential Impact of Education on Young People's Political Activism: Comparing Italy and the United Kingdom". *Comparative Sociology* 12: 1–30.

Grasso, M. T. (2014). "Age-Period-Cohort Analysis in a Comparative Context: Political Generations and Political Participation Repertoires". *Electoral Studies* 33: 63–76.

Inglehart, R. (1990). *Culture Shift in Advanced Industrial Society.* Princeton, Princeton University Press.

Inglehart, R. and G. Catterberg (2002). "Trends in Political Action: The Developmental Trend and the Post-Honeymoon Decline". *International Journal of Comparative Sociology* 43: 300–16.

Kriesi, H. and D. Wisler (1996). "Social Movements and Direct Democracy in Switzerland". *European Journal of Political Research* 30(1): 19–40.

Lipset, S. and S. Rokkan (1967). *Party Systems and Voter Alignments: Cross-national Perspectives.* London, Collier-MacMillan.

Luke, D. (2004). *Multilevel Modelling.* London, Sage.

Mannheim, K. (1928). The Problem of Generations. *Essays on the Sociology of Knowledge.* London, Routledge.

Rosow, I. (1978). "What is a Cohort and Why?" *Human Development* 21: 65–75.

Spitzer, A. B. (1973). "The Historical Problem of Generations". *American Historical Review* 78: 1353–85.

Van Aelst, P. and S. Walgrave (2001). "Who is that (Wo)man in the Street? From the Normalisation of Protest to the Normalisation of the Protester". *European Journal of Political Research* 39: 461–86.

8 The future of political participation in Western Europe

Studies of voter turnout and party membership often suggest that Western publics are becoming increasingly disengaged from conventional politics. At the same time, scholars studying 'unconventional' participation claim that a new form of political engagement is on the ascendant, and will continue to rise as younger, more 'cognitively mobilised' (Inglehart 1990) 'critical citizens' (Norris 1999, 2011), with 'new' value priorities, shun 'elite-directed' forms of engagement in favour of more 'elite-challenging' ones (Inglehart 1977, 1990; Inglehart and Catterberg 2002). The literature develops conflicting narratives on political engagement, a problem which is exacerbated by the fact that theorists from the two schools often talk past each other. In this context, Chapter 4 aimed to paint as unified a picture as possible of Western European participation patterns over the last thirty years or so. It examined over-time patterns for all the available survey indicators of both conventional and unconventional participation, side-by-side. The ten countries studied by this research are undergoing similar processes of modernisation, and are all post-industrial, democratic nations. The modernisation account suggests that the same forces are driving both the established trend of lowering levels of elite-directed activism and that of increasing elite-challenging activism. The implication is that conventional participation should continue to decline, whereas unconventional participation should continue to rise as younger cohorts replace older ones in the population. Moreover, this pattern should be recognisable across advanced democratic countries. The patterns observed should be broadly similar in the ten countries analysed in this study, since they are all advanced industrial democracies.

However, the results presented in previous chapters show that in some countries conventional participation is rising. There are also several declining patterns for unconventional participation, particularly in the post-1990 period. The evidence presented here does not support the idea that the same modernising forces are affecting the various Western European nations in relatively similar ways. It is not a universal trend that elite-challenging participation is becoming increasingly more popular and conventional participation less so. One piece of evidence running counter to this theory is that within the same time intervals, the proportion of individuals participating in many of the political activities analysed is increasing in some countries but decreasing in others. These activities include party membership, party work, union membership, unpaid voluntary work for a union, joining unofficial strikes, demonstrating, boycotting, signing a petition, joining environmental or animal rights organisations, doing unpaid voluntary work for the environmental or animal rights organisations, joining development or human rights organisations, doing unpaid voluntary work for development or human rights organisations. Significantly, in subsequent time periods and within the same countries, participation in 'elite-challenging' activities initially goes up, but then goes down again. This shows that unconventional political participation is not continuing to rise across countries and across the various indicators.

The results presented here suggest that nation-specific political contexts are more important than the 'logic of post-industrialism' (Heath *et al.* 1990) in explaining the observed cross-national variation in over-time patterns of political participation, both conventional and unconventional. The substantial cross-national variation suggests that nation-specific contexts and the actions of parties, the dynamic interaction between political actors and social groups, have an important role to play in explaining the divergent participation trajectories of different nations. Moreover, this evidence does not show elite-challenging activities continuing to rise.

Chapter 5 turned to analysing cohort differences for conventional political participation. It examined whether younger cohorts are less likely than older cohorts to engage in these activities. Thus, it investigated whether generational replacement could explain why 'elite-directed' participation is declining in some countries. As Hooghe (2004: 333) points out: "An implicit assumption in most of the current literature on youth and politics is that youth studies have a wider relevance for the field of political science in general". This suggests that the political orientations of older cohorts, which are shaped in earlier formative periods, are in turn carried along throughout their life-cycles (Jennings 1987). This means that the political behaviours of older adults today reflect their formative experiences in past historic periods, rather than any specific influence of the present political context. Meanwhile, the present political context might be shaping the underlying political orientations of younger adults, as the effect of "these structural transformations is not just easier to detect and observe, it might also have a stronger impact as they were experiences in the formative period of their lives" (Hooghe 2004: 333). As Franklin (2004: 216) expands:

> the future lies in the hands of young people. Young people hold the key to the future because they are the ones who react to new conditions. Older people are, on the whole, too set in their ways ... so most long-term change comes about by way of generational replacement.

In this respect, the results presented in Chapter 5 showed that younger cohorts are, in most countries, less likely than older cohorts to join a party and to vote in national elections. Generation effects are more important than age effects in explaining observed differences in party memberships between cohorts. In France, Germany, Ireland and Great Britain young people are also significantly less likely than people in the middle age group to vote. However, the presence of cohort effects net of period and life-cycle effects suggests that turnout will probably continue to fall in these countries in the future as older cohorts who vote at higher levels are replaced by younger cohorts who vote at lower levels. However, the results show that younger cohorts are not significantly less likely than older cohorts to engage in all types of conventional political activities. Indeed, with the exception of Britain, younger cohorts are actually more likely than older cohorts to contact politicians.

Importantly, the results presented in Chapter 5 show that education plays a mediating role for conventional participation. For party membership, this means that in the absence of the expansion in education witnessed since the 1960s, cohort differences between younger and older cohorts for this activity could have possibly been even more marked. The '80s and '90s cohorts are more likely to contact a politician than older cohorts, which can be accounted for by their relatively higher levels of education (Grasso 2013a). However, this is generally not true of the baby-boomers. This suggests that while the pre- and post-WWII cohorts tend to be more involved in activities pertaining to parties and elections than younger cohorts, that younger cohorts tend to be more involved in more 'consultative' types of conventional political participation. These consultative forms may have risen to prominence as a result of the trends towards more managerial-style politics in many Western European countries, as suggested by some authors (e.g. Mair 2006).

Therefore, these results confirm the findings in previous research that cohort effects have a determinant role to play in explaining why party membership and turnout are falling in many Western nations. However, the configuration of cohort effects would also seem to suggest that other conventional activities, such as contacting politicians, should not be falling in the future. This is based on the fact that younger cohorts tend to be more active than older cohorts with respect to this particular mode of engagement.

The results also showed that while there is still a gender bias for party membership and contacting a politician, that men and women tend to vote at about the same levels. In most countries there are class inequalities in conventional participation, with working class individuals participating less than others. These effects are somewhat weaker for party membership in countries with traditionally strong left-wing subcultures. The analysis also showed that high levels of politicisation on the left-right spectrum increase the chances of joining a party, but that the effect of ideological politicisation is somewhat weaker for contacting a politician and almost negligible for voting across countries. This is consistent with the fact that smaller numbers of individuals join parties. Only the very ideologically polarised join parties, whereas voting is something that almost everyone does, including individuals with more moderate political views. Finally, it was shown that the effect of having different types of political values varies idiosyncratically across countries and conventional activities: voting, joining a party and contacting a politician do not seem to be practiced disproportionately by individuals with specific sets of socio-political values.

In terms of the wider implications, following modernisation, similar processes affecting all Western European democracies in roughly the same way should be driving younger cohorts to shun 'elite-directed' actions. This means that cohort effects should be similar across different types of 'conventional' indicators and that they should be relatively similar across countries. However, the evidence presented here shows that this is not true of all the different types of conventional activities. The evidence presented here is consistent with Mair's (2006) argument that politicians are increasingly becoming more open to consultation and other procedural mechanisms in order to 'engage' the citizenry while at the same time parties decline in importance and turnout and party membership falls since politicians refrain from ideological discourse and therefore downplay the 'popular' component of democracy leading individuals to perceive party politics as irrelevant to their lives since no "issues of vital concern [are] presented" (Boechel 1928: 517). Political context theories emphasise the importance of the actions of parties, politicians and the cost-benefit analysis of individuals, in other words, the interaction between the supply and demand side aspects of political participation, to explain why we should observe different patterns. Therefore, theories suggesting that the nature of democratic politics is changing to one where parties and elections are less important but where procedural, consultative aspects of democracy are emphasised would not be in conflict with these results showing that the '80s and '90s cohorts participate in certain conventional activities more than older cohorts, regardless of the depressing effect of their young age.

Since it was shown in Chapter 4 that aggregate party membership fell in every country except Spain between 1978 and 2000, this would suggest that cohorts coming of age in periods where parties were declining in importance could have been 'impressed' by this experience, and joined parties at lower rates than older cohorts, who came of age during the heyday of party politics. This interpretation would therefore indicate that cohort effects on party membership are relatively similar to those uncovered by Franklin (2004) for turnout: younger cohorts, learning the habit of voting in less competitive contexts, were habituated into voting at lower rates than earlier, more civic, cohorts, therefore explaining aggregate turnout decline. In this sense, the decline of party membership could be explained by the intersection of both period and cohort effects. As parties become less prominent, young people socialised in these periods join parties at lower rates than older cohorts, thus resulting in the decline of party membership in the population as a whole, as older cohorts are replaced by younger cohorts which do not join parties. However, the question remains as to what caused parties to decline in importance in the first place. It is unclear what is prior: declining rates of party membership in the population could lead parties to become less important and for younger cohorts to participate less; however, the actions of parties themselves, making it less appealing for people to join them, could instigate the declining levels of party membership, which in turn would result in younger cohorts getting involved with parties less than their predecessors. Theories concerning the changing nature of democratic politics such as Mair's (2006) would emphasise the role of parties and politicians as the seeds for this change, whereas modernisation theories such as Inglehart's (1990) would identify the rising levels of education and 'cognitive mobilisation' in the population, leading individuals to reject 'elite-directed' modes of participation as being the initial drivers of this transformative process. It is not in the scope of this study to adjudicate between these two explanations, but simply to suggest that whereas the political context explanation can account for why younger cohorts are less likely than older cohorts to join parties and vote, but are at the same time more likely to engage in other conventional or elite-directed modes of participation, the modernisation hypothesis would suggest that younger cohorts should be less likely to participate in all types of conventional political activities relative to older cohorts. As such, at least based on the evidence offered in this study, explanations which focus on the changing political context would seem to better conform to the patterns uncovered.

Chapter 6 turned to examining whether younger cohorts are more likely than older cohorts to engage in various types of unconventional or 'elite-challenging' participation. The results showed that the baby-boomers are in most countries more likely than the post-WWII cohort to demonstrate and sign a petition and, to a lesser extent, to join a boycott. Differences between each of the '80s and '90s generations and the post-WWII cohort were much less marked than those between the baby-boomers and the post-WWII cohort for these activities. Where differences between the '80s/'90s cohort and the post-WWII generation were significant, they were generally accounted for by higher education levels of those cohorts. The same was not generally true of the baby-boomers. Therefore, the argument that all the younger cohorts should be engaging in elite-challenging activities more than older cohorts and that this should not be attributable to education alone is not universally supported with respect to protest activism based on the evidence presented here, and more so for demonstrating.

This suggests that formative experiences which set the baby-boomers apart from later cohorts are probably what explains their higher participatory patterns, as suggested by Della Porta and Diani (2006). Moreover, it appears that the fact that "subsequent political contexts differed greatly" (Della Porta and Diani 2006: 65) has had a depressing impact on the likelihood of cohorts coming of age in later periods to demonstrate and participate in other protest activities. Therefore, the results presented in Chapter 6 showed that the context of formative years matters and that the baby-boomers are still 'the protest generation'. Differences between the '80s generation and the post-WWII cohort were more marked in later periods for boycotting and for petitioning, but even here differences between the baby-boomers and the post-WWII cohort were greater. Again, education plays a mediating role for participation, but less so for the baby-boomers than the other cohorts.

Including education in the models showed that taking their higher education level into account, the '90s generation was less likely than the post-WWII generation to boycott. As for participation in social movement organisations (SMOs), in no country is any one of the younger cohorts more likely than the post-WWII cohort to participate in new social movements (NSMs). In four countries, younger cohorts are less likely than the post-WWII cohort to participate in SMOs. Gender inequalities are negligible in this mode of engagement.

Results showed that participation in NSMs appears to be strongly biased against people in manual occupations. Since their flagship concerns are meant to be those of the 'new middle class' perhaps this is not so surprising (Grasso and Giugni 2013, Grasso and Giugni 2015, Grasso and Giugni 2016). Moreover, in Denmark and Sweden, Italy and Spain, and as was the case for party membership (Chapter 5), having a manual occupation did not have a negative effect on demonstrating and boycotting, suggesting that at least in those countries with traditionally strong left-wing subcultures class inequalities in participation are weak for these repertoires and, therefore, that 'unconventional' participation might provide such generally under-represented groups with more opportunities for say on the running of society, or at the very least 'oppositional space' in the democratic arena. Class inequalities were also negligible for petitioning in six out of ten countries, although this is probably due to the fact that this activity is more or less universal due to its cheapness and ubiquity. Moreover, while men are more likely to demonstrate, this effect is reversed or no longer significant for boycotting and petitioning in the later period.

Strong left-wing identifiers were in all cases more likely to engage in protest activities than others. However, unlike with conventional participation, strong right-wing identifiers were, in several countries, less likely than others to engage in elite-challenging participation. Additionally, while left-libertarians are more likely than the other economic-social value groups to engage in protest activism in the earlier period, right-libertarians are about as likely to join boycotts and to petition for the later period. This suggests that other values may have become more prominent levers than economic considerations for engagement in these activities in more recent years. Therefore, in this limited respect, there is some evidence that, as suggested by Inglehart (1990: 374), the meaning of 'Left' may have changed in more recent years to include value considerations, and that "except in the very general sense ... the traditional and contemporary meanings of 'Left' are very different".

Taken together, the results presented in Chapter 6 suggested that the baby-boomers are rather distinctive in being significantly more likely than the post-WWII generation to engage in the various types of protest activities and more so since their higher levels of participation are not generally accounted for simply by their higher levels of education relative to this older cohort. Thereby, the evidence presented in this chapter showed that at least for protest activism, the baby-boomers' formative experiences in the radicalising period of the late 1960s and 1970s left a lasting imprint on their political behaviour patterns (Grasso 2014). However, neither the baby-boomers nor, the even younger '80s and '90s cohorts are more likely than the post-WWII cohort to participate in NSMs. Similarly to the results presented in Chapter 5 for conventional participation (where it was shown that younger cohorts were more likely than older cohorts to contact a politician), this suggests that modernisation arguments purporting that similar influences should be drawing younger cohorts to engage more in elite-challenging participation and less in elite-directed activities than older generations, do not hold across indicators included in these two groups. Therefore, it seems that other, more specific mechanisms might fare better for explaining generational differences in participation.

By analysing cohort differences across Western Europe for eight indicators of political participation side by side in Chapter 7, we provide a more unified and consistent account of these patterns. The results presented in Chapter 7 showed that the patterns suggested by the country-by-country analyses in Chapters 5 and 6 held across Western Europe. More specifically, Chapter 7 showed that younger cohorts are less likely than the post-WWII cohort to join a party and vote, but that they are more likely than older cohorts to contact a politician. As such, younger cohorts are not less likely than older cohorts to participate in all types of 'elite-directed' participation as modernisation arguments would suggest. Moreover, for unconventional participation, younger cohorts are more likely than older cohorts to engage in protest activism, but, amongst the younger cohorts, the baby-boomers are more likely than the '80s and '90s cohorts to demonstrate and occupy, and more likely than the '90s generation to participate in NSMs and to join a boycott. However, based on modernising trends and post-materialist value-change driving rising levels of elite-challenging participation, one would expect each younger cohort to participate in these sorts of activities more than the previous one, or at least at about the same level. Younger cohorts were less likely than older cohorts to participate in NSMs (or SMOs). This indicated that, across Europe, younger cohorts are not more likely than older cohorts to participate in all types of 'elite-challenging' participation. Moreover, generalised additive models were applied to test the sensitivity of results to the cohort categorisation applied in this study. The theoretical considerations which contributed to this cohort schema were upheld by the observed patterns for non-linear smoothed cohort effects. Therefore, the results from Chapter 7 further suggested that formative experiences matter: the baby-boomers, coming of age in the radicalising period of the late 1960s and 1970s, stand out as 'the protest generation' (Grasso 2011, Grasso 2014). They are more likely than any of the other cohorts to demonstrate, boycott and occupy. But they are also more likely than all the other cohorts to contact a politician. Moreover, while members of the post-WWII generation are those most likely to join a party, vote and participate in NSMs, the baby-boomers are nonetheless more likely than both the '80s and '90s generation to engage in these activities.

To summarise, this study examined whether Western European publics are experiencing a decline in 'conventional' or 'elite-directed' political participation, associated with political parties and electoral politics, and a rise in 'unconventional' or 'elite-challenging' participation, associated with protest activism and the emergence of NSMs since the mid-to-late 1960s. The research investigated whether empirical evidence conforms to the expectations of prominent theories which cite intergenerational replacement as an explanation for changing patterns of political participation in advanced, post-industrial Western democracies, by investigating if younger cohorts (the baby-boomer, '80s and '90s generations) are less likely to participate in 'conventional' activities in favour of 'unconventional' activities, relative to older cohorts (the pre- and post-WWII generations). The research analysed ten advanced, post-industrial Western European democracies: Belgium, Denmark, France, Germany, Great Britain, Ireland, Italy, the Netherlands, Spain and Sweden and showed that there is substantial cross-national variation in patterns of participation. Against expectations, 'conventional' political participation is rising in some countries. In many countries, 'unconventional' participation remains stable or declines post-1990. This means that rather than modernisation affecting all countries in the same way, nation-specific political contexts have a role to play for explaining over-time changes in patterns of participation. Moreover, generational differences in participation did not conform to the standard expectations in the literature. Younger cohorts are more likely than older cohorts to participate in certain types of 'conventional' or 'elite-directed' activities (contacting a politician), whereas they are less likely than older cohorts to participate in certain kinds of 'unconventional' or 'elite-challenging' participation (NSM-organisation involvement). Amongst the three youngest cohorts, the (older) baby-boomers, coming of age in the radicalising period the late 1960s and 1970s, and not the '80s or '90s generation, are the most likely to demonstrate and engage in other protest activities. This means that 'elite-challenging' participation will not continue to rise. Moreover, generalised additive models plotting the non-linear smoothed cohort effects tested the sensitivity of results to the cohort schema applied in this study, showing that they are robust. Therefore, we conclude that across Western Europe the baby-boomers are still 'the protest generation'. As such, this study provides further evidence to show that the formative experiences of specific generations in different socio-historic political contexts matter, and differentiate generations in their patterns of political participation many years later.

In light of this, future research should continue to keep the various indicators of political participation in disaggregated form as far as possible. Rather than assuming that diverse activities fall in the same broad groupings, such as conventional or unconventional participation, and that therefore they will be subject to similar age, period and cohort effects, this is something which should, as far as possible, be tested empirically (Caren *et al.* 2011). Therefore, rather than applying predefined theoretical classifications and constructing scales, it would be preferable to examine different activities in their own right. This is more so, since participation is historically specific and the meanings and contextualisation of different modes of engagement evolve over time and vary between countries. Additionally, rather than aggregating data and looking at patterns for the whole of Western Europe, or the totality of 'post-industrial' democracies, cross-national differences should be examined first, and rather than simply analysing data via pooled regression analysis, the correct multi-level models should be specified to take into account, via random effects, those variables which vary at the country level (Grasso 2014). Moreover, in future research, explanations for country-level variations could be investigated by including higher-level predictors in such models. Additionally, variables capturing different aspects of the political context at the time of socialisation of different cohorts, and also capturing key elements that could be contributing to the observed variation in period effects, could be included. Other variables could include party ideological distance, the polarisation of the electorate, and many other 'opportunity structure' factors which have traditionally been discussed in the literature on NSMs (Grasso and Giugni 2013, Giugni and Grasso 2015a, Giugni and Grasso 2015b, Grasso and Giugni 2016).

Another key point which was emphasised in this research is that only indicators of actual participation should be included in studies of participation. Protest potential questions tell us more about the education levels and tolerant attitudes of individuals than about whether respondents have or will actually participate in the various political activities. And since younger cohorts tend to be more highly educated and to have more tolerant outlooks, these types of indicators could easily overestimate their propensity for actual participation (Grasso 2011).

Moreover, integrating data from other sources, such as protest event-analysis and interviews with protesters at demonstrations (Van Aelst and Walgrave 2001) and the more recently developed protest survey data,[1] to study demonstrators and cohort differences in this salient type of 'unconventional' participation could be a fruitful avenue for future research (see for example Saunders, Grasso *et al.* 2012).

With respect to indicators that were not investigated in detail in this study, the question of union membership and whether this should count as a *political* activity should be examined in a cross-nationally comparative context. The question of whether union members are strongly politicised, and whether there are important cross-national and cohort differences in this respect, is an area which could open up interesting avenues for future research. Additionally, one could investigate the intensity of participation rather than its incidence, or the number of different activities individuals engage in, regardless of the specific domain. Moreover, the availability of new data not only provides exciting opportunities for further research on generational differences in participation, but also for examining how cohorts differ in terms of their political attitudes and how these relate to their participatory propensities. Future studies should examine in greater detail the relationship between political values, including post-materialism, and various types of political activism, but also politicisation on the left-right spectrum and the question of whether having progressive values continues to be a strong predictor of protest (but see also Giugni and Grasso 2016 on the effect of activism on values).

Finally, there are a number of areas of crucial substantive interest that have been successfully uncovered through the detailed empirical analyses of political participation in Western Europe carried out in the course of this study. This final section therefore draws together the various (and often conflicting) narratives on political participation in the classic and contemporary literature with a particular focus on the salient role of generational differences. We summarise the key substantive conclusions of this study and contextualise them in relation to the broader patterns of participation in Western societies. We also bring to the fore the fundamental problems with some of the central assumptions traditionally held by scholars of political participation. In turn, challenging these assumptions and their corollary implications provides the basis for a wider discussion of the considerable implications of the results of this study for what we might expect in terms of the future of political participation in post-industrial societies.

The patterns of participation of Western European publics have undergone widespread changes since the 1960s. The two key patterns identified in the literature in this respect are the decline of participation in 'conventional' activities associated with political parties and electoral politics (Blais *et al.* 2004; Dalton and Wattenberg 2000; Franklin 2004; Gray and Caul 2000; Heath and Taylor 1999) and the rise of 'unconventional' repertoires including protest activism and participation in SMOs (Inglehart 1977, 1990; Inglehart and Catterberg 2002; Norris 2002; Topf 1995). While citizens' willingness to engage in party-mediated activities is said to have deteriorated in recent decades (Mair 2006; Rogers 2005; Schmitt and Holmberg 1995; Wattenberg 2002), novel channels of participation are seen to have flourished in what has been heralded as 'the social movement society' (Meyer and Tarrow 1998) developing out of the student revolts of *Mai 1968*. While turnout decline has been well-documented and political parties are said to have been 'haemorrhaging members' (Mair and Van Biezen 2001), those participatory repertoires – marches, rallies, demonstrations, occupations, sit-ins and other forms of public protest – once perceived to be the sole remit of 'anti-state rebels' (Norris *et al.* 2005) are said to have become widespread and 'normalised' (Van Aelst and Walgrave 2001) in contemporary Western democracies.

Given the character of these transformations, it is perhaps unsurprising that generational replacement is often cited as the key mechanism underpinning these wide-ranging changes in the participation patterns of Western European publics. As Franklin (2004: 216) points out: "older people are, on the whole, too set in their ways to be responsible for social and political change, so most long-term change comes about by way of generational replacement". A substantial literature shows that generations are distinguished by their political attitudes and behaviour (e.g. Abramson and Inglehart 1992; Andersen and Fetner 2008; Heath and Park 1997; Mattei *et al.* 1990). The decline in 'conventional' participation is often understood as the result of older, more civic and participatory cohorts being replaced in the population by younger cohorts participating at lower levels (Putnam 2000). Franklin's (2004) account emphasises the importance of changes in institutional arrangements (and primarily the lowering of the voting age) for the resulting lower levels of turnout amongst more recent cohorts of voters. Additionally, other explanations for this phenomenon have also been offered in the literature (Blais *et al.* 2004; Fieldhouse *et al.* 2007; Plutzer 2002). Moreover, Hooghe (2004: 332) points out how "turnout figures are not the only indicators corroborating the observation that the relation between young people and institutionalised party politics is under serious stress"; younger cohorts are also less likely to be party members, to closely identify with parties and to engage in other 'conventional' activities.

At the same time, 'unconventional' participation is seen to be in continuous expansion as a result of the entry into the political arena of younger, more highly educated and protest-prone cohorts since the mid-to-late 1960s. Barnes and Kaase (1979) were the pioneers of this new area of study. Through the analysis of novel and rich data, their seminal work examined the potential for protest amongst the publics of five advanced industrialised nations. They found that 'unconventional' political participation was "characteristic of youth" and "reinforced by increasing levels of education" (Barnes and Kaase 1979: 524). This led them to "interpret this increase in potential for protest to be a lasting characteristic of democratic mass publics and not just a sudden surge in political involvement bound to fade away as time goes by" (1979: 524). They argued that Western societies were "facing a generational impact that will be increasingly apparent as the well-educated young march down the corridors of time" while also acknowledging "the potential bias introduced ... by tacitly assuming that we are mostly dealing with generational changes and not life-cycle phenomena" and by not being able to "safely exclude the possibility of substantial period effects contaminating ... findings" (1979: 524).

Bridging the two narratives, Inglehart and Catterberg (2002: 302) have recently argued that: "a major change is taking place.... As younger, better-educated, and more Postmaterialist cohorts replace older ones in the adult population, intergenerational population replacement will tend to bring a shift toward increasingly participant publics".

Similarly, Norris (2002: xi) argues that "it is all too easy to equate change with decline". She suggests instead that, citizens, and young ones in particular, are simply shifting from "the politics of loyalties" to "the politics of choice"; from 'citizen-oriented' to 'cause-oriented' repertoires of political participation. In summary, the argument is that while 'elite-directed' (conventional) participation declines, 'elite-challenging' (unconventional) participation will continue to rise in post-industrial nations since younger, more 'cognitively mobilised' 'postmaterialist' cohorts prefer to participate via this repertoire (Inglehart 1977, 1990; Inglehart and Catterberg 2002).

However, "younger cohorts" will be made up of different individuals at different points in time and "younger cohorts" observed at one point in time will be the "older cohorts" of subsequent studies. In his seminal essay on *The Problem of Generations*, Mannheim (1928: 232) argued that "youth experiencing the same concrete historical problems may be said to be part of the same actual generation". These experiences are understood to crystallise and differentiate generations in the population even as they mature through the life-course. Similarly to Mannheim (1928), Becker (1990: 2; 1992: 222) defined a generation as "the grouping ... characterised by a specific historical setting and by common characteristics". As Van Den Broek (1995: 4) explains, Becker "contended that the formative periods of members of successive cohorts took place in historical eras that differed to such an extent that five distinct generations emerged, diverging in biographical characteristics, value orientations and behavioural patterns". For Becker, these generations were the pre-war generation (born between 1910 and 1930), the silent generation (1931–1940), the protest generation (1941–1955), the lost generation (1956–1970) and the pragmatic generation (born after 1970).

In his classic study on the ageing of the American protest generation, Jennings (1987: 368) explained how:

Individuals coming of age during periods of pronounced stress and drama, epochal events or rapid socio-economic change are often said to be uniquely identified in a political sense – hence such labels as the 'depression generation', the 'silent generation', and 'the protest generation'.

He added: "in many respects the so-called protest generation provides an acid test of the [generational] thesis, for during its formative time it possessed strong political preferences, shared experiences, a common enemy, direct political action, and solidarity" (Jennings 1987: 368).

The question was thus "how this cohort, distinguished by its espousal of causes and its forceful efforts to achieve results, would fare as it marched through time" (Jennings 1987: 367). Following Mannheim's (1928) account of political generations as distinguished by their formative experiences in divergent socio-historic contexts at the time of socialisation, and in respect to Jenning's (1987) crucial question, I hypothesised in this study that the baby-boom generation, coming of age in the tumultuous period of the late 1960s and 1970s, would still be 'the protest generation' and exhibit distinctive participatory proclivities departing from those of cohorts coming of age in radically different historical phases, net of life-cycle and period effects.

Importantly, Mannheim (1928: 226) also pointed out how: "nothing is more false than the usual assumption uncritically shared by most students of generations, that the younger generation is progressive and the older generation eo ipso conservative". He argued instead:

> whether youth will be conservative, reactionary or progressive depends (if not entirely, at least primarily) on whether or not the existing social structure and the position they occupy in it provide opportunities for the promotion of their social and intellectual ends.
>
> (Mannheim 1928: 226)

At the time of the Political Action Study, Barnes and Kaase (1979) were examining a particularly special "younger cohort": the baby-boom generation coming of age in the tumultuous socio-historical period of the late 1960s and 1970s. Crucially, the fact that the baby-boom generation was so large, and that the key works predicting an intergenerational shift in political participation (Barnes and Kaase 1979; Inglehart 1977) emerged when this cohort was still young, led scholars to confuse the distinctive political participatory proclivities of 'the protest generation' with an emerging societal trend, one that would be extended and expanded by each successive younger cohort. Today, the baby-boomers are no longer young, and new cohorts, such as the generations coming of age in the 1980s and then 1990s, have subsequently taken their place as the "younger cohorts" in society.

Della Porta and Diani (2006: 1) described how: "in the late 1960s, the world was apparently undergoing deep, dramatic transformations, even a revolution, some thought". Events such as

American civil rights and antiwar movements, the Mai 1968 revolt in France, students' protests in Germany, Britain, or Mexico, the worker-student coalitions of the 1969 'Hot Autumn' in Italy ... all these phenomena ... suggested that deep changes were in the making.

(Della Porta and Diani 2006: 1)

In turn, these "social transformations and events of particular relevance ... produced an irreversible change in conceptions of social and political life, and that a new generation of citizens ... was formed" (Della Porta and Diani 2006: 69). Therefore, "It would thus be possible to speak of a 1960s generation, just as one speaks of generations when referring to the events of 1848, of the post-Victorian era, or of the Great Depression of the 1920s and 1930s" (Della Porta and Diani 2006: 69).

Taking as a starting point these arguments in the literature, this study investigated to what extent the baby-boomers, experiencing their formative years in the tumultuous late 1960s and 1970s, are still distinctive in their patterns of political participation relative to previous and later generations. More generally, this study analysed whether the evidence for generational differences in various types of political activities in Western Europe conformed to the patterns expected by prominent theories which cite generational replacement as an explanation for declining levels of 'conventional' participation and rising 'unconventional' participation in post-industrial democracies.

In this respect, this study showed that the divergent formative experiences of generations in subsequent historical contexts distinguish them in their patterns of political involvement many years later. The fact that conventional political participation is declining sharply in some countries (France, Germany, Ireland and Great Britain) but not so dramatically in others, and that younger cohorts, particularly the '80s and '90s generations, are less likely to vote and to join parties than older cohorts, suggests that the changes in the role of parties and the character of elections in the period of their formative years, have negatively affected the political socialisation of these younger generations, leaving a lasting negative 'imprint' on their patterns of participation.

If parties no longer perform the function of representing citizens' interests and of inspiring people with their grand-narratives for social progress, then it is not surprising that younger generations perceive voting or joining a party as ineffective means for achieving collective objectives (Grasso 2016). This means that if the present political conditions do not change and therefore new generations of young people continue to experience their political socialisation in contexts where joining political parties or voting are, often correctly, perceived as ineffective vehicles for change, it is very likely that conventional political participation will continue to fall as older, more participatory, cohorts die out and are replaced by new cohorts socialised in radically different political contexts (Grasso 2011, Grasso 2013b).

We know from previous studies that political habits are formed in young adulthood and persist through the life-cycle (Plutzer 2002). Older cohorts are more participatory because, unlike younger cohorts, they were socialised at times when parties and voting mattered and therefore they formed participatory political habits at a young age. Moreover, the evidence uncovered in this study that younger cohorts are more likely than older cohorts to contact a politician can be seen as adding further evidence to this point if contacting politicians is taken as a sign of dissatisfaction with representatives and the political system. Future research should examine whether those individuals who engage in this activity express attitudes which suggest that they are dissatisfied with party politics. Future studies should also investigate whether, as was found here, new data confirm that the youngest cohorts continue to be the least likely to vote and join parties. This would suggest that, in the absence of a radical reorganisation of political life, 'conventional' participation is set to continue to fall in the future. If younger cohorts increasingly disengage from formal politics this should signal to politicians that they must exit 'the beltway' – if they want future popular engagement.

Furthermore, Mannheim's (1928) idea that formative experiences in a specific political context leave a lasting imprint on generational patterns of participation sits well with the key finding from this study that the baby-boomers are distinguished from other cohorts by virtue of still being a highly participatory 'protest generation'. This theory can account for why the '80s and '90s cohorts do not match the baby-boomers in their levels of unconventional participation despite the fact that they are younger and also have higher education levels (Grasso 2013a).

The formative years of the baby-boomers (1966–1977) were marked by high levels of political militancy and ideological polarisation across Western Europe. Left-wing movements and parties were strong and young people for the first time emerged as a force in society. One need not even look at far as the *Mai 1968* uprisings in Paris to see that the late 1960s and 1970s were a period of social upheaval when many structural transformations were coming to the fore. The Cold War was in full sway and youth organisations emerged to challenge the perceived hypocrisy of both ideological blocs.

The baby-boomers also experienced rising societal affluence, the boom of mass production and the expansion of higher education. For the first time, young people from various social groups came together, sharing ideas and experiences, but also fighting together to redress common grievances. In particular, this generation did not have obvious conventional routes (the voting age was still twenty-one) to challenge the traditional structures of authority which confronted it. And in a sense, challenging what was already there in itself demanded that the methods employed be also new. However, this period of unbridled optimism soon dissipated, and the late 1970s brought with them economic crisis and mass youth unemployment.

The socialisation experiences of the '80s generation were thus quite different from those of the baby-boomers. Several scholars labelled them 'the Lost Generation' since the unfavourable societal conditions at the time of their youth meant that they were unable to enjoy many of the advantages of the previous generation. Moreover, by the time the '90s generation was coming of age the political landscape had changed a great deal with the end of the Cold War. The Left was very weak across Western Europe and parties recoiled from grand-ideological narratives, preferring instead to focus on more technocratic questions, characteristic of what Francis Fukuyama termed the phase of 'the End of History'. Given the very different historical contexts of socialisation of these three younger cohorts, it should come as no great surprise that the baby-boomers are still 'the protest generation'.

Crucially, the fact that the baby-boom generation was so large, and that the key works predicting an intergenerational shift in political participation (Barnes and Kaase 1979; Inglehart 1977) emerged when this cohort was still young, seems to have led scholars to confuse the distinctive political participatory proclivities of 'the protest generation' with an emerging societal trend, one that would be extended and expanded by each successive younger cohort, as argued by Inglehart and Catterberg (2002). Today, the baby-boomers are no longer young, and new cohorts, such as the generations coming of age in the '80s and '90s, have subsequently taken their place as the "younger cohorts" in society. The results of this study thus also suggest that, unless a new 'protest generation' emerges, unconventional participation may also begin to decline as the baby-boomers come to be replaced by less protest-prone cohorts in the population.

Even if unconventional participation does not decline in the future, it remains unclear how demonstrating, signing a petition, joining a boycott or becoming a member of an environmental/animal rights or third world development organisation can be seen as effective as a functioning representative system in equally reflecting the political demands of the demos and in promoting social change and reform. First, there are concerns that, being disproportionately practiced by highly educated, wealthy middle-class activists, these forms of activism promote political agendas that are not actually representative of public demands and therefore that the move from 'conventional' to 'unconventional' participation may further exacerbate political inequalities in society (Grasso 2016).

Political parties have traditionally been understood as the essential vehicles for representative democratic government (Schattschneider 1942). This is since they articulate collective interests on behalf of the various social groups in society (traditionally, social classes) and translate them into political programmes and decision-making. It does not follow that as citizens adapt to new conditions in modern societies, unconventional participation will come to fulfil the essential democratic representative functions which conventional political participation has traditionally channelled. Therefore, the decline of conventional political participation remains a grave concern for democratic practice despite any gains in unconventional participation.

As the patterns of participation of Western European publics have undergone widespread changes since the 1960s, the two most significant patterns identified have the decline of participation in 'conventional' activities associated with political parties and electoral politics, and the rise of 'unconventional' repertoires, including protest activism and participation in social movement organisations (SMOs) (Giugni and Grasso 2015a). Across post-industrial Western democracies, a process of societal modernisation is considered the driving force of these twin trends. This book studied this phenomenon of changing patterns of political participation and argued that there are strong reasons to be worried about the health of democracy in advanced industrial societies. The evidence presented in this book shows that while 'conventional' or 'formal' political participation is set to continue to decline in the future, 'unconventional' or 'informal' political participation cannot make up for this loss in democratic capability. First, this is since protest and participation in SMOs cannot replace a functioning democratic system. Second, since informal political participation is also likely decline in the future once the active, politicised baby-boomers age. The health of democracy in advanced industrial societies can only be rescued by a new, politicised activist generation. Only time will tell if the current context of deepening global inequality in the aftermath of the 2008 financial crisis will lead to the emergence of a new 'protest generation'.

Note

1 The 'Caught in the Act of Protest: Contextualizing Contestation' project (08-ECRP-001) collected (and continues to collect) these types of data at protests across Europe. See the project website for more details: www.protestsurvey.eu/.

References

Abramson, P. and R. Inglehart (1992). "Generational Replacement and Value Change in Eight Western European Societies". *British Journal of Political Science* 22(2): 183–228.

Andersen, R. and T. Fetner (2008). "Cohort Differences in Tolerance of Homosexuality: Attitudinal Change in Canada and the United States, 1981–2000". *Public Opinion Quarterly* 72(2): 311–30.

Barnes, S. and M. Kaase (1979). *Political Action: Mass Participation in Five Western Societies*. Thousand Oaks, CA, Sage.

Becker, H. A. (1990). Dynamics of Life Histories and Generations Research. *Life Histories and Generations*. H. A. Becker. Utrecht, ISOR.

Becker, H. A. (1992). A Pattern of Generations and its Consequences. *Dynamics of Cohorts and Generations Research*. H. A. Becker. Amsterdam, Thesis Publishers.

Blais, A., E. Gidengil and N. Nevitte (2004). "Where Does Turnout Decline Come from?" *European Journal of Political Research* 43: 221–36.

Boechel, R. (1928). *Voting and Non-Voting in Elections*. Washington, DC, Editorial Research Reports.

Caren, N., R. A. Ghoshalb, *et al.* (2011). "A Social Movement Generation Cohort and Period Trends in Protest Attendance and Petition Signing". *American Sociological Review* 76(1): 125–151.

Dalton, R. and M. Wattenberg (2000). *Parties without Partisans: Political Change in Advanced Industrial Democracies*. Oxford, Oxford University Press.

Della Porta, D. and M. Diani (2006). *Social Movements: An Introduction, 2nd Edition*. Oxford, Blackwell.

Fieldhouse, E., M. Tranmer and A. Russell (2007). "Something about Young People or Something about Elections? Electoral Participation of Young People in Europe: Evidence from a Multilevel Analysis of the European Social Survey". *European Journal of Political Research* 46: 797–822.

Franklin, M. N. (2004). *Voter Turnout and the Dynamics of Electoral Competition in Established Democracies since 1945*. Cambridge, Cambridge University Press.

Giugni, M. G. and M. T. Grasso (2015a). "Environmental Movements in Advanced Industrial Democracies: Heterogeneity, Transformation, and Institutionalization". *Annual Review of Environment and Resources* 40: 337–61.

Giugni, M. G. and M. T. Grasso, Eds. (2015b). *Austerity and Protest: Popular Contention in Times of Economic Crisis*. Farnham, Surrey, Ashgate.

Giugni, M. G. and M. T. Grasso (2016). The Biographical Impact of Participation in Social Movement Activities: Beyond Highly Committed New Left Activism. *The Consequences of Social Movements*. L. Bosi, M. G. Giugni and K. Uba, Eds. Cambridge, Cambridge University Press.

Grasso, M. T. (2011). *Political Participation in Western Europe*. Nuffield College, University of Oxford. D. Phil. Thesis.

Grasso, M. T. (2013a). "The Differential Impact of Education on Young People's Political Activism: Comparing Italy and the United Kingdom". *Comparative Sociology* 12: 1–30.

Grasso, M. T. (2013b). "What Are the Distinguishing Generational, Life Course, and Historical Drivers of Changing Identities? Future Identities: Changing Identities in the UK – The Next 10 Years". *Foresight: The Future of Identity in the UK*. London, The Government Office for Science.

Grasso, M. T. (2014). "Age-Period-Cohort Analysis in a Comparative Context: Political Generations and Political Participation Repertoires". *Electoral Studies* 33: 63–76.

Grasso, M. T. (2016). Political Participation. *Developments in British Politics 10*. R. Heffernan, P. Cowley and C. Hay, Eds. Basingstoke, Palgrave Macmillan.

Grasso, M. T. and M. Giugni (2013). Anti-austerity movements: Old wine in new vessels? Working Paper, XXVII Meeting of the Italian Political Science Association (SISP), University of Florence. Florence, September 12–14.

Grasso, M. T. and M. G. Giugni (2015). Are Anti-Austerity Movements Old or New? *Austerity and Protest: Popular Contention in Times of Economic Crisis*. M. G. Giugni and M. T. Grasso, Eds. Farnham, Surrey, Ashgate.

Grasso, M. T. and M. Giugni (2016). "Do Issues Matter? Anti-Austerity Protests' Composition, Values, and Action Repertoires Compared". *Research in Social Movements, Conflicts and Change* 39.

Gray, M. and M. Caul (2000). "Declining Voter Turnout in Advanced Industrial Democracies, 1950–1997. The Effects of Declining Group Mobilisation". *Comparative Political Studies* 33: 1091–1122.

Heath, A. and A. Park (1997). Thatcher's Children? *British Social Attitudes: The End of Conservative values? (the 14th Report)*. R. Jowell. London, Sage: 1–22.

Heath, A. and B. Taylor (1999). New Sources of Abstention? *Critical Elections: British Parties and Elections in Long-Term Perspective*. G. Evans and P. Norris. London, Sage.

Heath, A., R. Jowell, J. Curtice and G. Evans (1990). "The Rise of the New Political Agenda?" *European Sociological Review* 6(1): 31–48.

Hooghe, M. (2004). "Political Socialisation and the Future of Politics". *Acta Politica* 39: 331–41.

Inglehart, R. (1977). *The Silent Revolution: Changing Values and Political Styles among Western Publics*. Princeton, Princeton University Press.

Inglehart, R. (1990). *Culture Shift in Advanced Industrial Society*. Princeton, Princeton University Press.

Inglehart, R. and G. Catterberg (2002). "Trends in Political Action: The Developmental Trend and the Post-Honeymoon Decline". *International Journal of Comparative Sociology* 43: 300–16.

Jennings, M. K. (1987). "Residues of a Movement: The Aging of the American Protest Generation". *The American Political Science Review* 81(2): 367–82.

Mair, P. (2006). "Ruling the Void? The Hollowing of Western Democracy". *New Left Review* 42: 25–51.

Mair, P. and I. Van Biezen (2001). "Party Membership in Twenty European Democracies, 1980–2000". *Party Politics* 7(1): 5–21.

Mannheim, K. (1928). The Problem of Generations. *Essays on the Sociology of Knowledge*. London, Routledge.

Mattei, F., R. G. Niemi and G. Powell (1990). "On the Depth and Persistence of Generational Change: Evidence from Italy". *Comparative Political Studies* 23(3): 334–54.

Meyer, D. and S. Tarrow, Eds. (1998). *The Social Movement Society: Contentious Politics for a New Century*. Lanham, MD, Rowman & Littlefield Publishers.

Norris, P., Ed. (1999). *Critical Citizens: Global Support for Democratic Governance*. Oxford, Oxford University Press.

Norris, P. (2002). *Democratic Phoenix: Reinventing Political Activism*. Cambridge, MA, Cambridge University Press.

Norris, P. (2011). *Democratic Deficit: Critical Citizens Revisited*. New York, Cambridge University Press.

Norris, P., S. Walgrave and P. Van Aelst (2005). "Who Demonstrates? Anti-State Rebels, Conventional Participants, or Everyone?" *Comparative Politics* 37(2): 189–205.

Plutzer, E. (2002). "Becoming a Habitual Voter: Inertia, Resources, and Growth in Young Adulthood". *American Political Science Review* 96: 41–56.

Putnam, R. (2000). *Bowling Alone: The Collapse and Revival of American Community*. New York, Simon & Schuster.

Rogers, B. (2005). "From Membership to Management? The Future of Political Parties as Democratic Organisations". *Parliamentary Affairs* 58(3): 600–10.

Saunders, C., M. T. Grasso, C. Olcese, E. Rainsford and C. Rootes (2012). "Explaining Differential Protest Participation: Novices, Returners, Repeaters and Stalwarts". *Mobilization* 17: 263–80.

Schattschneider, E. (1942). *Party Government*. New York, Greenwood Press.

Schmitt, H. and S. Holmberg (1995). Political Parties in Decline? *Citizens and the State*. D. Klingemann and D. Fuchs. Oxford, Oxford University Press.

Topf, R. (1995). Beyond Electoral Participation. *Citizens and the State*. D. Klingemann and D. Fuchs. Oxford, Oxford University Press: 52–91.

Van Aelst, P. and S. Walgrave (2001). "Who is that (Wo)man in the Street? From the Normalisation of Protest to the Normalisation of the Protester". *European Journal of Political Research* 39: 461–86.

Van Den Broek, A. (1995). Cultural Change: The Impact of Cohort Replacement and the Absence of Generations. *Workshop on "Generational Change in Post-War Europe", Second Conference of the European Sociological Association*. Budapest, 30 August–2 September, 1995.

Wattenberg, M. (2002). *Where Have All the Voters Gone?* Cambridge, MA, Harvard University Press.

Appendix
Analysing political participation and social change in Western Europe

This chapter provides a more detailed background to the methodology and data sources employed in this study. It discusses data sources employed, question wording and how the various variables of interest are measured. The chapter also further discusses the classification of cohorts. This classification is inspired by Mannheim's (1928) theory of generations, which is based on the socio-historic context of formative experiences. The 'identification problem' in age, period and cohort analyses and solutions employed in this study are also discussed. Finally, this chapter reflects on the issues involved in attempting to develop comparable models for analysing data from two different surveys conducted in repeated cross-sections, and the implications of the differences in question wording of the political action questions.

Data sources

The focus of this study is to analyse political participation in Western Europe over time; it analyses principally data from the European Values Study (EVS, 1981, 1990, 1999, WVS/EVS Integrated Dataset, 1981–2004) and European Social Survey (ESS, 2002, 2004, 2006, ESS 1–3 Cumulative Dataset). Due to voting age restrictions, and to make the samples comparable across forms of participation, all respondents under the age of eighteen were dropped from all datasets. Restricting the sample to individuals aged over eighteen means that everyone in the sample would have had at least some opportunity to engage in the various political activities.

Unless otherwise specified, the EVS country sample weights (s017a) with regional split-ups (since I include West Germany) are employed in the analyses. This is to compensate for small deviations in the resulting sample with respect to one or several dimensions considered important to get reliable results (e.g. sex-age distribution, education-level distribution). For the ESS, the design weights (dweight) are employed.

Since over-time data are necessary to investigate the evolution of patterns of participation, and in later chapters to disentangle age, period and cohort effects in the analyses, the EVS sample is restricted to those Western European democracies included in all three waves: 1981, 1990 and 1999. On this basis, the study excludes nations such as Austria and Norway, which would have otherwise fitted the theoretical characteristics of the 'most similar' nations.

The sample is also restricted to those countries totalling $N > 1,000$ respondents in at least two waves to allow enough data for the identification of age, period and cohort effects in the country-by-country analyses. For this reason, Malta and Northern Ireland are excluded from the study. The analyses of EVS political participation indicators for all ten countries are based on three surveys conducted in: (1) 1981 (1982 in Sweden); (2) 1989; (3) 1999 (1999–2000 in Ireland and Sweden).

Having restricted the sample to Belgium, Denmark, France, Germany (West, in the EVS), Great Britain, Ireland, Italy, the Netherlands, Spain and Sweden given the data limitations from the European Values Study discussed above, the study also examines the same set of ten countries with the ESS data. This is because the EVS over-time data are the key focus of this study for disentangling age, period and cohort effects. The analysis of ESS political participation indicators is based on three surveys from 2002, 2004 and 2006 (except for Italy, where there are no data for 2006).

Following Brady (1999: 737), throughout this study participants are identified as those who have said that they have actually participated in a specific activity. Moreover, this study requires data that cover several decades in order to examine age, period and life-cycle effects. As such, data from other cross-national surveys commonly used in analyses of political engagement were not viable options for this study. This is because no other surveys contained indicators of actual participation over a suitable time-span for all the key countries included in the sample. For example, the International Social Survey Programme (ISSP) dataset only includes questions concerning people's approval of different forms of political action over time. However, as discussed in Chapter 2, Brady (1999: 737) clearly points out that measuring attitudes towards participation of different types is simply not the same thing as whether people actually did that action (Dunn, Grasso and Saunders 2014). For example, liberal, educated people might be very tolerant of different types of political activity, and even fairly radical ones, but not choose to engage in these political activities themselves, or for that matter to participate in any political actions at all. Moreover, the Comparative Study of Electoral Systems (CSES, Module 1 (1996–2001), Module 2 (2001–2005)) only asks whether respondents contacted a politician over two time points (France and Italy are only included in one study). Since the ESS asks the same question in roughly the same years and includes all ten countries, the CSES indicator was not included here. The European Election Study asks whether respondents attended a European Election rally. However, since European Elections matter more in some countries than in others, this item is potentially biased. Therefore, this indicator is not included in this study.

Data from the Eurobarometer (EB) Trendfile 1970–2002 were also considered for this study, but were inadequate for the purposes here outlined in a number of ways. Two major European countries, Spain and Sweden, are only included in the final years. The dataset has an indicator for political discussion, but this does not allow for distinguishing between conventional and unconventional participation. Therefore, it was not included in this study. The EB includes some voting behaviour variables; however, these are focused on European Elections and so they were not included in this study for the same reasons cited above for the EES indicator for attending European Election rallies. Additionally, the Eurobarometer includes items on attitudes to politics (interest, efficacy) and party attachment. I follow Brady (1999: 737) here and do not consider these attitudes as measures of participation: attitudes to politics and feelings of partisanship might be highly correlated with political participation, but they are not measures of it. Attitudes do not relay the key piece of information for this study: whether an individual has actually participated in a political activity. Moreover, they do not tell us which *type* of activity people participated in.

Indeed, as studies have shown, people can be very interested in politics but not participate in political activities. For example, Van Deth (1990) links this to the literature on social capital and argues that people with high levels of resources, who are highly educated and follow politics in the papers and on the news, have a greater opportunity for other activities, particularly leisure ones, which do not include politics. In other words, political activity takes second place to other concerns and opportunities.

Further data sources

Chapter 4 maps patterns over time for various indicators of political participation. Here multiple data sources, in addition to EVS and ESS indicators, are employed. This includes three sources of aggregate-level (as opposed to individual-level survey data): two for turnout and a further one for party membership. The chapter also examines data for party membership from seven national election studies (Denmark, France, Germany, Italy, the Netherlands, Great Britain, Sweden) and, as discussed, the data from two cross-national surveys: the European Values Study (WVS/EVS Integrated Dataset, 1981–2004) and the European Social Survey (2002–2006 Cumulative Dataset). With the exception of Britain, the national election studies did not include other indicators of participation over time, so data from those studies were only used to examine party membership.

The turnout data contain observations for all legislative elections between 1945 and 2008, except for Spain, where elections begin in 1977. The data come from Franklin's (2004) turnout dataset, which originally contained data for elections from 1945 to 1999 in twenty-two advanced democracies. These original data were compiled by Franklin (2004) from Mackie and Rose's (1991) *International Almanac of Electoral History* and its various supplements as specified in Appendix B of Franklin's (2004) book. I updated these data with IDEA figures and also included Spain in the sample.

For comparability of the country-set across indicators of political involvement, and since in any case, compulsory voting does not ensure 100 per cent turnout (Hirczy 1994) Belgium is not excluded from the turnout dataset. Again, this study only looks at over-time patterns in turnout for the set of ten Western European countries included in this study.

The analysis of party membership in Chapter 4 is based on the EVS and ESS as well as the National Election survey data on self-reported party membership: Denmark (1971–1998), Germany (1965–1994), Netherlands (1971–1998), Great Britain (1964–2001) and Sweden (1979–1998) are from the European Voter Database; data for Italy (1968–2001) are from the ITANES; data for France (1978–2002) are from EPF 1978–1997 and PEF 2002 (CDSP). Moreover, Mair and Van Biezens's (2001) aggregate data on party membership in Europe for all ten nations are also employed in the analysis of over-time trends in this chapter. These data were compiled by the authors primarily using parties' own official records or estimates. Due to the small number of cases and respondents' own confusion about the meaning of party membership (Mair and Van Biezen 2001), since people can often equate membership with feelings of attachment, this is seen as an improvement on individual-level survey data for measuring over-time levels. However, these sorts of data may be sensitive to changes in the rules of party membership (paying fees, how many people are needed to form a local branch), as well as potentially excluding smaller parties. This means it remains important to compare the results for aggregate and survey data.

Indicators of political participation in the ESS and EVS surveys

Table A.1 lists all the indicators of political participation available in the WVS/ EVS Integrated Dataset, 1981–2004 (1981, 1990, 1999) and the European Social Survey 1–3 Cumulative Dataset (2002, 2004, 2006). Between them, the two surveys include twenty-five different indicators of political participation. These are listed as follows:

- party membership;
- unpaid work for a party/political group;
- member of a local political action group;
- unpaid work for local political action group;
- union membership;
- unpaid work for a union;
- voted in the last national election;
- contacted a politician or government official;
- member of environment, conservation, ecology/ animal rights organisation;
- unpaid work for environment, conservation, ecology/animal rights organisation;
- member of environmental protection, peace or animal rights;
- member of third world development or human rights organisation;
- unpaid work for third world development or human rights organisation;
- member of humanitarian aid, human rights, minorities/immigrants organisation;

Table A.1 Indicators of political participation in the EVS and ESS surveys

	Question type	In both surveys?	1981–1990/ 2002–2006?	EVS 1981	EVS 1990	EVS 1999	ESS 2002	ESS 2004	ESS 2006*
Political parties									
(EVS) A068 Belong to political party	Yes/No	X	X	X	X	X			
(ESS) MMBPRTY Member of a political party	Yes/No	X	X				X	X	X
(EVS) A085 Unpaid work for political party/group	Yes/No	X	X	X	X	X			
(ESS) WRKPRTY Worked in political party or action group last twelve months	Yes/No	X	X				X	X	X
(EVS) A069 Belong local political action group	Yes/No				X	X			
(EVS) A086 Unpaid work for local political action group	Yes/No				X	X			
Labour unions									
(EVS) A067 Belong to labour union	Yes/No	X	X	X	X	X			
(ESS) MBTRU Member of trade union or similar organisation	Yes/No	X	X				X	X	X
(EVS) A084 Unpaid work for labour union	Yes/No		X	X	X	X			
Other conventional participation									
(ESS) VOTE Voted in the last national election	Yes/No		X				X	X	X
(ESS) CONTPLT Contacted politician, government official last twelve months	Yes/No		X				X	X	X
Environment and animal rights									
(EVS) A071 Belong to environment, conservation, ecology, animal rights organisation	Yes/No		X	X	(X)	X			
(EVS) A088 Unpaid work for environment, conservation, ecology, animal rights org.	Yes/No		X	X	(X)	X			
(EVS) A071b Belong to animal rights organisation	Yes/No				X				
(EVS) A088b Unpaid work for animal rights organisation	Yes/No				X				
(EVS) A071c Belong to environment, conservation, ecology organisation	Yes/No				X				
(EVS) A088c Unpaid work for environment, conservation, ecology organisation	Yes/No				X				
(ESS) E7a: environmental protection, *peace* or animal rights?	Yes/No**						X		

Development and human rights

Variable	Coding							
(EVS) A070 Belong to third world development or human rights organisation	Yes/No	X		X	X	X		
(EVS) A087 Unpaid work for to third world development or human rights organisation	Yes/No	X		X	X	X		
(ESS) E6a: an organisation for humanitarian aid, human rights, minorities, or immigrants?	Yes/No**						X	

Women's groups and peace movement

Variable	Coding							
(EVS) A075 Belong to women's groups *and* (1) A092 Unpaid work for women's group	Yes/No			X	X			
(EVS) A076 Belong to the peace movement *and* (1) A093 Unpaid work for peace move.	Yes/No			X	X			

Other unconventional participation

Variable	Coding							
(EVS) E027 Attending lawful demonstrations	Have done/Might/Never	X	X	X	X	X		
(ESS) PBLDMN Taken part in lawful public demonstration last twelve months	Yes/No		X				X	X
(EVS) E026 Joining in boycotts	Have done/Might/Never	X	X	X	X	X		
(ESS) BCTPRD Boycotted certain products last twelve months	Yes/No		X				X	X
(EVS) E025 Signing a petition	Have done/Might/Never	X	X	X	X	X		
(ESS) SGNPTIT Signed petition last twelve months	Yes/No		X				X	X
(EVS) E029 Occupying buildings or factories	Have done/Might/Never		X	X	X	X		
(EVS) E028 Joining unofficial strikes	Have done/Might/Never		X	X	X	X		
(EVS) E030 Damaging things, breaking windows, street violence	Have done/Might/Never		X					
(EVS) E031 Personal violence	Have done/Might/Never		X					

Notes

Variable names/codes are from original documentation.

* Italy not included in ESS 2006.

** Individual variables for each that apply from each of: Member, Participated, Donated money, Voluntary work.

- member of women's groups;
- unpaid work for women's groups;
- member of peace movement;
- unpaid work for peace movement;
- attended lawful demonstration;
- joined a boycott;
- signed a petition;
- occupied buildings or factories;
- joined an unofficial strike;
- damaged things, broke windows, or street violence;
- personal violence.

This would appear encouraging for those interested in studying patterns of political participation over time. However, several indicators are not available in all the surveys, meaning that they cannot be used in the analyses for this study that are aimed at examining over-time patterns and disentangling age, period and cohort effects to isolate 'pure' generational differences. Therefore, this study only examines indicators available in the EVS 1981, 1990 and 1999 or in the ESS 2002, 2004 and 2006. For obvious reasons, when comparing results from the two surveys, the study can only examine indicators available in the EVS 1981, 1990 and 1999 and in the ESS 2002, 2004 and 2006. The right-hand columns of Table A.1 with the Xs show the studies in which each indicator is included. Belonging to and doing unpaid voluntary work for local political action groups, belonging to women groups and the peace movement as well as doing unpaid work for these 'new' organisations are only available in the 1990 and 1999 EVS; damaging things, breaking windows, street violence and the indicator for personal violence are only available in the EVS 1981. In the ESS, the items concerning membership in 'new' organisations were only available for 2002. As such, if data over three time points are required from either the EVS or ESS surveys, the previous list of twenty-five items slims down to the following list of fifteen indicators:

- party membership;
- unpaid work for a party/political group;
- union membership;
- unpaid work for a union;
- voted in the last national election;
- contacted a politician or government official;
- member of environment, conservation, ecology/animal rights organisation;
- unpaid work for environment, conservation, ecology/animal rights organisation;
- member of third world development or human rights organisation;
- unpaid work for third world development or human rights organisation;
- attended lawful demonstration;
- joined a boycott;

- signed a petition;
- occupied buildings or factories;
- joined an unofficial strike.

These fifteen indicators will be analysed in this study. As Table A.1 shows, in the EVS, joining an unofficial strike, occupying, demonstrating, boycotting and signing a petition are measured on a three-point scale where: 1 would never do, 2 might do, 3 have done. As mentioned above, this study is only interested in measuring *actual participation* and not 'action potential' or attitudes to participation. As such, each of the above five indicators of protest activism are recoded so that 1 means have done and 0 have not (and includes 2/3 above). In the EVS, party membership, union membership, membership and voluntary work for environment, ecology or animal rights groups, and membership and voluntary work for development or human rights groups were already dichotomous in the original dataset. Similarly, in the ESS all items were already dichotomous, with the exception of union membership which was coded as 1 current, 2 previous and 3 no; this was also recoded to a dichotomy as we are only interested in members at the time of study.

Moving on, Table A.2 shows that the degree of overlap between the two surveys is poor. The set of six indicators listed below are present in both surveys. As detailed further below, we will only compare results for four of these here (party membership, demonstrating, signing a petition, joining a boycott):[1]

- party membership;
- unpaid work for a political party or political action group;
- union membership;
- attended a lawful demonstration;
- signed a petition;
- joined a boycott.

Table 2.1 in Chapter 2 listed the indicators of participation in the EVS and ESS for which data are available for all three waves and subdivides them into two theoretical groupings based on the distinction between conventional, or traditional, and unconventional, or new, political participation. At this stage, it is important to reiterate once again that since this study is concerned with over-time change and with disentangling age, period and cohort effects, it only examines indicators of participation available in all three waves of the EVS (1981, 1990 and 1999) or in all three waves of the ESS (2002, 2004 and 2006). The cells in Table A.2 report the item wording from the EVS (and where they differ also from the ESS, the second, after the comma), as this has implications for the interpretation of results. Table A.2 also shows that while the EVS has many indicators of unconventional participation and 'new' memberships, it is poor on indicators of conventional political participation. The ESS is more balanced between the two types of indicators of participation but it has no over-time data for 'new' memberships and even for just the 2002 data, the indicators for 'new'

Table A.2 Overlap of indicators of political participation in EVS and ESS

'Conventional' or 'traditional'	EVS	ESS	'Unconventional' or 'new'	EVS	ESS
Belong to political party, Member of a political party	✓	✓	Belong to environment, conservation, ecology, animal rights organisation	✓	✓
Belong to a labour union, Member of a labour union	✓	✓	Belong to third world development, or human rights organisation	✓	✓
Unpaid work for political party or group, Worked in a political party or action group*	✓	✓	Unpaid work for environment, conservation, ecology, animal rights organisation	✓	✓
Unpaid work for labour union	✓		Unpaid work for third world development, or human rights organisation	✓	
Voted in the last national election		✓	Attended lawful demonstration, Taken part in lawful public demonstration	✓	✓
Contacted a politician or government official		✓	Signed a petition	✓	✓
			Joined a boycott, Boycotted certain products	✓	✓
			Occupied buildings or factories	✓	
			Joined an unofficial strike	✓	

Notes
This table only includes indicators of political participation available in EVS 1981, 1990 and 1999. The 1981 EVS also includes E030 'damaging things, breaking windows, street violence' and E031 'personal violence'. The 1990 and 1999 EVS also include indicators for belonging and unpaid voluntary work in 'new' organisations: women's groups (A075, A092) and the peace movement (A076, A093).
This table only includes indicators of political participation available in ESS 2002, 2004 and 2006; the ESS 2002 also includes other types of activities, such as deliberately buying products for political, ethical or environmental reasons, and other memberships, e.g. 'environmental, protection, peace and animal rights'.
* This is ambiguous, and therefore, it is unclear whether this indicator fits neatly into the 'conventional' category, as it could potentially refer to other 'new' political groups, such as peace, anti-nuclear, etc.

memberships include several different types of organisations in one item (e.g. environment *and* peace, or human rights *and* migrant organisations) and therefore are not comparable to those in the EVS.

From Table A.2 the least problematic indicator of conventional political participation available in both surveys is party membership. As discussed in Chapter 2, union membership is much more 'political' and therefore politicised in some countries than others and while Olson (1965) and Wilson (1974) included union membership in their classic works, other authors have expressed doubts about whether this should be considered as 'political' participation. Additionally, union membership is problematic since the risk set does not include the entire population so that we would have to restrict our analyses to the employed, making it difficult to disentangle age, period and cohort effects since most employed people would fall in the middle age group, making the sample unbalanced. For different reasons, the item for 'unpaid work for a political party or political group' (according to the EVS question wording) or 'worked in a political party or action group' (according to the ESS question wording) is also unsatisfactory since 'political or action groups' could refer to other 'new' or unconventional groups such as anti-nuclear or peace or gay rights or women's groups and therefore could potentially also be picking up on 'unconventional' political participation, and more so in the ESS. Therefore, when analysing cohort differences in conventional political participation, Chapter 5 and Chapter 7 focus on party membership (in both the EVS and ESS); we also look at voting and contacting a politician (only in the ESS).

Of the three indicators of 'unconventional' political participation available in both surveys, joining a boycott and signing a petition are individualised activities, while demonstrating is a social activity (see Table 2.1). As discussed in Chapter 2, Dekker *et al.* (1997) only include boycotting, demonstrating and occupying factories in their classification of unconventional participation. The authors exclude petitioning, as they say it is difficult to understand how this could be understood as a protest activity. Indeed, a similar point could be made about boycotting. One would not be wrong to wonder in what sense this type of activity is meant to influence a 'political outcome' at all. Given these considerations, this research focuses primarily on demonstrating as the 'ideal type' unconventional political activity when analysing cohort differences in participation in Chapters 6–7. However, results are also compared with signing a petition, boycotting (in both the EVS and ESS), and occupying and SMO participation (only in the EVS) to ascertain whether cohort effects are different for social vs individualised unconventional actions, and for activities vs organisations.

The dependent variables

There are strong theoretical and empirical reasons for examining individual activities in turn in Chapter 4. This allows to check for whether various activities understood as forming part of the 'conventional' repertoire are becoming less popular amongst Western European publics and also for whether the various activities classed as 'unconventional' are becoming more popular.

As explained, Chapters 5–7 disentangle age, period and cohort effects to analyse generational differences for the two different repertoires. However, an alternative approach to analysing each indicator of political participation on its own terms would be to construct two scales, one for conventional activism, and another for unconventional activism, to employ as dependent variables. However, as discussed in previous sections, there are strong theoretical reasons that suggest this is not a particularly good course of action. As noted in Chapter 2, it is widely assumed in the literature that the various unconventional or 'elite-challenging' activities are broadly equivalent. However, whilst the young and more highly educated cohorts are more predisposed to participating in these activities than older cohorts, it is also true that demonstrating was an activity that rose to particular prominence in the formative years of the baby-boomers. Therefore, if the impressionable years hypothesis is correct, then this generation might be particularly prone to this type of activity despite the ageing process and lower education levels relative to the '80s and '90s cohorts. Indeed, whether cohort differences in participation work as hypothesised in the literature for all those forms of participation broadly classed as 'unconventional' is a question which should remain open to empirical scrutiny. It is therefore important to distinguish between *types* of activity within the same broad theoretical repertoire. Moreover, as also discussed in Chapter 2, while demonstrating and signing a petition are both classified as 'unconventional', these activities are actually very different. First, one activity is social whereas the other is individualised. It could be added that one involves a higher degree of effort than the other and so forth. Hence, despite the tendency to group demonstrating, signing a petition and boycotting together because they do not pertain to traditional mobilising agencies or voting, there are good reasons to expect different patterns of participation and possibly different cohort effects for these activities.

There are several additional reasons that suggest constructing one scale for unconventional participation and another for conventional participation from the various indicators in each theoretical subset is not the ideal course of action. First, this study needs to compare results from two different surveys, the EVS and ESS. But as Table A.2 shows, the indicators included in these surveys are different sets. If scales were constructed for conventional and unconventional political participation from the different sets of indicators available from each repertoire in the two surveys, they would not be comparable measures. A scale for conventional participation from the EVS includes belonging to a party, belonging to a labour union, working for a party or group *and* unpaid work for a labour union, whereas the one from the ESS would be including belonging to a party, belonging to a labour union, working for a party or group, *and* voting and contacting a politician. Similarly, a scale for unconventional political participation from the EVS would include demonstrating, signing a petition, joining a boycott *and also* occupying buildings or factories, joining an unofficial strike, belonging to an environmental organisation, belonging to a development or human rights organisations, doing voluntary work for an environmental organisation, doing voluntary work for a development or human rights organisations.

This is clearly problematic. It would further perpetuate the problem already present in the literature, where scholars speak of 'conventional' or 'unconventional' political participation but refer to different activities. It is preferable to analyse voting or party membership or demonstrating or boycotting individually. In turn, this renders comparison of the available evidence more straightforward.

It is a more effective strategy to keep indicators separate and to focus only on people who actually said they did an activity when analysing participation, and more specifically, age period and cohort effects on participation. For example, while younger cohorts may be more 'cognitively mobilised' and more approving of different types of unconventional political activities, they might not necessarily also be more likely than older cohorts to engage in 'elite-challenging' or 'unconventional' activities. Moreover, this may vary by type of activity.

The age, period and cohort identification problem

The debate between life-cycle and generation theories makes it important to determine which effects underlie the observed cohort differences in participation. In order to assess the relative importance of age, period and cohort, the three effects must be disentangled. The problem here is that without restrictions, age (A), period (P) and cohort (C) models are not identifiable, since the three variables are exact linear functions of each other $(A = P - C)$. Further, their differences cannot be separated using a function $Y = f(C, P, A)$ (Mason and Fienberg 1985). As Glenn (2005: 6) points out, "the multiple correlation of each independent variable with the other ones is unity – the most extreme kind of collinearity that is possible".

Since the 1970s, several scholars have examined the problem of identification in age, period and cohort models to 'get around' the linear dependence of the terms (Converse 1976; Fienberg and Mason 1979, 1985; Glenn 1976; Grasso 2014; Mason and Fienberg 1985; Mason *et al.* 1973; Palmore 1987; Tilley 2001, 2002; Tilley and Evans 2014; Smets and Neundorf 2014). One way of achieving identification, by what is often a very strong theoretical assumption, lies with establishing that only two of the three variables affect the outcome (Firebaugh and Davis 1988; Glenn 1994). This is not an option for this study, however, since there are reasons to believe that all three of age, period and cohort effects are at play for political participation.

An alternative approach would be to constrain the effect of one of the three variables to be proportional to some other substantive variable. For example, by assuming that the effect of cohort is proportional to cohort size (Fienberg and Mason 1985). Heckman and Robb (1985) call this the 'proxy variable approach' since one of age, period or cohort terms is represented by some other variable. O'Brien (2000) refers to this as the age, period, cohort-characteristic model. Typically, the constraint is justified by specifying the mechanism by which the variable used to replace or constrain one of the age, period or cohort variables captures the effect of one of these in the postulated mechanism (Heath and Martin 1996). For example, Blossfeld (1986) used two variables representing labour market conditions in a certain year instead of period to analyse the way in which a changing labour market structure affects career opportunities. Another approach is to replace age with a categorical life-cycle variable to identify age, period and cohort models in studies of political behaviour. However, EVS and ESS do not contain the appropriate variables over time to create suitable life-cycle variables. One other approach to capture period effects could be to substitute years for the relevant variables. However, in our case, period effects are understood to be multifaceted and complex and as such they cannot be captured by specific variables to substitute for year of survey in the age-period-cohort models.

A further approach which does not involve variable substitution, as suggested by Mason *et al.* (1973) involves the assumption that two age parameters, two period or two cohort parameters are equal (Harding and Jencks 2003; Knoke and Hout 1974). Nakamura (1986) employed a sophisticated version of this method, using a Bayesian approach for specifying restrictions. As Tilley (2001) points out, the problem with this approach is that if we accept this critical assumption, there is no possibility of interaction between age, period and cohort effects in this model. A further problem with this approach is that it is often difficult to find restrictions that can be firmly theoretically justified, and as Glenn (1976) shows, the wrong assumptions can have major effects on parameter estimates. In this study, it is not feasible for the purposes of the research to make any of these assumptions. Converse (1976) and Glenn (1976) emphasise the importance of looking at the data and using side-information before applying any 'statistical fixes'.

A promising alternative to the above solutions was employed by Tilley (2001, 2002), who used generalised additive methods (or GAMs) to study the effects of age, period and cohort effects on partisanship. While this method has never been applied to the study of political participation, Beck and Jackman (1998: 596) have argued that since "GAMs strike a sensible balance between the flexibility of nonparametric techniques and the ease of interpretation and familiarity of linear regression", they should be applied more widely in the social sciences. Generalised additive models (Hastie and Tibshirani 1986, 1990) are generalised linear models with a linear predictor involving a sum of smooth functions of covariates (Wood 2006). This sort of model allows for flexible specification of the dependence of the response on the covariates by specifying the model only in terms of smooth functions (Tilley, 2002; Wood, 2006). However, the flexibility and convenience comes at the cost of two new theoretical problems: how to represent the smooth functions and how smooth they should be (Tilley, 2002; Wood, 2006). The smooth function employed can vary from a moving average, to Lowess, to cubic smoothing splines. Tilley (2001) argues that the advantage of the latter technique is that it minimises the compromise between fit and smoothness as one can adjust this through setting the desired degrees of freedom. In Chapter 7, this study applies generalised additive models as a sensitivity test to ensure results are robust to alternative measures from the cohort classification schema from the age-period-cohort models.

While generalised additive models are applied in Chapter 7 as a sensitivity analysis, the solution applied in Chapters 5–7 in order to break the linear dependence of age, period and cohort and to identify the models is to categorise the age and cohort variables based on theory (cf. Glenn 1976). The categorisation of the period variable is readily available from the data structure (repeated cross-sections) and as such consists of survey waves/studies. Generation effects are captured by the cohort or political generations variable. Finally, age is classified into three categories (age groups), which approximate life-cycle stages. This categorisation of the variables allows for model identification.

While some information is lost by categorising cohorts and age, these restrictions are what allows for identification. Moreover, the GAMs are applied as a sensitivity test to visualise the smoothed cohort effects (cf. Tilley 2002) and check that the cohort patterns are broadly similar to those from the age-period-cohort models with the categorical variable. This sensitivity analysis shows that the categorisation is a good approximation of non-linear effects, and that the results are not a spurious result of the cohort schema applied.

Table A.3 shows the classification of cohorts and their age in the different survey waves from both the EVS and ESS included in this study. As each column shows, examining at data over time allows for following cohorts as they age. This allows for identification of age, period and cohort effects. Next, we examine the age-group coding.

Age-group coding and life-cycle theories

The EVS sample consists of a total of 40,836 respondents aged 18–90 years of age for the three survey waves (1981, 1990 and 1999) for the ten Western European countries included in this study. Respondents younger than eighteen years of age were excluded from the sample to maintain comparability with results from turnout studies and ensure that individuals had at least some opportunity to engage in various political acts. Respondents born before 1909 were also excluded from the sample to fit with the cohort classification schema based on historical events. The oldest people in survey year 1999 are aged ninety; eighty-one in 1989; seventy-two in 1981. The variable for age is used to distinguish between life-cycle stages, splitting the sample into three age groups. The coding scheme applied (creating three roughly equal-sized groups) is 18–33 years of age: young (14,640 respondents); 34–50 years of age: middle (12,546 respondents); and 51+ years of age: old (13,650 respondents). Similarly, the ESS sample consists of a total of 50,464 respondents aged 18–97 years for the three survey waves (2002, 2004 and 2006) for the ten Western European countries included in this study. Again here, respondents younger than eighteen were excluded from the final sample for analysis (to maintain comparability with results from turnout studies and to ensure that individuals had at least some opportunity to engage in various political acts) and those born before 1909 (in keeping with the cohort classification schema) so that the oldest people in survey year 2002 are aged ninety-three; ninety-five in 2004; and ninety-seven in 2006. Again, the variable

Table A.3 Cohort classification based on socio-historic period of formative years, EVS and ESS

	Pre-WWII	Post-WWII	Baby-boomers	'80s generation	'90s generation	% (N)
Formative years*	1929–1945	1946–1965	1966–1977	1978–1988	1989–2001	
Year of birth	1909–1925	1926–1945	1946–1957	1958–1968	1969–1981	
EVS 1981, 1990, 1999						
Age in 1981 EVS	56–72	36–55	24–35	13–23***	0–12**	30 (12,274)
Age in 1990 EVS	64–81	44–63	32–43	21–31	8–20***	39 (15,839)
Age in 1999 EVS	74–90	54–73	42–53	31–41	18–30	31 (12,723)
% (N)	14 (5,583)	29 (11,926)	23 (9,529)	23 (9,517)	11 (4,281)	100 (40,836)
ESS 2002, 2004, 2006						
Age in 2002 ESS	77–93	57–76	45–56	34–44	21–33	34 (18,380)
Age in 2004 ESS	79–95	59–78	47–58	36–46	23–35	34 (18,329)
Age in 2006 ESS	81–97	61–80	49–60	38–48	25–37	32 (17,315)
% (N)	5 (2,657)	27 (13,441)	22 (11,306)	23 (11,800)	22 (11,260)	100 (50,454)

Notes

* Each respondent is assigned to a particular political generation based on the historic formative period during which they have spent the majority of their formative years (i.e. at least six out of eleven 15–25 years during that period).
** The sample only contains respondents aged 18 and over as such there are no data in this cell.
*** The sample only contains respondents aged 18 and over and as such respondents from the '90s generation are aged 18–20 in 1990; similarly, respondents from the '80s generation are aged 18–23 in 1981.

for age is used to distinguish between life-cycle stages, splitting the sample into three age groups. The same age-group coding scheme as discussed for the EVS above is applied for the ESS. The sample totals are: young (12,803 respondents); middle (17,627 respondents); and old (23,577 respondents).

Based on life-cycle theories, the 'young' age group is meant to reflect the first life-cycle stage. This is when individuals are still developing their sense of identity, are either still in education or at an early career stage and are still looking for a partner or have only just recently entered a stable relationship. The 'middle' age group is meant to reflect the second life-cycle stage. This is when individuals enter a stable career stage and generally have (and bring up) children. The 'old' age group is intended to reflect the third life-cycle stage. This is when individuals are about to leave or have left employment and their children have left the home. The core idea behind life-cycle theories lies in stressing the importance of a person's social-connectedness and maturity in influencing political behaviours and allegiances. Older people are generally understood to be more embedded in certain social locations and social networks. They tend to have a more stable employment situation than young people and are thus also clearer on their socio-economic positioning and their political interests. They are therefore more likely to be able to tell which party is best placed to fight for their economic interests, for example, allowing them to have the information relevant for supporting one's becoming a party member. On the other hand, young people, since they hold fewer commitments, are generally not responsible for a family, and have more fluid social connections and networks, tend to be less risk-averse and also to have more time on their hands. They are therefore seen to be more likely to attend demonstrations, or engage in direct action against the authorities, compared to more institutional types of engagement.

Of course, the meaning of different 'life-cycle stages' also varies with time, and indeed today, people stress the importance of 'life-course' perspectives emphasising the changing dynamics of the stages of life in modern societies. People often point out how 'youth' has expanded today; others point out how this concept only emerged in the 1960s. Moreover, one could object that the age groups are imprecise and by nature too broad, and indeed that there are important differences between individuals of eighteen years of age and individuals of thirty years. Similarly one could object that grouping individuals aged fifty-one and those aged ninety-seven is too gross a categorisation of 'life stage'. However, given that the focus of this study is to study generational differences, this broad categorisation of life-cycle is necessary if the model is to be identifiable. It is not the goal of this research to investigate life-cycle effects on participation in detail. To identify the model and have relatively stable estimates, these broader age groups are necessary in order that each cell in Table A.3 has a sensible number of cases by country for the various types of political activities examined here. In particular, for certain activities such as party membership which involve relatively few people, this is crucial. Therefore, this categorisation of age group is necessary to identify cohort and age effects and disentangle them from period effects in the models employing the EVS data. Since the aim is to compare results from these models with those employing the ESS data, exactly the same categorisation is employed for this other dataset.

Achieving identification within the constraints of data limitations

Applying this categorisation of age into age groups (or life-cycle stages) allows for the identification of the age-period-cohort models in this study (Grasso 2011). This is since, as shown in Table A.4, with the exception of the '90s generation in the ESS, in each survey year, each age group includes individuals from at least two different cohorts. For the '90s generation in the ESS (with the exception of 2002) identification is achieved since this cohort is split over two different age groups in 2004 and 2006. As discussed, this categorisation means that even in the cells with the smallest number of cases, and particularly in the crucial cells for identification in the EVS data from Table A.4 (the post-WWII cohort in the 51+ age group in 1981; the pre-WWII cohort in the 51+ age group in 1999; and the '80s generation in the 18–33 age group in 1999) there are enough cases for each age group and cohort in a given year and country. So for example, for Italy, there are 101 cases for individuals in the post-WWII cohort in the 51+ age group in 1981. There are ninety-seven cases for individuals in the pre-WWII generation in the 51+ age group in 1999. And there are 153 cases for individuals in the '80s generation in the 18–33 age group in 1999. Similarly, for the ESS, in the key cell for identification in this model (see above), there are eighty-five cases for individuals in the '90s generation in the 34–50 age group in 2002, in Britain; ninety in Germany. Moreover, of course, longitudinal panel data would be the ideal way to properly separate age period and cohort effects, since one could follow the same individuals as they move through their life-cycle. However, assuming random samples of the population in each survey wave, and given that these types of repeated cross-sectional data are the best data available for examining the research questions of interest in this study, this is in practice the only available option available to the researcher for achieving age-period-cohort model identification within the practical constraints of data limitations. Additionally, in Chapter 7, generalised additive models are applied as a sensitivity test to show that the results from the models in Chapters 5–7, applying these categorisations of cohorts and age groups, are robust.

Other independent variables

This section discusses the independent and control variables from the age-period-cohort models presented in Chapters 5–7. A dummy variable for gender is included. Traditionally, it has been suggested that men are more likely to be involved in political activities than women due to gender roles and the fact that men have traditionally been more exposed to the public sphere. However, this may be different for younger people and the more recent generations, given advances in gender equality. A dummy variable capturing whether individuals

Table A.4 Cohorts by age group in each survey year, EVS and ESS

	Pre-WWII	Post-WWII	Baby-boomers	'80s generation	'90s generation	Total
Formative years	Until 1945	1946–1965	1966–1977	1978–1988	1989–2001	
Year of birth	1909–1925	1926–1945	1946–1957	1958–1968	1969–1981	
Age group						
EVS 1981–1999						
1981 18–33 years			2,755 (85%)	2,697 (100%)		5,452
1981 34–50 years		2,942 (79%)	498 (15%)			3,440
1981 51+ years	2,578 (100%)	804 (21%)				3,382
1990 18–33 years			266 (7%)	3,816 (100%)	1,430 (100%)	5,512
1990 34–50 years		1,580 (33%)	3,368 (93%)			4,948
1990 51+ years	2,141 (100%)	3,238 (67%)				5,379
1999 18–33 years				825 (27%)	2,851 (100%)	3,676
1999 34–50 years			1,979 (75%)	2,179 (73%)		4,158
1999 51+ years	864 (100%)	3,362 (100%)	663 (25%)			4,889
Total	5,583	11,926	9,529	9,517	4,281	40,836
Age group						
ESS 2002–2006						
2002 18–33 years					3,726 (100%)	3,726
2002 34–50 years			1,905 (48%)	4,122 (100%)		6,027
2002 51+ years	1,142 (100%)	4,722 (100%)	2,028 (52%)			7,892
2004 18–33 years					3,094 (82%)	3,094
2004 34–50 years			1,293 (34%)	3,953 (100%)	702 (18%)	5,948
2004 51+ years	819 (100%)	4,675 (100%)	2,538 (66%)			8,032
2006 18–33 years					2,430 (65%)	2,430
2006 34–50 years			619 (17%)	3,725 (100%)	1,308 (35%)	5,652
2006 51+ years	696 (100%)	4,044 (100%)	2,923 (83%)			7,663
Total	2,657	13,441	11,306	11,800	11,260	50,464

completed education before the age of sixteen is also included in the models (Grasso 2013). There were no other education variables for the three survey waves in the EVS; the analyses rely on the item that asks 'at what age did you complete your education?' to test the argument in the literature that people with fewer years of formal education tend to be less politically involved since they have lower levels of political knowledge and interest, and thus fewer relevant resources. Moreover, this variable also captures 'cognitive mobilisation': "though formal education is by no means the same thing as cognitive mobilisation, it is probably the best readily available indicator" (Inglehart 1990: 337). While the ESS also includes more detailed education variables, in order to make the EVS and ESS models comparable the item which asks how many years of formal education someone has completed is also employed here. In this respect, ten years are taken to be equivalent to sixteen years of education since most individuals begin formal schooling at age six; the variable is dichotomised as with the EVS variable. Education is thus measured in broadly equivalent terms for the two surveys. Figure A.1 and Figure A.2 compare these measures by plotting the proportion of individuals in each cohort with low education (i.e. those leaving school before or at the age of sixteen in the EVS and those completing ten or fewer years of formal education in the ESS) for respectively, the EVS and the ESS. As can be seen in the figures there are only minor differences between the two measures in some countries, reflecting slightly different national educational

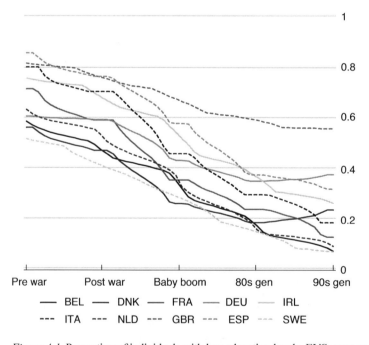

Figure A.1 Proportion of individuals with low education levels, EVS, over generation.

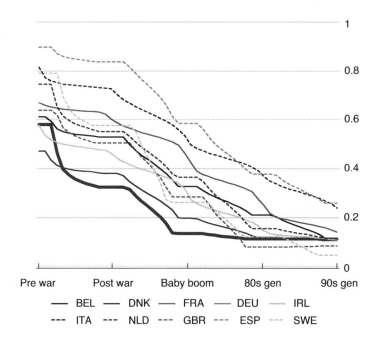

Figure A.2 Proportion of individuals with low education levels, ESS, over generation.

structures (e.g. GCSEs in Britain). Figure A.1 and Figure A.2 also show that there are some clear cohort differences in education levels and thus provide a strong motivation for including this variable in the models in order to examine the extent to which education level mediates cohort differences in political participation.

A dummy variable for manual occupation is also included to test for whether there are class inequalities in participation. While a more fine-tuned measure of SES or class schema would have been ideal, this was the only option available to render the EVS and ESS models comparable. The EVS only includes the ISCO-88 (ILO 1990) occupational classification variable for the 1999 wave. Therefore, the only useful EVS measures were two variables categorising the professions of the individual (x036) or the chief wage earner in the household (x043) according to the following schema:

1   employer/manager of establishment with 100 or more employees;
2   employer/manager of establishment with fewer than 100 employees;
3   professional worker/middle level non-manual office worker;
4   junior level non-manual;
5   foreman and/or supervisor;
6   skilled manual;
7   semi-skilled manual worker;

8   unskilled manual;
9   farmer: has own farm;
10   agricultural worker;
11   member of armed forces;
12   never had a job.

The ESS included the ISCO-88 in all three studies, and as such the *iskoegp* program[2] was employed to recode this into the EGP-schema (Erikson *et al.* 1979):

1   higher controllers;
2   lower controllers;
3   routine non-manual;
4   self-employed with employees;
5   self-employed without employees;
6   manual supervisor;
7   skilled manual;
8   semi-skilled and unskilled manual;
9   farm labourer;
10   self-employed farmer.

Given that these two schemas are still very different, the working class dummy variable from the EVS was developed by assigning value 1 to respondents in the following occupational categories (and if they had a missing value, that of the chief wage-earner):

6   skilled manual;
7   semi-skilled manual worker;
8   unskilled manual.

And for the ESS the working class variable was developed by assigning a value of 1 to respondents in the following EGP classes:

7   skilled manual;
8   semi-skilled and/or unskilled manual.

Table A.5 shows the proportion of respondents in the working class based on these new variables in the ESS and EVS surveys and compares them to estimates from a third survey, the EU-SILC (using the same occupational categories). This table shows that with the exception of the Netherlands and Great Britain (where the EVS estimates are much larger than those for the ESS and the EU-SILC), the proportion of respondents in the working class is roughly similar in the EVS and ESS surveys for comparable time points. As such, this suggests that the new variable measuring whether an individual belongs to the working class for the two surveys is comparable.

Table A.5 Proportion of respondents in working class in EVS, ESS and EU-SILC

	EVS 1981–1999	EVS 1999	ESS 2002	ESS 2006	EU-SILC 2006**
Belgium	38	30	34	29	37
Denmark	39	32	34	29	30
France	29	28	29	28	38
Germany	33	32	31	30	30
Ireland	43	30	29	26	34
Italy	32	30	30	34*	45
Netherlands	34	33	20	23	24
Great Britain	50	50	30	30	30
Spain	44	55	44	42	48
Sweden	30	33	35	28	26

Notes
* Data for 2004.
** Estimates from EU-SILC 2006.

Three further independent variables measuring ideology and political values are included in the models. One is for left-wing ideological polarisation (values 1 and 2 on a 1–10 left-right scale on the EVS; and values 0 and 1 on a 0–10 left-right scale in the ESS). The other is for right-wing ideological polarisation (values 9 and 10 on a 0/1–10 left-right scale). The third is a categorical variable for 1 left-libertarian, 2 left-authoritarian, 3 right-libertarian and 4 right-authoritarian value orientations. Details of how this variable was coded are presented in Table A.6. These variables will allow for testing the arguments in the literature that individuals who are more left wing or more left-libertarian tend to be more politically active since they have an interest in reform and social change, rather than maintaining the status quo (as those on the right). The political values categorical item is constructed from various attitudinal questions on economic attitudinal (as opposed to the left-right self-placement scale) and social values items. The same value questions were not available from both surveys and the ESS had only two useful items. Table A.6 provides a detailed account of how this variable was constructed for both surveys. Moreover, the results from the analyses in Chapter 5–7 show that results for the EVS and ESS measures are remarkably similar and therefore this suggests that even though the specific items are not identical, the variables are nonetheless reflecting of very similar value dimensions. For the left-right scale, instead, the questions from the EVS (1) and ESS (2) are virtually identical:

1   *In political matters, people talk of "the left" and "the right". How would you place your views on this scale, generally speaking? 1 = Left, 2, 3, 4, 5, 6, 7, 8, 9, 10 = Right.*
2   *In politics people sometimes talk of "left" and "right". Using this card, where would you place yourself on this scale, where 0 means the left and 10 means the right?*

Table A.6 Libertarian-authoritarian/left-right variable coding

---

EVS 1981–1999
Left-libertarian=Left-right scale >=5 & Libertarian-authoritarian scale >=0.5
Left-authoritarian=Left-right scale >=5 & Libertarian-authoritarian scale <0.5
Right-libertarian=Left-right scale <5 & Libertarian-authoritarian scale l>=0.5
Right-authoritarian=Left-right scale <5 & Libertarian-authoritarian scale <0.5

Libertarian-authoritarian scale (where 0=auth, 1=lib), Cronbach's alpha: 0.5577
Based on the relevant value items available for all ten countries for 1981–1999:

A125: On this list are various groups of people. Could you please sort out any that you would not like to have as neighbours?

People of a different race (1 mentioned, 0 not mentioned) – recoded 1=0, 0=1

A129: On this list are various groups of people. Could you please sort out any that you would not like to have as neighbours?

Immigrants (1 mentioned, 0 not mentioned) – recoded 1=0, 0=1

D018: If someone says a child needs a home with both a father and a mother to grow up happily, would you tend to agree or disagree? (0 Tend to disagree, 1 Tend to agree) – recoded 1=0, 0=1

D019: Do you think that a woman has to have children in order to be fulfilled or is this not necessary? (0 Not necessary, 1 Needs children) – recoded 1=0, 0=1

D022: Do you agree or disagree with the following statement: marriage is an outdated institution (0 Disagree, 1 Agree)

D023: If a woman wants to have a child as a single parent but she doesn't want to have a stable relationship with a man, do you approve or disapprove?

(0 Disapprove, 1 Approve, 2 Depends) – recoded 0/2=0, 1=1

A048: Do you approve or disapprove of abortion under the following circumstances?

When the woman is not married 0 Disapprove, 1 Approve

A049: Do you approve or disapprove of abortion under the following circumstances? When a married couple does not want to have any more children 0 Disapprove, 1 Approve

Left-right values scale (where 1=right, 10=left), Cronbach's alpha: 0.6065
Based on the relevant value items available for all ten countries for 1981–1999:

E035: Now I'd like you to tell me your views on various issues. How would you place your views on this scale? 1 means you agree completely with the statement on the left; 10 means you agree completely with the statement on the right; and if your views fall somewhere in between, you can choose any number in between. Sentences:

Incomes should be made more equal vs We need larger income differences as incentives recoded 1=10, 2=9, 3=8, 4=7, 5=6, 6=5, 7=4, 8=3, 9=2, 10=1

E036: Private ownership of business should be increased vs Government ownership of business should be increased

E037: People should take more responsibility to provide for themselves vs The government should take more responsibility to ensure that everyone is provided for

Table A.6 Continued

E038: People who are unemployed should have to take any job available or lose their unemployment benefits vs People who are unemployed should have the right to refuse a job they do not want

E039: Competition is good. It stimulates people to work hard and develop new ideas vs Competition is harmful. It brings the worst in people

ESS 2002–2006
Left-libertarian=GINCDIF=1/2 & FREEHMS=1
Left-authoritarian=GINCDIF=1/2 & FREEHMS=2/5
Right-libertarian=GINCDIF=3/5 & FREEHMS=1
Right-authoritarian=GINCDIF=3/5 & FREEHMS=2/5
Based on (the only relevant value-) items in the ESS 2002–2006:

Left-right values
GINCDIF, Government should reduce differences in income levels
1 Agree strongly, 2 Agree, 3 Neither agree nor disagree 4 Disagree, 5 Disagree strongly

Libertarian-authoritarian
FREEHMS, Gays and lesbians free to live life as they wish
1 Agree strongly, 2 Agree, 3 Neither agree nor disagree, 4 Disagree, 5 Disagree strongly

These items were split based on cumulative % most closely approximating 50%:

GINCDIF	N	%	Cum %
(1) **Strongly agree**	**11,526**	**21.65**	**21.65**
(2) **Agree**	**23,910**	**44.91**	**66.55**
(3) Neither	8,206	15.00	81.97
(4) Disagree	8,033	15.0	97.05
(5) Strongly disagree	1,569	2.95	100.00

FREEHMS	N	%	Cum %
(1) **Strongly agree**	**18,278**	**34.25**	**34.25**
(2) Agree	23,972	44.92	79.16
(3) Neither	5,984	11.21	90.38
(4) Disagree	3,234	6.06	96.44
(5) Strongly disagree	1,90	3.56	100.00

Models in Chapter 5

The analysis is based on EVS and ESS data for the following indicators of conventional political participation: party membership (both from the EVS and ESS), voting at the last national election and contacting a politician (both ESS). Following a brief description of the data and the key relationships between the age, cohort and participation variables, the analysis applies logistic regression to assess the relative impact of age, period and cohort effects on different types of conventional political participation in each of the ten countries analysed in this study: Belgium, Denmark, France, Germany, Ireland, Italy, the Netherlands, Great Britain, Spain and Sweden. The focus of this investigation is to assess whether, cross-nationally and across different types of indicators of conventional participation, younger cohorts participate less than older cohorts, or whether age effects play a prominent role for explaining differences in conventional political participation between younger and older people. Education is included in sub-sequent models to ascertain whether higher levels of education amongst the younger cohorts mediate cohort differences in conventional participation. This is because it has been traditionally shown that education is a key determinant of political participation at the individual level. Finally, in the fully specified model, a dummy variable is included for male gender, to examine whether a gender bias remains in conventional participation. A dummy variable for whether a respond-ent belongs to manual occupations is also included, to check for inequality in conventional participation. Dummies are also included for whether individuals are highly politicised either on the left (1 means the respondent selected values 0 or 1/1 or 2 on the left-right scale) or on the right (values 9 and 10 on the left-right scale). This is to investigate whether more politicised individuals parti-cipate more than others in conventional activities. Finally, a categorical variable is included for political values, measured on both the left-right and libertarian-authoritarian dimension, to examine whether people with different sets of polit-ical values exhibit different patterns of participation.

Given Inglehart's (1977, 1990) understanding of 'post-material' struggles as those based around issues concerning gender, the environment, religion, homo-sexuality and abortion, over those pertaining to the left-right dimension, it would seem that both libertarian categories (left- and right-libertarians) should be less likely to participate in conventional activities than left- and right-authoritarians. This would suggest that post-material value commitments, as defined by Ingle-hart, lead individuals to shy away from bureaucratised, hierarchical, or in other words 'elite-directed' or conventional, political participation. 'Materialist values', meanwhile, lead individuals to engage in these actions. Moreover, this would sustain his view that the 'old', class-based, left-right conflict has been overcome by value-oriented struggles so that libertarian (post-material) indi-viduals should be equally less likely to engage in conventional political parti-cipation regardless of their left-right affiliations.

A number of the dependent variables categorised as 'conventional' based on standard theories for the purpose of the analysis in Chapter 4 are excluded from the analysis in this chapter. This is because of their problematic nature. The party work variables also mention political 'groups'. This term could potentially be understood to involve 'new groups', such as new social movements. In turn, this casts doubt on whether this variable should be understood as an indicator of con-ventional participation. Moreover, the sample sizes for this indicator are so small that nearly all effects would be statistically insignificant. Additionally, union membership is not examined in detail in this chapter. This is for both theoretical and methodological reasons. First, it is unclear whether union membership can be conceived of as an indicator of *political* participation in all the countries in the sample (see Chapter 2 for a discussion of this issue). Second, it is unclear whether union membership should be understood as an indicator of *conventional* political participation (as Inglehart suggests in his emphasis on elite-direction) for distinguishing between repertoires of action. Since union membership is generally only an opportunity for individuals in employment, the analyses would have to be restricted to this 'risk set'. However, given the resulting reduction in sample size and the fact that the vast majority of individuals in employment would be in the middle age group this course of action would not be particularly helpful for the analyses carried out in this chapter. The same applies for union work, which is thus not analysed in this chapter.

Models in Chapter 6

A detailed discussion of data sources, selection of key dependent variables and explanatory variables was provided above. This section briefly summarises the data and methodologies employed in this specific chapter. The analysis is based on EVS and ESS data for the following indicators of unconventional political participation: demonstrating, boycotting, petitioning (both from the EVS and ESS), and occupying and participation in new social movements (only EVS). After a brief description of the data and the key relationships between the age, cohort and participation variables, the analysis applies logistic regression to assess the relative impact of age, period and cohort effects on different types of unconventional political participation in each of the ten countries analysed in this study: Belgium, Denmark, France, Germany, Ireland, Italy, the Netherlands, Great Britain, Spain and Sweden. The focus of this investigation is to assess whether, cross-nationally and across different types of indicators of unconventional participation, younger cohorts participate more than older ones, or whether age effects play a prominent role for explaining differences in unconventional political participation between younger and older cohorts. Education is included in subsequent models to ascertain whether higher levels of education amongst the younger cohorts mediate cohort differences in unconventional participation, since it has been traditionally shown that education is a key determinant of political participation at the individual level. Finally, the fully specified model includes a dummy variable for male gender, to see if there is a gender bias as in unconventional participation, a dummy variable for whether a respondent belongs to manual occupations, to check for inequality also in unconventional participation; dummies for whether individuals are highly politicised either on the left (values 0/1 [EVS] or 1/2 [ESS] on the left-right scale) or on the right (values 9/10 on the left-right scale) to see whether more politicised individuals participate more than others in conventional activities and whether being left wing has a positive effect on unconventional participation as the literature has traditionally shown; and a categorical variable for four different combinations of political values measured on both the left-right and libertarian-authoritarian dimension. Given Inglehart's (1977, 1990) understanding of post-material struggles as those based around issues concerning gender, the environment, religion, homosexuality and abortion, and overcoming those pertaining to the left-right dimension, it would seem that both libertarian categories (left- and right-libertarians) should be more likely to participate in unconventional activities than left- and right-authoritarians. In other words, that post-material value commitments, as suggested by Inglehart (1977, 1990), lead individuals to engage in

Table A.7 The evolution of political participation? Levels of participation over time

	Party membership EVS and ESS						Work for a party/group EVS and ESS*					
	1981	1990	1999	2002	2004	2006	1981	1990	1999	2002	2004	2006
Belgium	3	6	7	8	7	7	2	2	3	6	4	6
Denmark	7	7	7	6	7	7	2	2	3	4	5	4
France	3	3	2	2	2	2	2	2	1	5	4	3
Germany	8	8	3	3	3	4	4	3	1	4	4	4
Ireland	4	4	4	5	6	5	2	2	2	5	5	4
Italy	7	5	4	4	4		5	3	2	3	4	
Netherlands	8	9	9	5	6	5	2	2	3	3	4	4
Great Britain	5	5	3	3	3	3	2	2	1	3	2	3
Spain	3	2	2	3	4	3	2	1	1	6	8	5
Sweden	13	10	10	8	7	6	2	4	4	5	3	5

	Union membership EVS/ESS**						Union work EVS			Cont. politician ESS*		
	1981	1990	1999	2002	2004	2006	1981	1990	1999	2002	2004	2006
Belgium	16	16	18	31	33	34	1	2	2	18	14	19
Denmark	44	50	54	68	65	64	3	3	4	18	20	19
France	10	5	4	8	6	7	3	2	1	17	15	15
Germany	16	15	7	16	11	10	2	2	0	13	11	13
Ireland	14	9	10	21	20	20	2	1	2	23	23	24
Italy	8	6	6	15	13		4	3	2	13	14	
Netherlands	15	20	22	22	21	18	1	2	2	15	13	14
Great Britain	21	14	8	18	15	16	1	1	2	19	16	18
Spain	6	3	4	8	8	9	2	1	1	12	13	12
Sweden	46	58	64	60	61	58	2	6	11	17	15	15

Unoff. strike EVS

	1981	1990	1999
Belgium	3	6	9
Denmark	10	18	22
France	11	10	13
Germany	2	2	2
Ireland	5	4	6
Italy	3	6	5
Netherlands	2	3	5
Great Britain	7	10	9
Spain	8	6	9
Sweden	2	3	5

Occupying EVS

	1981	1990	1999
Belgium	3	4	6
Denmark	3	2	3
France	8	8	9
Germany	2	1	1
Ireland	2	2	2
Italy	6	8	8
Netherlands	2	3	5
Great Britain	3	2	2
Spain	3	3	3
Sweden	0	0	3

Attending demonstrations EVS/ESS*

	1981	1990	1999	2002	2004	2006
Belgium	15	23	40	9	6	8
Denmark	20	28	29	8	5	7
France	28	33	39	17	12	14
Germany	15	21	22	11	9	7
Ireland	13	17	22	7	6	7
Italy	27	36	35	10	11	5
Netherlands	13	25	32	3	4	3
Great Britain	11	14	13	5	4	4
Spain	26	24	27	16	33	18
Sweden	15	23	36	6	7	5

Joining in boycotts EVS/ESS*

	1981	1990	1999	2002	2004	2006
Belgium	3	9	12	13	10	11
Denmark	10	11	25	23	29	25
France	12	13	13	26	30	27
Germany	8	11	10	25	21	23
Ireland	7	7	8	14	11	13
Italy	6	11	10	8	8	
Netherlands	7	9	22	11	9	10
Great Britain	8	14	17	27	21	25
Spain	9	5	6	7	14	10
Sweden	9	16	34	33	35	31

Signing petitions EVS/ESS*

	1981	1990	1999	2002	2004	2006
Belgium	25	48	72	34	22	30
Denmark	46	52	57	28	29	36
France	47	54	68	34	31	33
Germany	48	58	47	32	33	28
Ireland	30	42	61	27	22	24
Italy	43	48	55	19	15	
Netherlands	36	51	62	23	23	21
Great Britain	64	76	81	40	35	41
Spain	25	23	29	22	25	23
Sweden	54	72	87	41	49	45

continued

Table A.7 Continued

	Env. memb. EVS			Dev. memb. EVS			Env. work EVS			Dev. work EVS		
	1981	1990	1999	1981	1990	1999	1981	1990	1999	1981	1990	1999
Belgium	3	12	10	1	6	10	2	4	3	0	3	5
Denmark	6	15	13	4	3	4	0	1	2	1	1	1
France	2	4	2	1	3	1	1	2	1	0	1	1
Germany	3	9	3	1	2	1	1	3	1	1	1	0
Ireland	2	3	3	1	2	3	1	1	1	1	1	2
Italy	2	4	4	1	1	3	1	2	2	1	1	2
Netherlands	11	29	45	3	14	24	1	3	3	1	3	4
Great Britain	5	6	2	2	2	3	1	2	8	1	1	5
Spain	2	2	3	1	1	2	2	2	1	1	1	1
Sweden	3	15	12	3	9	16	4	3	4	2	3	5

Notes
* ESS items specify last 12 months.
** The ESS items for union membership also add 'or similar organisation?'

'elite-directing', or unconventional political participation. Moreover, this would sustain the view that the 'old', class-based, left-right dimension has been overcome by value-oriented struggles so that libertarian individuals should be equally as likely to engage in unconventional political participation regardless of their left-right affiliations. On the other hand, if other authors (Brooks and Manza 1994; Evans and De Graaf 1996) are right that post-materialism is a poor proxy for progressive liberalism, then left-libertarians should be significantly more likely than all the other three groups to engage in elite-challenging activism. The variable for NSM participation is constructed out of the four disaggregated indicators and takes a value of 1 where individuals engaged in any of the following four activities: joining/working for an environmental organisation, joining/ working for a development or human rights organisation. This variable is also employed in Chapter 7.

Models in Chapter 7

A detailed discussion of data sources, selection of dependent variables and explanatory variables was provided above. This section briefly describes the data and methodologies employed in this specific chapter. The discussion of the multi-level and generalised additive models employed in this chapter is provided below. The analysis in this chapter is based on EVS and ESS data for the following indicators of political participation as employed in the previous chapters: party membership (both from the EVS and ESS), voting at the last national election and contacting a politician (both ESS), demonstrating (both from the EVS and ESS), boycotting (both from the EVS and ESS), petitioning (both from the EVS and ESS) and occupying and NSM participation (both from the EVS; as discussed above the NSM indicator includes membership and unpaid work in both environmental and human rights organisations). As mentioned, this chapter applies multi-level models (which will be discussed in more detail below) to assess the relative impact of age, period and cohort effects on different types of conventional and unconventional political participation across Western Europe.

The central focus of this investigation is to assess whether, across Europe, younger cohorts participate less than older cohorts in conventional activities. This also means assessing whether older cohorts participate less than younger ones in unconventional activities, and also whether age effects play a prominent role for explaining differences in political participation between younger and older cohorts. Education is included in the relevant models since it has been traditionally shown that education is a key determinant of political participation at the individual level. A dummy variable is included for male gender, to ascertain how far a gender bias remains in either type of participation; a dummy variable is included for whether a respondent belongs to manual occupations, to check for inequality in the various types of participation; dummies are also included for whether individuals are highly politicised either on the left (1 means the respondent selected values 0 or 1/1 or 2 on the left-right scale) or on the right (values 9 and 10 on the left-right scale) to examine whether more politicised individuals participate more than others in different types of activities; and a categorical variable is present for political values measured on both the left-right and libertarian-authoritarian dimension to investigate whether people with different sets of political values exhibit different patterns of participation. Given Inglehart's (1977, 1990; Inglehart and Catterberg 2002) understanding that post-material struggles are those based around issues concerning gender, the environment, religion, homosexuality and abortion, over those pertaining to the left-right dimension, it would seem that, if his theory is correct, both libertarian categories (left- and right-libertarians) should be less likely to participate in conventional activities and more likely to participate in unconventional activities than left- and right-authoritarians. This would suggest that post-material value commitments, as Inglehart argues, lead individuals to shy away from bureaucratised, hierarchical – or 'elite-directed', conventional – political participation. In turn, materialist values should guide individuals to engage in these actions. On the other hand, following the same logic, post-materialist values should lead individuals to engage more in unconventional or 'elite-directing' political activities.

Multi-level models

Chapters 5–6 presented country-by-country analyses. The chapters showed that within each political activity, cohort effects followed broadly the same pattern across Western Europe. The effects of age and the other explanatory variables were also similar between countries. However, the relationship between time and participation varied between countries. This means that the observations cannot simply be pooled into one logistic regression model, where it is assumed that the coefficients for survey year apply equally to each country. Ignoring the hierarchical structure of the data, that respondents are nested in countries, would underestimate the standard errors and therefore potentially lead to Type I errors (Snijders and Bosker 1999). A further approach would be to pool the observations into one logistic regression model and interact country with year. However, such a fixed effects approach ignores the random variability associated with group-level characteristics (Luke 2004). Therefore, in order to deal with the hierarchical nature of the data *and* to model the cross-national variability in the relationship between time and participation, logistic multi-level models with random effects for survey year are fitted. This forms the first part of the analysis in this chapter; which then moves on to the GAMs. The mixed-effects model being fit is:

$$\log\left[\frac{p}{1-p_{ij}}\right] = \gamma_{00} + \gamma_1 X_{ij} + ... + \gamma_z\ Year_{ij} + \delta_{0j} + \delta_{zj}\ Year_{ij} + \varepsilon_{ij}$$

$\gamma_{00} + \gamma_1 X_{ij} + ... + \gamma_z\ Year_{ij}$ represents the fixed effects and $\delta_{oj} + \delta_{zj}\ Year_{ij} + \varepsilon_{ij}$ represents the random effects. The *j* subscripts indicate that parameters vary between countries, whereas the *ij* subscripts indicate that each variable varies between respondents and countries. γ_{00} is the constant; $\gamma_1 X_{ij} + ...$ denotes all explanatory variables that, with the exception of the survey year dummies (γ_z Year$_{ij}$), are included solely as fixed effects in the model. ε_{ij} is the individual-level error, δ_{oj} represents the random variability associated with group-level characteristics and δ_{zj} Year$_{ij}$ represents the random effects for the year of survey dummies. Fitting a random slope for survey year thus takes into account the variability in the relationship between time and participation between countries which was uncovered in the analyses in Chapters 5 and 6. It is important to note that δ_{oj}, δ_{zj} and ε_{ij} are each separately independently normally distributed with mean zero and some variance parameter that is estimated.

Generalised additive models

Generalised additive models (GAMs) and generalised non-parametric models (GNMs) are similar to generalised linear models (GLMs) in that Y can be replaced with a linear predictor transformation and the appropriate link function included. Like GLMs, these models can be fit when the outcome variable is not continuous. This makes them useful for the purposes of this research, since all the dependent variables are binary. Generalised semi-parametric additive models are hybrids of the general additive model and linear regression – some terms enter non-parametrically while others enter linearly:

$$Y_i = a + f_k(X_{ik}) + \beta_r X_{i1} + \ldots + \beta_r X_{r+1} + \varepsilon_i$$

The semi-parametric model is useful if categorical variables need to be included. However, while this method allows us to capture the non-linearity of cohort effects without being restricted to specific cohort categorisations, it also has its own drawbacks. Unlike the multi-level random effects model employed in the previous section, the drawback of the GAMs is that random coefficients cannot be used for period. This means that the estimates could be somewhat biased, since it has been established that period effects vary between countries. However, GAMs still provide a helpful graphical representation of the smoothed effects of cohort on political participation. Moreover, because GAMs require a large number of data for computational purposes, these analyses cannot be conducted country-by-country given the sample sizes available in the EVS and ESS surveys. Unfortunately, this means it is not possible to test for country-by-country specificities in terms of eye-balling the smoothed cohort effects. More specifically, the model applied in this section of the analysis is the following:

$$\log\left(\frac{\pi}{1-\pi}\right) = a + s \ (Year \ of \ birth) + \beta_1 \ Young + \beta_2 \ Old + \beta_3 \ Year_1 + \beta_4 \ Year_3$$

This model allows for plotting of the smoothed cohort effects while also identifying the model, despite only having few time points available in the data. Ideally, it would have been helpful to apply a more fine-tuned age categorisation in this model. However, the demands of identification and data limitations mean

Table A.8 Multi-level parameter estimates for conventional and unconventional participation, EVS/ESS

	Party-EVS	Party-ESS	Voting-ESS	Contpol-ESS	Demo-EVS
	Model 3	*Model 3*	*Model 3*	*Model 3*	*Model 3*
Fixed effects	*Estimate (s.e.)*	*Estimate (s.e.)*	*Estimate (s.e.)*	*Estimate (s.e.)*	*Estimate (s.e.)*
Constant γ_{00}	−2.57(.19)***	−2.84(.18)***	−2.44(.19)***	−1.54(.10)***	−0.70(.11)***
Cohort					
Pre-WWII	0.05(.08)	0.19(.08)*	−0.42(.06)***	−0.43(.07)***	−0.25(.06)***
Post-WWII *r.c.*					
Baby-boomers	−0.29(.08)***	−0.27(.06)***	−0.30(.05)***	0.24(.04)***	0.27(.05)***
80s generation	−0.70(.12)***	−0.68(.11)***	−0.61(.07)***	0.12(.06)	0.07(.07)
90s generation	−1.02(.17)***	−1.08(.18)***	−0.89(.09)***	0.00(.08)	0.03(.09)
Age group					
18–33	−0.24(.09)**	0.08(.16)	−0.33(.06)***	−0.31(.07)***	0.01(.05)
34–50 *r.c.*					
51+	−0.09(.08)	0.17(.09)	0.28(.06)***	0.01(.05)	−0.11(.05)*
Survey year					
1981/2002*	−0.04(.11)	−0.01(.06)	0.05(.07)	0.09(.05)	−0.57(.10)***
1989/2004* *r.c..*					
1999/2006*	−0.14(.12)	0.00(.06)	−0.00(.06)	0.03(.05)	0.17(.07)*
Education (low)	−0.60(.06)***	−0.28(.05)***	−0.56(.03)***	−0.54(.03)***	−0.75(.03)***
Male	0.70(.05)***	0.58(.04)***	0.10(.03)***	0.36(.02)***	0.56(.03)***
Working class	−0.47(.05)***	−0.37(.05)***	−0.44(.03)***	−0.40(.03)***	−0.23(.03)***
Left	1.11(.07)***	0.95(.08)***	0.11(.06)	0.37(.05)***	1.11(.05)***
Right	0.74(.09)***	0.90(.08)***	0.49(.08)***	0.26(.06)***	−0.26(.07)***
Political values					
Left-libertarian *r.c.*					
Left-authoritarian	−0.24(.07)***	−0.26(.06)***	−0.10(.03)**	−0.22(.03)***	−0.67(.07)***
Right-libertarian	−0.24(.07)***	−0.16(.08)*	0.14(.05)**	−0.01(.04)	−0.60(.04)***
Right-authoritarian	−0.12(.07)	−0.10(.06)	−0.11(.04)**	−0.13(.04)***	−0.81(.04)***
Random effects	*Variance (std. d.)*	*Variance (std. d.)*	*Variance (std. d.)*	*Variance (std. d.)*	*Variance (std. d.)*
Between-country var σ_u^2	0.29(.54)	0.20(.44)	0.29(.54)	0.06(.25)	0.08(.29)
Survey year					
1981/2002*	0.07(.26)	0.01(.11)	0.03(.18)	0.01(.12)	0.08(.28)
1989/2004* *r.c.*					
1999/2006*	0.11(.33)	0.01(.09)	0.03(.17)	0.01(.11)	0.03(.18)
AIC	14,780	18,207	42,175	42,930	36,824
BIC	14,978	18,410	42,377	43,113	37,020
LogLikelihood	−7,367	−9,080	−21,064	21,442	−18,389
Deviance	14,734	18,161	42,129	42,884	36,778

Notes
Significance levels:
* $p \le 0.05$.
** $p \le 0.01$.
*** $p \le 0.001$.

emo-ESS	Boycott-EVS	Boycott-ESS	Petition-EVS	Petition-ESS	NSM-EVS	Occupy-EVS
Model 3	*Model 3*	*Model 3*	*Model 3*	*Model 3*	*Model 3*	*Model 3*
stimate (s.e.)	*Estimate (s.e.)*	*Estimate (s.e.)*	*Estimate (s.e.)*	*Estimate (s.e.)*	*Estimate (s.e.)*	*Estimate (s.e.)*
2.26(.25)***	−1.61(.14)***	−0.95(.22)***	−0.67(.22)**	−0.48(.15)**	−1.35(.24)***	−3.56(.27)***
0.59(.14)***	−0.35(.09)***	−0.67(.08)***	−0.27(.04)***	−0.59(.06)***	−0.12(.07)	−0.46(.14)**
0.52(.06)***	0.24(.07)***	0.20(.04)***	0.27(.04)***	0.33(.03)***	−0.14(.07)*	0.56(.11)***
0.32(.09)***	0.08(.09)	0.15(.06)*	0.17(.06)**	0.30(.05)***	−0.24(.09)**	0.17(.14)
0.12(.12)	−0.24(.12)*	−0.03(.08)	−0.03(.07)	0.21(.07)**	−0.50(.12)***	−0.13(.20)
0.26(.10)**	−0.02(.06)	−0.06(.06)	−0.21(.04)***	−0.02(.05)	−0.06(.07)	−0.02(.10)
0.10(.07)	−0.22(.07)**	0.00(.05)	−0.12(.04)**	−0.06(.04)	−0.04(.07)	−0.02(.12)
0.01(.14)	−0.50(.16)**	0.03(.09)	−0.49(.10)***	0.11(.08)	−0.78(.14)***	−0.19(.11)
0.17(.13)	0.30(.14)*	−0.02(.06)	0.38(.12)**	0.05(.07)	−0.02(.17)	−0.20(.11)
0.62(.05)***	−0.67(.04)***	−0.65(.03)***	−0.63(.03)***	−0.58(.03)***	−0.79(.05)***	−0.43(.07)***
0.29(.03)***	0.45(.04)***	−0.07(.02)**	0.19(.02)***	−0.08(.02)***	−0.02(.04)	0.62(.06)***
0.29(.04)***	−0.33(.05)***	−0.48(.03)***	−0.26(.03)***	−0.38(.03)***	−0.58(.05)***	0.20(.06)**
1.10(.06)***	1.09(.06)***	0.48(.05)***	0.70(.05)***	0.48(.05)***	0.43(.07)***	1.27(.07)***
0.02(.10)	−0.30(.11)**	−0.20(.07)**	−0.10(.05)	−0.12(.06)*	−0.21(.09)*	−0.22(.19)
0.50(.04)***	−0.82(.06)***	−0.53(.03)***	−0.49(.03)***	−0.45(.03)***	−0.33(.06)***	−0.72(.08)***
0.51(.06)***	−0.57(.05)***	−0.18(.04)***	−0.25(.03)***	−0.26(.04)***	−0.20(.05)***	−0.59(.08)***
0.93(.06)***	−0.88(.06)***	−0.53(.04)***	−0.42(.03)***	−0.55(.03)***	−0.30(.05)***	−1.08(.10)***
ariance (td. d.)	*Variance (std. d.)*	*Variance (std. d.)*	*Variance (std. d.)*	*Variance (std. d.)*	*Variance (std. d.)*	*Variance (std. d.)*
0.56(.75)	0.15(.39)	0.45(.67)	0.45(.67)	0.20(.45)	0.54(.04)	0.58(.76)
0.19(.43)	0.24(.49)	0.07(.27)	0.10(.31)	0.06(.24)	0.18(.42)	0.04(.20)
0.15(.39)	0.18(.42)	0.03(.18)	0.13(.36)	0.05(.22)	0.26(.51)	0.05(.21)
25,151	21,941	44,914	45,412	56,695	21,669	10,281
25,354	22,137	45,116	45,608	56,898	21,867	10,477
−12,553	−10,948	−22,434	−22,683	−28,325	−10,812	−5,118
25,105	21,895	44,868	45,366	56,649	21,623	10,235

eference categories: Post-WWII cohort (2); 34–50 age group (2); 1990/2004 (2), therefore, 1981/2002 is the ıverse of the period effect 1981–1990/2002–2004; Left-libertarian (1); Edu (low) is a dummy variable where means the respondent left school before the age of 17 or completed less than eleven years in FTE; Working ass is a dummy variable where 1 means the respondent is an unskilled, semi-skilled or skilled manual worker; eft and right are dummy variables derived from the left-right scale, respectively, values 0/1 and values 9/10.

this is not a viable option for getting at reliable estimates in this specific case. The important component to note in the model above is the *s (Year of birth)* term, or the $f_k(X_{ik})$ term in the general model presented earlier. This is the smooth function that replaces the linear function. It is non-parametric and it permits one to plot the smooth non-linear cohort effect since year of birth is estimated as smoothly changing.

While there are different smoothing functions which could be applied,[3] here smoothing splines are applied since they offer the best compromise between fit and the degree of smoothness (Tilley 2002: 126). The age and year dummy variables are included linearly, and as such this is a semi-parametric model. The term which replaces Y on the left-hand side shows that this is a generalised additive model for binary response variables, in other words, a logistic, generalised (semi-parametric) additive model where π is the probability that the response variable is 1 rather than 0.

Conclusions

This Appendix has discussed the key methodological and data issues involved in measuring and analysing political participation in a comparative framework. It has provided details omitted from the chapters to make them more accessible as to the identifying strategies and more advanced statistical models underpinning the investigation.

Notes

1 See the end of this section for why I do not analyse union membership and party work in Chapters 5–7.
2 The *isko* package (developed by John Hendrickx, Management Studies Group, Wageningen University, The Netherlands) consists of a series of programs to recode ISCO-88 codes into other occupational scales. These programs are STATA versions of the SPSS recode files by Harry B.G. Ganzeboom and Donald J. Treiman, which are available at www.fss.uu.nl/soc/hg/ismf. The *iskoegp* program transforms ISCO-88 codes into a ten-category EGP scale (cf. Erikson *et al.* 1979) – see schema on page above. Note that the *iskoegp* program requires the specification of variables indicating whether or not the respondent is self-employed and whether the respondent is a supervisor.
3 There are two packages in *R* which can be used to fit generalised additive models: these are the *mgcv* and the *gam* package which uses either Lowess and/or smoothing splines and allows one to choose the span of degrees of freedom. As Tilley (2002: 126) points out,

> choosing the number of degrees of freedom to use is a matter of judgement informed to some extent by theoretical expectations, but also results from analysis using several different values.... There is a trade off between variance and bias; high levels of smoothing give a fit with arrow confidence intervals; low levels of smoothing have larger confidence intervals but reflect changes in the data more accurately.

As such, I use the *mgcv* package which (only) fits smoothing splines and selects the smoothing parameter by generalised cross-validation since they offer the best compromise between fit and the degree of smoothness.

References

Beck, N. and S. Jackman (1998). "Beyond Linearity by Default: Generalised Additive Models". *American Journal of Political Science* 42: 596–627.

Blossfeld, H.-P. (1986). "Career Opportunities in the Federal Republic of Germany: A Dynamic Approach to the Study of Life-Course, Cohort, and Period Effects". *European Sociological Review* 2(3): 208–25.

Brady, H. (1999). Political Participation. *Measures of Political Attitudes*. J. Robinson, P. Shaver and L. Wrightsman. Burlington, VA, Academic Press.

Brooks, C. and J. Manza (1994). "Do Changing Values Explain the New Politics? A Critical Assessment of the Postmaterialist Thesis". *The Sociological Quarterly* 35(4): 541–70.

Converse, P. (1976). *The Dynamics of Party Support: Cohort-analysing Party Identification*. Beverly Hills, CA, Sage.

Dekker, P., R. Koopmans and A. van den Broek (1997). Voluntary Associations, Social Movements and Individual Political Behaviour in Western Europe. *Private Groups and Public Life: Social Participation and Political Involvement in Representative Democracies*. J. Van Deth. Abingdon, Routledge.

Dunn, A., M. T. Grasso and C. Saunders (2014). "Unemployment and Attitudes to Work: Asking the 'Right' Question". *Work, Employment, and Society* 28: 904–25.

Erikson, R., J. H. Goldthorpe and L. Portocarero (1979). "Intergenerational Class Mobility in Three Western European Countries: England, France, and Sweden". *British Journal of Sociology* 30: 415–51.

Evans, G. and N. D. De Graaf (1996). "Why are the Young More Postmaterialist? A Cross-National Analysis of Individual and Contextual Influences on Postmaterial Values". *Comparative Political Studies* 28(4): 608–35.

Fienberg, S. E. and W. M. Mason (1979). "Identification and Estimation of Age-Period-Cohort Models in the Analysis of Discrete Archival Data". *Sociological Methodology* 10: 1–67.

Fienberg, S. E. and W. M. Mason (1985). Specification and Implementation of Age, Period and Cohort Models. *Cohort Analysis in Social Research*. W. M. Mason and S. E. Fienberg. New York, Springer-Verlag.

Firebaugh, G. and K. Davis (1988). "Trends in Antiblack Prejudice, 1972–1984: Region and Cohort Effects". *American Journal of Sociology* 94(2): 251–72.

Franklin, M. N. (2004). *Voter Turnout and the Dynamics of Electoral Competition in Established Democracies since 1945*. Cambridge, Cambridge University Press.

Glenn, N. (2005). *Cohort Analysis, 2nd Edition.* London, Sage.

Glenn, N. D. (1976). "Cohort Analysts' Futile Quest: Statistical Attempts to Separate Age, Period and Cohort Effects". *American Sociological Review* 41(5): 900–4.

Glenn, N. D. (1994). "Television Watching, Newspaper Reading, and Cohort Differences in Verbal Ability". *Sociology of Education* 67: 216–30.

Grasso, M. T. (2011). *Political Participation in Western Europe*. Nuffield College, University of Oxford. D. Phil. Thesis.

Grasso, M. T. (2013). "The Differential Impact of Education on Young People's Political Activism: Comparing Italy and the United Kingdom". *Comparative Sociology* 12: 1–30.

Grasso, M. T. (2014). "Age-period-cohort Analysis in a Comparative Context: Political Generations and Political Participation Repertoires". *Electoral Studies* 33: 63–76.

Harding, D. and C. Jencks (2003). "Changing Attitudes Towards Pre-Marital Sex: Cohort, Period and Aging Effects". *Public Opinion Quarterly* 67: 211–26.

Hastie, T. and R. Tibshirani (1986). "Generalized Additive Models". *Statistical Science* 1: 297–318.

Hastie, T. and R. Tibshirani (1990). *Generalized Additive Models*. London, Chapman and Hall.

Heath, A. F. and J. Martin (1996). Changing Attitudes Towards Abortion: Life-cycle, Period and Cohort Effects. *Understanding Change in Social Attitudes*. B. Taylor and K. Thomson. Dartmouth, Aldershot.

Heckman, J. and R. Robb (1985). Using Longitudinal Data to Estimate Age, Period, and Cohort Effects in Earnings Equations. *Cohort Analysis in Social Research*. W. Mason and S. E. Fienberg. New York, Springer-Verlag: 137–50.

Hendrickx, J. (2002). "*Isko* Package". Wageningen University, the Netherlands, Management Studies Group.

Hirczy, W. (1994). "The Impact of Mandatory Voting Laws on Turnout – a Quasi-experimental Approach". *Electoral Studies* 13(1): 64–76.

ILO. (1990). *International Standard Classification of Occupations: Isco-88*. Geneva, International Labour Office.

Inglehart, R. (1977). *The Silent Revolution: Changing Values and Political Styles among Western Publics*. Princeton, Princeton University Press.

Inglehart, R. (1990). *Culture Shift in Advanced Industrial Society*. Princeton, Princeton University Press.

Inglehart, R. and G. Catterberg (2002). "Trends in Political Action: The Developmental Trend and the Post-Honeymoon Decline". *International Journal of Comparative Sociology* 43: 300–16.

Knoke, D. and M. Hout (1974). "Social and Demographic Factors in American Party Affiliations, 1952–1972". *American Sociological Review* 39: 700–13.

Luke, D. (2004). *Multilevel Modelling*. London, Sage.

Mackie, T. and R. Rose, Eds. (1991). *The International Almanac of Electoral History*. Basingstoke, Macmillan.

Mair, P. and I. Van Biezen (2001). "Party Membership in Twenty European Democracies, 1980–2000". *Party Politics* 7(1): 5–21.

Mannheim, K. (1928). The Problem of Generations. *Essays on the Sociology of Knowledge*. London, Routledge.

Mason, K. O., W. M. Mason, H. H. Winsborough and W. K. Poole (1973). "Some Methodological Issues in Cohort Analysis of Archival Data". *American Sociological Review* 38(2): 242–58.

Mason, W. M. and S. E. Fienberg (1985). *Cohort Analysis in Social Research: Beyond the Identification Problem*. New York, Springer-Verlag.

Nakamura, T. (1986). "Bayesian Cohort Models for General Cohort Table Analysis". *Annals of the Institute of Statistical Mathematics* 38: 352–70.

O'Brien, R. (2000). "Age Period Cohort Characteristic Models". *Social Science Research* 29: 123–39.

Olson, M. (1965). *The Logic of Collective Action*. Cambridge, MA, Harvard University Press.

Palmore, E. (1987). "When Can Age, Period and Cohort be Separated?" *Social Forces* 57(1): 282–95.

Smets, K. and A. Neundorf (2014). "The Hierarchies of Age-period-cohort Research: Political Context and the Development of Generational Turnout Patterns". *Electoral Studies* 33.

Snijders, T. and R. Bosker (1999). *Multilevel Analysis: An Introduction to Basic and Advanced Multilevel Modelling*. London, Sage.

Tilley, J. (2001). Social and Political Generations in Contemporary Britain. *Nuffield College*, University of Oxford. D. Phil.

Tilley, J. (2002). "Political Generations and Partisanship in the UK, 1964–1997". *Journal of the Royal Statistical Society, Series A (Statistics in Society)* 165(1): 121–35.

Tilley, J. and G. Evans (2014). "Ageing and Generational Effects on Vote Choice". *Electoral Studies* 33(19–27).

Van Deth, J. W. (1990). Interest in Politics. *Continuities in Political Action: A Longitudinal Study of Political Orientations in Three Western Democracies*. M. Jennings and J. W. Van Deth. Berlin, De Gruyter and Aldine: 275–312.

Wilson, J. Q. (1974). *Political Organisations*. Princeton, Princeton University Press.

Wood, S. N. (2006). *Generalized Additive Models: An Introduction with R*. London, Chapman and Hall.

Index

Page numbers in *italics* denote tables, those in **bold** denote figures.

period effects: on boycotting 130; vs cohort effects 38, 76; on demonstrating 115; examples 4; modelling the impact of 121; on party membership 89, 94; on petition signing 143; on SMO participation 150

petition signing 66, 135–50; cohort differences 143, 173; ESS data **67**, **144–5**, *148–9*, *152*, *178–9*; EVS data **67**, **142–3**, *146–7*, *151*, *178–9*, **189**; historical perspective 135

Pilcher, J. 27

Pitkin, H. 1

Plutzer, E. 35

political disengagement: evidence of in Western democracies 26; young people and 26–8

political habits, evidence for the resilience of 35

political organisations: definition 15; 'old' vs 'new' 15–16; vs social movement organisations 16

political participation: activities 19; categorisations 17–18; conflicting narratives 6–9; defining 13–17; evolution of 28–9; the future of in Western Europe 192–207; indicators *18*, 19; individual-level influences and aggregate-level change 21–2; levels of over time *236–8*; measuring 19–20; predictors 22–3; relationship to democracy 4–6; resources, attitudes and cross-national differences 22–3; socio-economic predictors 22

political parties: managerial transformation of 29, 30; targeting of campaign strategies 34

political socialisation, key moment 40

political values: and boycotting 135; and demonstrating 125, 172; and NSM/SMO participation 155, 182; and party membership 94; party membership and 167; and petition signing 150

political values and, voting 100, 167

politicians: openness to consultation 103; professionalisation 104; public perception 1, 22

politics, 'spectator sport' analogy 29

population replacement, and intergenerational change 113–14

post-materialism 35, 38, 125, 164

post-war generation, classification 36

post-WWII generation, classification 36

pragmatic generation, classification 36

pre-war generation, classification 36

pre-WWII generation: classification 36; shared experience 41

'The Problem of Generations' (Mannheim) 27

progressive liberalism 38, 125

protest, function of 31

protest activism: cohort differences 186–7; examples 17; rise in 1

'protest generation' 3, 6–7, 36–7, 44, 113, 130, 164, 172, 207; classification 36; *see also* baby-boomers

protest movements, growth of 14

protest politics, Norris on the rise in 32

purposes of this study 21

research into participation, challenges for 19

Right-authoritarian values 94, 105, 125

Right-libertarian values 94, 125, 135, 150

Robb, R. 221

Rodgers, W. L. 121

Rosow, I. 182

Russell, A. T. 35

satisfaction, influence on participation patterns 23

silent generation, classification 36

SMOs (social movement organisations): and the 'new middle class' 114; vs traditional political organisations 16; *see also* NSM/SMO participation

social capital 14

social change: drivers of 1; social class and 31

social class: and boycotting 135; and contacting a politician 105; and demonstrating 172; and voting 100

social deprivation hypothesis 23

social forms of participation 17

Spain: boycotting 64, 66, 130, 132; civil war 41; demonstrating 64, 121, 124–5; gender bias in party membership 89; occupation and party membership 94; party membership 54–5, 89; party-mediated participation patterns 58; period effects on party membership 89; political values and party membership 94; proto-fascist regime 41; SMO participation patterns 69; social class and voter turnout 100; strikes and building occupation patterns 62; union membership and unpaid work 58; voting 54, 97

Taylor & Francis eBooks

Helping you to choose the right eBooks for your Library

Add Routledge titles to your library's digital collection today. Taylor and Francis ebooks contains over 50,000 titles in the Humanities, Social Sciences, Behavioural Sciences, Built Environment and Law.

Choose from a range of subject packages or create your own!

Benefits for you

» Free MARC records
» COUNTER-compliant usage statistics
» Flexible purchase and pricing options
» All titles DRM-free.

Free Trials Available
We offer free trials to qualifying academic, corporate and government customers.

Benefits for your user

» Off-site, anytime access via Athens or referring URL
» Print or copy pages or chapters
» Full content search
» Bookmark, highlight and annotate text
» Access to thousands of pages of quality research at the click of a button.

eCollections – Choose from over 30 subject eCollections, including:

Archaeology	Language Learning
Architecture	Law
Asian Studies	Literature
Business & Management	Media & Communication
Classical Studies	Middle East Studies
Construction	Music
Creative & Media Arts	Philosophy
Criminology & Criminal Justice	Planning
Economics	Politics
Education	Psychology & Mental Health
Energy	Religion
Engineering	Security
English Language & Linguistics	Social Work
Environment & Sustainability	Sociology
Geography	Sport
Health Studies	Theatre & Performance
History	Tourism, Hospitality & Events

For more information, pricing enquiries or to order a free trial, please contact your local sales team:
www.tandfebooks.com/page/sales

Routledge
Taylor & Francis Group

The home of
Routledge books

www.tandfebooks.com